C000285307

"Darlene Lancer understands the DNA c
personality disorder, including their relatior
personal experience make this a book not to be
with NPD, whether you're staying or leaving the relationsnip.
~ Randi Kreger, Author of *Stop Walking on Eggshells*

"Darlene Lancer's book will help you regain your sense of self and restore belief in yourself again. It will help you make sense of the nonsensical experiences with a narcissist or person with high narcissistic traits."
~ Lisa A. Romano, Life Coach,
Bestselling Author of *The Codependency Manifesto*

"A must-have manual that will enlighten you and provide concrete steps to make you narcissist-proof moving forward, liberating you to finally create the mutually loving relationship you long for."
~ Katherine Woodward Thomas,
NYT Bestselling Author of *Calling in "The One"*

"Darlene Lancer's expertise on narcissism and its impact on relationships is unequalled. She understands the differences in our brains, and has insight that all could benefit from."
~ Hackie Reitman, M.D., *DifferentBrains.org*

"I am extremely impressed with this book and highly recommend it to anyone who has a narcissist in their life. Instead of demonizing narcissists, Lancer focuses on changing the relationship dynamics, offering hope and healing for anyone dealing with a narcissist."
~ Beverly Engel, Author of *Escaping Emotional Abuse:
Healing from the Shame You Don't Deserve*

"Lancer is not only a scholar of codependency and narcissism, she's been a victim of narcissism and healed from it. I'm grateful for her expertise and personal wisdom and highly recommend her books to my clients."
~ Jean 'Shayna' Lester, LMFT, Prison Chaplain and Spiritual Director

"Darlene Lancer has written an insightful and comprehensive book that is transformative for loved ones of narcissists. Like her books on shame and codependency, she remarkably breaks down deep psychological concepts into empathetic and practical strategies for anyone wanting to improve their relationship and/or decide whether to leave."
~ Sherry Gaba, LCSW, Author of *Love Smacked* and host of *The Fix Podcast*

Also By Darlene Lancer

DATING, LOVING, AND LEAVING A NARCISSIST

ESSENTIAL TOOLS FOR IMPROVING OR LEAVING NARCISSISTIC AND ABUSIVE RELATIONSHIPS

DARLENE LANCER

Copyright © 2022 Darlene Lancer, JD, LMFT

All rights reserved. No part of this publication may be reproduced, stored in a retrieval system, or transmitted by any means—electronic, mechanical, photographic (photocopying), recording, or otherwise—without prior permission in writing from the author.

The information in this book is intended to be educational and not for diagnosis, prescription, or treatment of any mental health disorder. Without a personal, individual, professional consultation with you, the author is unable to give you professional psychological advice. Hence, you understand that the material contained herein is general, and the author disclaims any personal liability, directly or indirectly for suggestions and information in this book. Darlene Lancer is an affiliate Amazon advertiser and receives fees for linking to Amazon.com.

Cover image by Nadia Forkosh
Cover design by Simon Hough
Printed in the United States of America
First Printing 2022
ISBN No. 978-0-578-37318-8
Carousel Books
Santa Monica, California
www.whatiscodependency.com

PREFACE

People the world over share with me the heartache from relationships with parents, partners, siblings, or lovers who have emotionally abandoned or abused them. I know how victims feel, having had a similar mother, spouse, brother, and boyfriend. Uniformly, they yearn for love that lies out of reach and vacillate between hope and pain, love and resentment, and staying or leaving. They live with anxiety and grow accustomed to self-sacrifice and emotional and, at times, physical abuse. Loving someone who is unable to show love or who alternates between care and abuse is confusing and heart-wrenching. It's also addictive.

My eBook, *Dealing with a Narcissist: 8 Steps to Raise Self-Esteem and Set Boundaries with Difficult People,* helped thousands of people understand and improve their relationship with a narcissist — or anyone who is antagonistic, selfish, and highly defensive. They often feel hurt and frustrated by the disregard for their feelings and needs and betrayed by the loving person they once knew who disappeared over time. Constant conflict, rejection, control, and criticism undermined their self-worth. Many gave up their studies, careers, hobbies, family ties, or friends and sank further into despair.

Leaving the relationship isn't an option for everyone. Some partners lack the courage, but many don't hesitate to say they love the narcissist and prefer to stay, if only they were more appreciated and respected. For other people, their priorities are parenting, financial concerns, co-parenting with an ex, or maintaining family ties. Whatever you choose to do, rebalancing the power in the relationship will facilitate either option as well as restore your mental and physical health.

I relate to the experiences of my readers and clients. My recovery started in 1979 when I sought help for an abusive, personality-disordered, alcoholic husband. I'd given up so much of myself in my relationship that I became isolated from friends and family. I didn't know that my self-worth was nil and was surprised to learn that *I had a problem*. I had stopped trying new things and couldn't take pleasure in activities by myself — even watching television! I lost touch with my feelings and never considered my needs. Bit by bit, I was dying inside, so slowly that I didn't notice.

I had a bad case of the "if only's" — "if only he would change." Instead of initiating, I reacted. Instead of setting limits, I accepted his blame and sought to understand and help him. I excused broken promises, rationalized, and continued to adapt. It never occurred to me to put my energy into developing myself; instead, I tried harder to make things work.

After seeking help, I discovered that I was the one who had to change. I steadily grew my self-esteem, became more assertive, and set boundaries. I took responsibility for my happiness and no longer reacted to my husband. In short, I recovered my "Self." By accessing my power, his power over me diminished. The entire relationship improved. Eventually, I realized that I deserved more than my husband could provide and left my marriage and profession as an attorney to become an author and psychotherapist, what I'd always wanted to do and more suited to my real Self.

If you're under the spell of an abuser, your perceptions and autonomy are compromised. To change, it's essential to see reality for what it is. Recent research on narcissism and huge demand for a paperback prompted me to share new information and substantially expand the eBook, add new sections, and also cover dating and ending a relationship with a narcissist.

I've been empowering people to unshackle and stand up for themselves for over three decades. I trust that you, too, will reclaim yourself and your power by following the suggestions in this book. I sincerely hope that my words, training, research, and personal and professional experience embolden your heart and soul and lead you back to your Self.

Darlene Lancer

CONTENTS

INTRODUCTION

This is a workbook designed to both inform and help you take action, build your self-esteem, and improve your communication skills and relationship, whether the person you love fully qualifies as a narcissist or not. Doing the exercises can increase your confidence and relationship satisfaction, help you resolve any ambivalence about staying in your relationship, and provide you with strength if you decide to leave.

The term "narcissism" is commonly used to describe personality traits among the general population. However, there are specific criteria for diagnosing narcissistic personality disorder. This book can help you decide whether your loved one meets those criteria. Regardless, the same guidelines and suggestions apply and also pertain to a relationship with a spouse, child, friend, parent, sibling, or other relative or co-worker.

Gaining an in-depth comprehension of the disorder, its cause, and underlying features are the focus of the first three chapters. The different types of narcissists, including narcissistic parents, and their behaviors, motivations, and traits are covered. Narcissistic defenses and all varieties and even the subtlest forms of abuse are explained.

Chapters 4 and 5 look at the typical personality of people who love narcissists. Some aspects of this profile may not fit you, but understanding yourself is where your personal growth lies.

Chapters 6-9 center on the relationship, starting with dating and loving a narcissist. Many partners of narcissists have repeatedly been emotionally abandoned. By examining the signs and attraction to narcissists, you can avoid repeating that pattern. Issues such as control, intimacy, emotional unavailability, love-bombing, ghosting, and gaslighting are covered. Chapter 7 explores whether a narcissist is capable of love and how to make a determination. Chapters 8 and 9 are about taking action. A blueprint is laid out for you to follow in order to change your reactions, the relationship dynamics, and the balance of power. Chapter 9 details specific steps, a game plan, and scripts you can practice to effectively communicate and set boundaries with a narcissist, plus advice for navigating couples therapy.

Chapters 10-12 discuss leaving your relationship and moving on. They cover how to decide, why it's so difficult, what to expect, such as hoovering, flying monkeys, and divorce tactics, plus practical strategies you can implement. Finally, the stages of recovery are set forth along with valuable guidance for creating a single life that may include dating and therapy.

Throughout this book, there are 21 "*Innercises*" designed to identify your beliefs and behaviors that keep you stuck in an abusive relationship. There are also checklists, strategies, and things you can do to better your relationship with yourself and the narcissist. To be gender-neutral, I refer to "narcissist" and "your partner." As you read try substituting the name of your loved one. Some of the narcissistic behaviors described may not pertain to him or her. Use suggestions that apply and overlook those that don't. If you review any sections that are difficult to absorb later, you may find them more meaningful.

A book does not replace professional advice or counseling with a psychotherapist who is familiar with narcissistic relationships. You may need support to hold your ground if abuse increases as the narcissist tries to reassert power. But there's a lot you can do on your own and witness positive results. If you're being physically abused, get help immediately.

By persevering, you'll start to feel more connected to yourself and less reactive to the narcissist. You'll be able to handle situations with greater wisdom, ease, and effectiveness. Putting the suggestions into practice will yield positive changes in you and, in time, your relationship. In fact, you might see a difference in all your relationships. I sincerely believe that reading this book and doing the exercises will enlighten and en-*courage* you to take the steps to enhance your well-being and your relationship.

Chapter 1

WHAT IS NARCISSISM?

We use the term "narcissism" to describe personality traits of inordinate self-love, arrogance, and vanity. Havelock Ellis (1859–1939) was the first to use the term in a psychological context (1898). Freud later wrote about primary narcissism as an initial developmental stage. He used that term to describe the egocentricity of young children before they learn reciprocity and the value of others' perspectives. Narcissism also describes adults who lack those traits. When narcissism is pervasive and enduring, it constitutes a personality disorder, according to the American Psychiatric Association's *Diagnostic and Statistical Manual of Mental Disorders* (DSM),[1] discussed later on in this chapter.

Ellis referred to the Greek myth of Narcissus and Echo as told by the Roman poet Ovid.[2] This poignant myth crystallizes the tragic problem of relationships with narcissists. Narcissus was a beautiful hunter who broke the hearts of many women who loved him. Arrogant and aloof, he viewed them with disdain.

Meanwhile, the beautiful forest nymph Echo had incurred the ire of the goddess Juno for talking too much. Juno punished Echo by depriving her of free expression. From then on, she could utter only the words she had just heard from others.

Echo spotted Narcissus and became infatuated with the handsome young man. She followed him, longing for his attention, but he was fixated on himself. She wanted to call out to him, but of course, she couldn't. One day, Narcissus became separated from his hunting companions and called out, "Is anyone there?" Echo repeated his words. Startled, he said, "Come here," which she echoed. Echo jubilantly rushed to Narcissus, only to be spurned by his words: "Hands off! May I die before you enjoy my body."[3] Humiliated and rejected, Echo fled in shame. Nevertheless, her love for Narcissus grew.

Witnessing this, Nemesis, the goddess of revenge, decided to punish Narcissus by putting a spell on him. When Narcissus noticed his reflection in a pool of water, unaware it was his own. Love overtook him. He became absorbed with his beauty and convinced he'd finally found someone worthy of his love.

Unable to get Narcissus's attention, Echo's obsession and depression grew. Over the years, she lost her youth and beauty, pining away for the unattainable Narcissus. He eventually committed suicide, consumed by his impossible love, leaving only a flower in his name. Echo wasted away, leaving only her echoing voice.

As in the myth, narcissists and their partners become sadly locked in a painful drama. The relationship brings anguish for both. Neither feels satisfied nor sufficiently loved. But the narcissist feels superior and irreproachable and hence lays the blame on their Echo partner, who too often, readily agrees.

Narcissists project their shortcomings on their partners, whom they depend upon to reflect their positive self-image. They're arrogantly dismissive and rude. Echo can't speak or advocate for herself (regardless of her gender). She lacks her own voice and can only mimic the words of others, whom she idealizes. The children and partners of narcissists share Echo's experience of feeling rejected, invisible, and unheard. They long to be seen, to have their needs met, and their love returned. Even though Narcissus and Echo both long for love, Narcissus can neither give love nor receive the love that Echo offers.

THE CONTINUUM OF NARCISSISM

All personality traits, including narcissism, range on a continuum from mild to severe and from primitive to mature. Narcissism can be healthy, or sub-clinical in a self-centered person with some narcissistic traits, or diagnostic of full-blown narcissistic personality disorder (NPD). But even NPD ranges from mild to severe. Stories on the Internet about narcissists often describe people with extreme NPD who may also have sociopathic traits.

Early in my recovery from codependency, I dreamt that I needed to be more narcissistic. The problem was that my opinion of myself wasn't high enough. Codependents must learn to think more highly of themselves, grow their self-esteem, and set boundaries that reflect self-care. They may consider that to be selfish or overly self-involved, but this is different from narcissism. Narcissists do the opposite. Most narcissists rarely look at themselves, take responsibility, or feel a need to improve. Doing so or seeking help would be an admission of imperfection — that they're flawed. Instead, they blame others.

Freud identified a natural, narcissistic stage of child development when toddlers feel they own the world. They can suddenly walk and want to explore everything. Freud noted that a certain amount of self-focus and self-regard is essential to a healthy ego structure. During normal development, a child advances from this primary narcissism to the oedipal phase when they can desire others and eventually mature to form mutually reciprocal relationships. Those who are unable to progress in their ability to love remain highly sensitive to wounding, have unstable relationships, and employ destructive and psychotic defenses not grounded in external reality. Mature individuals can idealize and love romantic partners. Many immature people fall somewhere in between; they're defensive and have unstable boundaries with others.

Psychoanalyst Heinz Kohut (1913–1981) believed that healthy narcissism begins in infancy and continues to develop throughout our lives. Interruption of that development accounts for pathological narcissism. Individuals with NPD get arrested in early development and don't mature beyond it. Another psychoanalyst, Otto Kernberg (b. 1928), disagreed with this Kohut's model. He viewed pathological narcissism as distinct from both primary and healthy narcissism, which he referred to as self-esteem.

People with too much or too little egocentricity are at greater risk for psychological disorders. With healthy narcissism, you can feel confident without arrogance. It enables you to have sufficient pride and self-investment to fuel self-efficacy to accomplish your goals. Jack Welch, Oprah, Intel founder Andy Grove, and George Soros are all successful individuals who exemplify healthy narcissism. They're charismatic, confident leaders who developed their talents, persevered to pursue their goals, and are empathic, socially skillful, authentic, generous, assertive, and hold others accountable.

Such self-esteem enhances your life, creativity, resilience, and mood. You expect to succeed and likely will, and you can also tolerate disappointment and failure. You're not defensive and can accept feedback. You ask for and pursue what you want and enjoy your activities and achievements. Your self-regard empowers you to confront abuse and disrespect. Feeling worthy, you don't hesitate to say no and set boundaries. Still, however, you have empathy and consideration for others. Even though you strive to attain your wants and needs, you don't manipulate, control, seek revenge, envy, or exploit other people.

Only about 6 percent of the population could be diagnosed with NPD, with males accounting for 50-75 percent of the cases.[4] Some researchers believe that earlier studies were inaccurate and that the prevalence is only about 1 percent. The personality disorder wasn't categorized as a disorder by the American Psychiatric Association until 1980 because psychologists and psychiatrists felt that too many people shared some of the traits and it was difficult to diagnose.

THE CAUSE OF NARCISSISM

Narcissists can be hard to empathize with, but they didn't choose to be that way; they bear scars from childhood. Kohut believed that insufficient nurturing from their mothers (or other early caregivers) arrested their natural development. Without empathic parental interactions, they lacked modeling, which stunted their emotional capacity to empathize. Empathetic matching of feelings is also essential for the healthy development of the self. Instead of feeling loved and accepted for who they were, they grew up praised only for their performance and for being the best, creating a belief that their true self was unlovable. Who they were and what they did were never good enough.

Kernberg emphasized the significance of veiled parental aggression expressed with harshness or criticism stemming from anger, envy, hate, or indifference. Such parents may be domineering, exploitative, or manipulative causing a humiliating "narcissistic injury" to their children's vulnerable feelings and needs. Feeling shamed and powerless, children create an ideal one that is superior to other people to protect their self-image. They then strive to achieve their perfectionistic ideal in ways that reflect their personality and skills. But because narcissists' achievements and beliefs aren't connected to their true self, they need constant validation for their fabricated self.

Social learning theorists argue that narcissism results from a lack of modeling and overindulgent parenting, which teaches children to feel superior and entitled irrespective of their behavior.[5] However, studies show that leniency can similarly result in healthy narcissism. But when psychological control is present, such as guilt induction and withdrawal of love, children don't develop a solid self because they're focused on gaining external approval.[6] They learn that love and involvement depend on conforming to parental needs and expectations and don't receive support for an emerging, autonomous self. Another view is that narcissism can result when a child is extremely close to an overly indulgent mother who encourages dependency, incompetence, and lack of self-reliance.

Some families have a pervasive attitude of superiority over other people, which children adopt. Other parents provide material benefits to their children, but the family lives in an emotional vacuum. The children feel emotionally abandoned and ignored. As adults, they may not remember feeling unhappy or lonely because they were involved with school, siblings, or friends, but they also don't recall any parental understanding or warmth. Whether critical, indulgent, or emotionally absent, different theories portray a mother (or another primary caregiver) unable to experience her child as a separate individual and to provide sufficient empathy, mirroring, or opportunity for idealization.

Studies have shown that results vary depending upon a child's personality. Although parenting styles affect the development of healthy narcissism, the effect on the development of unhealthy narcissism depends on the child's initial proclivity towards narcissism.[7] Although more research is needed, twin studies reveal a strong genetic component in narcissistic behaviors; the correlation ranges from 37 to 77 percent with a median of 47 percent.[8]

DIAGNOSTIC CRITERIA FOR NPD

Nonprofessionals often label people who show just a few narcissistic traits as having NPD, but just because someone is vain, arrogant, or selfish does not make them a narcissist. The clinical diagnostic criteria for NPD as specified in DSM are summarized as follows:

Individuals with NPD lack empathy, need admiration from others, and are grandiose (sometimes expressed only in fantasy), as indicated by at least five of the following nine characteristics:

1. Have a grandiose sense of self-importance and exaggerate achievements and talents
2. Dream of unlimited power, success, brilliance, beauty, or ideal love
3. Lack empathy for the feelings and needs of others
4. Require excessive admiration

5. Believe they're special and unique and can only be understood by, or should associate with, other special or high-status people (or institutions)
6. Unreasonably expect special and/or favorable treatment or compliance with their wishes
7. Exploit and take advantage of others to achieve personal ends
8. Envy others or believe others are envious of them
9. Have "an attitude" of arrogance or act that way

The range of NPD varies in severity from narcissists with only five of the diagnostic traits to those who strongly manifest all nine symptoms. Narcissists who have an excessive sense of entitlement and are exploitative of others make the most difficult partners. To measure narcissistic traits, you can take a quiz called the Narcissistic Personality Inventory,[9] but it's not determinative of whether you have NPD.

TYPES OF NARCISSISTS

Some narcissists emphasize one personality trait more than others. One person with a jovial personality might always show-off and need to be the center of attention, while another narcissist might be a vindictive bully, a demander of special treatment, an imperious authoritarian, or an exacting know-it-all, succinctly articulated by Madonna: "Listen, everyone is entitled to my opinion."

Regardless of the type relationships with narcissists are hurtful. Identifying the type of narcissist, however, can help you know whom you're dealing with and what to expect. Researchers have identified four major types: grandiose, vulnerable, communal, and malignant. Others are listed below.

The Grandiose Narcissist

For years, research mainly focused on the familiar, exhibitionistic narcissists who seek the limelight. The DSM describes these types as "Exhibitionist Narcissists." Some public figures and celebrities exemplify these extroverted narcissists who are grandiose and crave attention. Psychologist and radio host Dr. Wendy Walsh said, "Narcissistic personality disorder is not only accepted in the entertainment industry, it's often a requirement."[10] They're the boastful *grandiose* narcissists — public figures and big stars in films. You can spot those charming, attention-seeking extroverts, whose vanity and boldness are at times obnoxious and shameless. They're described in the DSM.

They're self-absorbed, entitled, callous, exploitative, authoritarian, and aggressive. Some are physically abusive. These unempathetic, arrogant narcissists think highly of themselves but spare no disdain for others. Helped by their extroversion, they report high self-esteem and satisfaction with their lives despite the pain they cause others. They outwardly seek acclaim and domination. Even in love, they seek power. Many maintain relationships, notwithstanding the lack of intimacy and the unhappiness of their partners, who are easily seduced by their charisma and boldness.

These narcissists want to be the center of attention. They like to talk about themselves, and your job is to be a good audience. Not only do they command your attention, but they also try to impress you by bragging about their accomplishments. All this suggests that they're trying to convince themselves that their hidden self-loathing and feelings of inferiority don't exist. To compensate, they embellish their stories, seek to associate with high-status people and institutions, and harbor disdain for those seen as inferior.

The Vulnerable Narcissist

Psychoanalyst James Masterson (1926–2010) identified a "closet narcissist" as someone with a deflated, inadequate self-perception, a sense of depression, and inner emptiness.[11] This subtype has also been referred to as a "covert narcissist" or "introverted narcissist," and on the surface may be hard to identify. Researchers now call them "vulnerable narcissists."

Like their grandiose kin, vulnerable narcissists are self-absorbed, entitled, exploitative, unempathetic, *manipulative,* and aggressive. But, despite sharing core traits, in a behavioral sense, the vulnerable narcissist is the antithesis of the exhibitionist narcissist. They may appear shy, humble, or anxious and believe they're uniquely sensitive. They have difficulty managing their perceptions, moods, and emotions.

All narcissists react poorly to criticism, but the vulnerables have the thinnest skin of all. They require reinforcement for their grandiose self-image and are highly defensive when perceived criticism triggers their negative opinion of themselves. While exhibitionist narcissists claim your attention, vulnerables fear criticism so much that they shy away from attention, yet feel slighted when they don't get it. Instead of working the room, they're self-absorbed.

Gratification for vulnerable narcissists can be indirect through their emotional investment in people they admire. Some play the role of victim and martyr. They take things personally and feel special, distrustful, mistreated, unappreciated, and misunderstood. Although they devalue themselves, they dream of greatness and wonder why people don't understand them and appreciate their specialness. They often feel that the world at large hasn't sufficiently recognized their uniqueness. Lacking the aggressiveness of the exhibitionistic narcissist, they're more prone to depression and feeling like things are falling apart.

Normal introverts are generally good listeners, but not vulnerable narcissists. They consider others boring or ignorant. Instead of bragging openly, they display a reserved smugness and judge everyone as inferior. They might act aloof and disinterested or make dismissive or discounting gestures, like looking away, sighing, yawning impolitely, or acting bored.

Rather than giving orders, vulnerable narcissists get their way indirectly through quiet cruelty and manipulative, passive-aggressive behavior. They may often be late, forgetful, make empty promises, and take pleasure in disappointing you. Or they may agree to plans but then never follow through or pretend that they never agreed in the first place.

Instead of the aggressive and exploitative nature of extroverted narcissists, vulnerables have feelings of neglect or belittlement, hypersensitivity, anxiety, and delusions of persecution. They add self-pity to their toolkit to control you and get attention. Rather than put you down directly, they play the victim even when they've gotten their way and are more likely to express envy. They have an attitude that "life is unfair"; others' achievements are attributed to privilege, while their failings are other people's fault.

You can get sucked into trying to console and help this manipulative martyr but to no avail. They exploit your empathy with sob stories of their misfortunes. You feel sympathetic and want to rescue them from their misery, but end up self-sacrificing and feeling responsible for their feelings and care. They manipulate you with their dependency, which may include threats of suicide or self-destructive behavior. Beware of flattery about how important you are to them and isolation from your other friends and family.

In contrast to grandiose narcissists, vulnerable narcissists lack positive relationships. They're threat-oriented and distrustful, not bold and domineering. Their attachment style, discussed in chapter 2, is more avoidant and anxious. To a much greater degree, they lack autonomy, have imposter syndrome, display a weak sense of self, and feel self-alienated and unable to master their environment.[12] They withdraw from others with hostile blame and resentment, internalizing their narcissism. Rather than feeling confident and self-satisfied, vulnerable narcissists are insecure and unhappy with their lives. They experience more distress, anxiety, guilt, depression, hypersensitivity, and shame.

Vulnerables are conflicted, holding both inflated and negative irrational views of themselves, the latter of which they project onto other people, their lives, and the future. Their negative emotionality can lead to a bitter *neurotic* aversion to personal growth.

The Communal Narcissist

This third type of narcissism can be difficult to identify. It was named only recently. Communal narcissists value warmth, agreeableness, and relatedness. They see themselves and want to be seen as being extremely trustworthy and supportive, and they try to achieve this through friendliness and kindness.

Like the grandiose narcissist, they're outgoing. But rather than be seen as the smartest and most powerful, a communal narcissist wants to be seen as the most giving and helpful. A communal narcissist's vain selflessness is no less selfish than a grandiose narcissist. They have similar motives for grandiosity, esteem, entitlement, and power, although each employs distinct behaviors to achieve them.

Even though they may appear to genuinely care for others and be active in philanthropy or a helping profession, their endeavors are motivated by their need for recognition, power over others, or egotistical pride. They behave self-righteously superior or moralistic, or as an exploited, resentful victim of all their unrequited giving. They may give without asking permission. When the hypocrisy of the communal narcissist becomes evident, however, they suffer a bigger fall than a grandiose narcissist would.

The Malignant Narcissist

Someone with narcissistic traits who behaves in a malicious, aggressive, and hostile manner is considered to have malignant narcissism. "Malignant narcissists" are at the extreme end of the continuum, exhibiting signs of antisocial behavior. They're cruel and vindictive when they feel threatened or don't get what they want. Malignant narcissists are paranoid, immoral, and sadistic. They're not bothered by guilt and enjoy creating chaos, taking people down, and inflicting pain. They can be so competitive and unprincipled that they engage in antisocial behavior. Paranoia puts them in a defensive-attack mode as a means of self-protection. These narcissists aren't necessarily grandiose, extroverted, or neurotic, but are closely related to sociopathy, described below.[13]

Other Classifications of Narcissists

Psychologist Theodore Millon (1928–2014) classified five other types of narcissists:[14]

1. **The Unprincipled Narcissist:** This type lacks a conscience and acts in an immoral, shady, or dishonest manner when dealing with others, whom the narcissist also tries to outsmart.
2. **The Amorous Narcissist:** Amorous narcissists are the consummate Don Juan or Mati Hari, using charm and seduction to lure their sexual conquests, whom they exploit and discard. Some lie and con, all to enhance their egos and their power.
3. **The Compensatory Narcissist:** This type lives in an imaginary world, where they're perpetually center stage, seeking admiration for fabricated or exaggerated accomplishments.
4. **The Fanatic Narcissist:** Fanatic narcissists suffer from paranoia and low self-esteem, which motivates them to seek recognition and admiration.
5. **The Elitist Narcissist:** These narcissists presume special status for their imagined achievements and live a self-inflated, "as-if" life that bears little resemblance to reality. They're opportunists and are constantly aggrandizing and marketing themselves to gain prestige and climb the corporate or social ladder. They're competitive and think nothing of trampling over others to achieve their ends.

Addicts Aren't Necessarily Narcissists

Addicts are characteristically self-centered, and so they may also display the symptoms of narcissism. Addiction is a disease marked by obsession and compulsive behavior regarding what the addict craves, which takes precedence over the feelings and needs of other people. Rather than boasting and acting needless, many addicts are needy and dependent. If they don't also have NPD, their behavior can change when they're abstinent or sober and in recovery from their addiction.

Narcissists Aren't Necessarily Sociopaths

The more extreme the narcissism, the more the personality disorder begins to resemble Antisocial Personality Disorder (APD), commonly known as sociopathy – the condition of someone who is a sociopath. The diagnosis also includes psychopaths because they have many traits in common. There is an axiom that sociopaths are *made*, while psychopaths are *born*, meaning the latter has a genetic cause, and the former stems from environmental factors such as childhood abuse, neglect, and addiction in the family.

The diagnostic criteria for APD specify that individuals must have a conduct disorder before the age of 15 and show disregard for and violation of the rights of others, plus at least three of the following traits:

1. Dishonesty, such as lying, using aliases, or conning for personal gain or pleasure
2. Impulsivity
3. Irritability and aggression with repeated fights or assaults
4. Reckless disregard for the safety of self and others
5. Repeated violation of criminal laws
6. Failure to meet adult responsibilities such as sustained work and paying bills
7. Lack of sincere guilt or remorse — indifference to or rationalizing the harm they cause

Although not required for the diagnosis, sociopaths and psychopaths, like narcissists, are also arrogant and contemptuous of other people. If the likelihood of being caught were low, all three would cheat on a test. Like narcissists, sociopaths and psychopaths can be aggressive and have interpersonal problems. They lack the somewhat hereditable trait of "agreeableness," as scored on the Big Five Personality Test,[15] which requires compliance and being trustworthy, unselfish, kind, direct, and modest — all important to sustain relationships. They also share a lack of empathy, as they're exploitative, entitled, unreliable, self-centered, insincere, dishonest, and needing control.

All three lack emotional empathy, but narcissists score highest on cognitive empathy.[16] The fact that these people are insensitive to others' feelings while retaining the ability to assess others' emotions allows them to strategically manipulate people and ignore the harm they inflict. When researchers showed subjects different facial expressions, narcissists and psychopaths generally felt positive looking at sad and angry faces, but in particular, psychopaths liked seeing fearful faces and felt negative seeing happy images.[17]

When malignant narcissists and sociopaths are abusive, they believe they're justified and deny responsibility for their behavior. They lack insight and emotional empathy and responsiveness. However, high-functioning, intelligent individuals can feign appropriate emotional reactions; these are learned behaviors and not sincerely felt. Narcissists who have fewer and less severe symptoms, along with "narcissistic" people who don't have full-blown NPD, can have insight, guilt, and remorse. They care about their families and the ability to emotionally connect, as well as love.

Psychopaths are considered to be more heartless, dangerous, and aggressive than sociopaths. They have malformed or damaged brains in the area responsible for emotional regulation and impulse control. They're unable to form real relationships other than superficial ones with people they can exploit. Their emotional range is limited to anger, although they can be glib and charming. They can maintain some semblance of work. In contrast to sociopaths and narcissists, psychopaths are calculating and might plan an attack for months. A narcissist is more likely to react sooner, using intimidation and lies. Narcissists often deceive themselves when they lie, while sociopaths consciously lie with intention.[18]

Unlike most narcissists, sociopaths can't fit into society or maintain a job, and although they can form attachments, their family life is chaotic. They're more impulsive and prone to rage than psychopaths, and thus their crimes are more random and unplanned. They're lazy and try to swindle, steal, or exploit others financially. In tests, sociopaths scored higher than narcissists in immorality, erratic lifestyle, sexual activity, aggression, poor well-being, and antisocial behavior.[19]

While people with APD qualify as narcissists, not all narcissists are sociopaths. Narcissists' main satisfaction is the validation of others. In contrast, sociopaths and psychopaths are indifferent to approval, making them more dangerous. They'll take greater risks and are more cunning and manipulative because their ego isn't always at stake. They might cheat even when there's more risk involved. If found out, people with APD feel no guilt and don't care, whereas narcissists will blame others or rationalize their actions.

Additionally, narcissists' anxiety and insecurity make them more fragile. Sociopaths don't have any real personality. They're the ultimate con artists and can take on any persona that suits them. They may be harder to spot because they're not trying to impress you, get attention, or win your approval unless it serves their agenda. Instead of bragging, their conversation might center on you rather than on themselves, and they can even be self-effacing and apologetic when doing so serves their goal.

Finally, although all three may be motivated to win at all costs, narcissists are more interested in what you think of them. They need others' admiration. This makes them dependent on others and capable of being manipulated. While narcissists can be exploitative, they often work hard to achieve their aims or perfection and they're able to sustain monogamous relationships. They're less likely to divorce their spouse than a sociopath, who might leave or vanish if they're exposed or don't get what they want.

THE CORE OF NARCISSISM

Using new techniques, recent studies have attempted to isolate a singular, unifying trait among narcissists. Researchers examined narcissism by testing distinct personality traits. Two models have recently emerged: one is based on personality and the other on an integrative, transactional approach.

The Trifurcated Model

The trifurcated model shows that narcissism centers on three personality traits: agentic extraversion, disagreeableness, and neuroticism.[20] ("Agentic" refers to extroverts who are authoritative, bold go-getters who pursue acclaim, achievement, and leadership.)

Trifurcated Model of Narcissism (TMN)

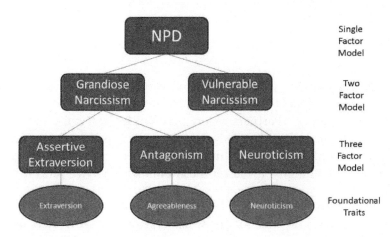

Disagreeableness is the only personality trait common to both types among the Big Five personality traits.[21] Vulnerable and grandiose narcissists express antagonism differently. The former are more hostile and distrustful, while the latter are more immodest and domineering. The trifurcated model illuminates the core of narcissism to be *interpersonal antagonism, a trait* shared by grandiose and vulnerable narcissists. It's characterized by manipulativeness, hostility, entitlement, callousness, and anger.[22]

The Spectrum Model

In contrast, the spectrum model shows that narcissism exists on a spectrum from grandiose to vulnerable.[23] The model demonstrates how NPD varies in severity and how traits manifest.

Narcissists' differing personalities express diverse qualities at various times. This model captures a fluid, functional analysis that is representative of real life. It displays both types of narcissism as sharing a common core of *entitled self-importance.*

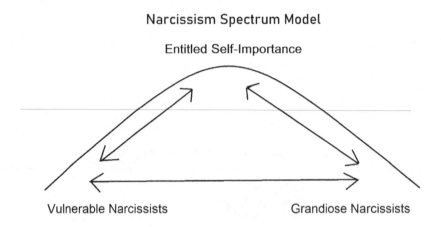

Narcissism Spectrum Model

Entitled Self-Importance

Vulnerable Narcissists   Grandiose Narcissists

This core consists of arrogance, self-involvement, and entitlement. Narcissists believe that they and their needs are special and take precedence over those of others. Partners report that entitlement is the most toxic element in their relationships. More entitlement and risk-taking increase professional and interpersonal difficulties. The diagram shows that the greater the vulnerability, the lesser the grandiosity and vice versa.

Distinguishing Types of Narcissists

If you have a hard time identifying which type of narcissist you're dealing with, it might be because grandiose narcissists present a mixed bag. They oscillate between states of grandiosity and vulnerability. Greater grandiosity indicates greater instability and likelihood of fluctuation. For example, grandiose narcissists may show vulnerability and emotionality (usually anger) when their success is thwarted or their self-image is under attack. While they feel and function better than vulnerable narcissists and can be socially engaging when they choose, their antagonism and entitlement create problems and jeopardize relationships. Little evidence exists to show that vulnerable narcissists exhibit grandiosity.[24]

In sum, narcissism ranges on a spectrum from domineering and extraverted to introverted and neurotic. The core traits of narcissism are antagonism, self-importance, and entitlement. These result in narcissists being disagreeable and uncooperative partners both at home or at work. Because other personality types can be antagonistic, the spectrum model is useful in that it identifies self-important entitlement as the core of narcissism, contrasting it with sociopathy, borderline personality disorder,[25] and other personality disorders.

Chapter 2

NARCISSUS: UNDERSTANDING A NARCISSIST

Narcissists' tendency toward grandiosity, controlling their feelings (not to be confused with healthy self-control), and exercising power over others doesn't help them cope with life's issues because these behaviors are defensive and not connected to their true self. Although many narcissists may seem to have strong personalities, in the end, they all are very vulnerable.

What they present is their protective armor, built up over years of denial. Internally, they suffer from profound alienation, emptiness, powerlessness, and lack of meaning. As prisoners of their need for specialness and perfection, they're not free to be spontaneous, make mistakes, behave foolishly, weep, or experience love and joy. The pursuit of their *ideal* self weakens their true self; but narcissists don't have much of a self at all. They live within their imagination, sealed off from a healthy social life and real intimacy. Sadly, they're unable to appreciate the love they do get, and they alienate those who give it.

They have disdain for any sign of weakness or vulnerability because they were shamed for those childhood feelings. To them feeling vulnerable not only suggests weakness and inferiority but also heightens their awareness of their need for someone and their anticipation of being hurt, rejected, controlled, or humiliated as they once were. Thus, vulnerable feelings, particularly shame, sadness, loneliness, and fear, are intolerable. They relegate them to their unconscious and eliminate uncomfortable feelings by demonstrating independence, courage, and strength — ideals with which they identify. In the process, they bury their true self, which would be more balanced. They don't often experience depression unless they suffer a major loss.

Gender Differences

Male narcissists outnumber female narcissists nearly three to one. Due to cultural biases, male narcissists are more assertive than their female counterparts and more likely to strive for wealth, power, and success in their work. The distrustful male child, in reaction to emotional abandonment and humiliation by his parents, determines that self-sufficiency is the highest goal: "I will need nothing from anyone." As adults, they get what they want through influence and money without needing to be in the humiliating position of asking for help or being indebted or dependent on anyone who might hurt or control them. Research also indicates that men are more likely than women to exploit others and feel self-entitled.[26]

Narcissism is on the rise in women, as is narcissism in general.[27] Female narcissists may be caregiving, covert or communal narcissists or compensatory narcissists who see themselves as playing the leading role. For example, she may behave like the has-been star Norma Desmond in the movie and play, *Sunset Boulevard*, singing, "With One Look." Both genders are equally exhibitionistic and self-absorbed. Women generally focus more on their appearance. They might dress provocatively and have exaggerated confidence in their looks or talents.

Female narcissists may insist on designer clothes, the best dermatologist, hairdresser, and perhaps plastic surgeon. They enjoy selfies, being professionally photographed, and spend an inordinate amount of time on hair, make-up, and clothes. More than males, female narcissists express entitlement by believing, "I deserve the best, and you owe me." One wife expected her husband to draw her bath at a precise temperature, take her only to five-star restaurants, and have his car stocked with anything she might need. He felt whatever he did was not right or enough. Because of their unrealistic, selfish expectations, these women may complain like martyred victims. ("It's always my fault," or "I can't do anything right.")

Both male and female narcissists employ forms of seduction such as flattery and flirtation, which allow them to attract a partner while retaining control. More often men give gifts and women dress provocatively.

UNDERLYING FEATURES

Aside from symptomatic behavior discussed in the next chapter, understanding some of the underlying features of narcissism can help you envision what drives a narcissist in their thinking and actions.

Shame and Impaired Self-Esteem

People think "high self-esteem" is optimal. But esteem that relies on others' opinions isn't *self-esteem*. It's "other-esteem," which isn't viable or healthy. So, I describe self-esteem as either healthy or *impaired*.

Ranking narcissists' self-esteem as high is misleading because it's generally inflated and unrelated to objective reality. Additionally, it's fragile and easily deflated. Healthy self-esteem is stable and not so reactive to the environment. It's non-hierarchical and not based on feeling superior to others, nor is it associated with aggression and relationship problems. People with healthy self-esteem aren't aggressive and have fewer relationship conflicts. They're able to compromise and get along.

The fact that narcissists brag, exaggerate, and lie about their greatness suggests that they're trying to convince themselves or have successfully hidden their feelings of self-loathing and inferiority. Underneath their bravado lies *toxic, internalized shame,*[28] that's often unconscious. Shame makes narcissists feel insecure and inadequate – vulnerable feelings that they deny to themselves and others. This is one reason that they can't take criticism, responsibility, dissent, or negative feedback, even when meant to be constructive. Instead, they demand unconditional, positive regard from others.

Their extravagant plans, inflated accomplishments, and self-serving self-descriptions are attempts to transcend feelings of shame, to cover up that they're flawed, inadequate, or a failure. They may embarrass family and friends with their boasting or obnoxious sense of entitlement, such as monopolizing the conversation, interrupting others, or being rude to waiters and clerks. This entitled attitude, however, is an attempt to compensate for unconscious feelings of deprivation and inferiority, which become intolerable when their needs aren't met or their self-bestowed privileges respected. To obtain what they want, they might exploit others, regardless of the consequences.

Some narcissists can be exceptionally beautiful, talented, powerful, or successful in their field. Many narcissists work hard to prove themselves and achieve celebrity, wealth, influence, and/or prestige. They appear enviably calm, confident, in control, or superior, aloof, and unresponsive. Nonetheless, they're insecure and extremely dependent upon success, prestige, and others' validation. Even narcissists who achieve recognition and success can't enjoy it because what they've accomplished is never good enough.

Due to their inner shame, they're hypersensitive to any imagined slight or perceived challenge to their illusion of being the best. They dread being considered a fraud, having their shortcomings revealed, their opinions or authority questioned, or their self-esteem or pride tarnished.

Impaired View of Self and Others

How you develop as a whole person, separate from others, depends on the caretaking you received in the earliest months and years of your life. Good enough parenting and mirroring from a parent help develop your identity. How you perceive yourself and others is integrally related. Narcissists have difficulty seeing themselves and others accurately as explained below, which seriously impairs their relationships.

Whole Object Constancy

Object constancy is your ability to see yourself (self-constancy) and another person (object constancy) in a whole, cohesive and realistic manner with positive and negative traits at the same time. Toddlers develop this perspective by experiencing that mommy (or daddy) will always be there and sufficiently meet their needs. This security enables a child to trust their mother and retain her loving, maternal feelings when she's gone. Her consistency allows him to develop a constant good image of her.

Self and object constancy permit you to accept and value yourself and others despite imperfections. It mitigates the panic and fury you might feel when you're hurt or your needs aren't met. Try recalling the good traits of people close to you even when you're angry at them. You can then forgive your own mistakes and flaws and theirs because you realize that the good outweighs the bad. Rather than rage or have a toddler-worthy temper tantrum, you're able to talk about your feelings. Without this capacity, you're unable to love or even like yourself or others as whole persons. Yet, by clearly seeing the whole person, you may determine that the bad outweighs the good.

Narcissists, to varying degrees, lack self and object constancy. Their self-identity fluctuates and depends on other people. Thus, they scan the environment and manipulate interactions to feel okay. To them, the environment is responsible for their good feelings as well as their profound feelings of emptiness. They project negative aspects of themselves and responsibility for their behavior onto other people so they can maintain their idealized, grandiose self-image. They deny, distort, and devalue facts, attributes, and feelings that contradict or weaken their feelings of superiority and perfection. Their reality differs from yours, and you can't convince them otherwise.

Splitting

When mothers insufficiently care for and attune to their babies, infants experience strong feelings of dread and negativity. Mommy becomes bad and abandoning, and instead of developing whole-person perceptions and object constancy, infants develop the defense of splitting between what they perceive as a good and bad mommy. Splitting keeps the "good" and loved aspects of a parent separate from the "bad" and hated aspects of him or her. Mommy can be idealized and loved without the negative feelings intruding, or she can be devalued and the good feelings are repressed.

In relationships, splitting manifests as seeing yourself or your partner as being wonderful one moment and then being terrible next. At times, you and your partner may idealize and then devalue each other when either of you are disappointed. When this splitting happens, it's impossible to see ourselves or others as a realistic combination of positive and negative qualities, because it impairs our ability to hold conflicting views or perceive things from different perspectives. We see things as black or white, good or bad.

Narcissists split in predictable ways. In a narcissist's mind, things are good or bad with no middle ground. They always believe they're either succeeding or failing, and their mood fluctuates accordingly. They make no room for mistakes or mediocrity, a mindset that primes them for rage. Similarly, when they feel slighted or disappointed with you, you rapidly lose all positive qualities and become dispensable. You're nothing but bad. When they can't maintain their grandiose self-image, you become the source of their unworthiness and bad feelings. Some narcissists have explosive tempers and can resort to violence when trying to escape from the negativity they feel inside.

The partners of many narcissists can also have these problems. You might deny the bad aspects of your partner when you're getting along and see only the good. You don't see the whole person and excuse abusive behavior. Then you're hurt and disappointed when you're attacked. Your splitting may not be as extreme as the narcissist's, but your impaired perceptions make seeing the other person accurately difficult, and this inhibits your ability to leave. Moreover, like the narcissist, your insecurities make you sensitive to any real or perceived rejection or rupture in the connection.

Disagreements are painful. Emotional distance, which is common, can trigger jealousy, anxiety, sadness, neediness, and pleasing behavior to re-establish your sense of security, albeit a fleeting and unstable one. When you feel abandoned, you may cycle through grief reactions. If these continue for a long time, you can become depressed, and feel shamed, lost, and empty.

Objectification

Narcissists act as though the world revolves around them. They're in their own reality and see you only as an extension of themselves, an object to satisfy their needs and wants. Your inner world is unattainable to them and of little interest; relationships become functional transactions oriented to maintain *their* inner world, their ego, and their self-regulation.

Objectification is seeing or treating someone or an animal as a nonliving object. Originally, it applied to viewing women as "sex objects," but it goes beyond sex and gender. Objectification can lead to instrumentality, which is treating a person or a group as an object of subjugation. When narcissists instrumentalize, they subordinate the needs, interests, and experiences of those whom they've objectified. Their partners are used to satisfy their purposes, needs, and wants. These narcissists deny their partners' subjective experience and individuality. One client grumbled that he felt his wife treated him like an ATM. In the extreme, objectification can lead to concepts such as ownership (slavery), exchangeability, disposability, and dehumanization.

Objectification isn't always oriented toward others, however. To some extent narcissists and their partners treat themselves as objects, denying their true needs, wants, and emotions. For example, some people have repetitive, unnecessary plastic surgeries because they prize their appearance above all. Narcissists deny their own emotional needs; some partners do, too, and believe their sole purpose is to serve their family or mate.

Emptiness and Insatiability

Narcissists lack a positive emotional connection to themselves, which hampers their ability to connect emotionally with others. They're emotionally depressed inside and see themselves only as seen through the eyes of others. Their undeveloped self and inner emptiness render them dependent on others to fill the void and affirm their impaired self-esteem and fragile ego. Lacking healthy self-confidence, they fear that they're undesirable. Despite their boasting and self-flattery, they crave constant attention, respect, and admiration.

Psychoanalysts have used the term "narcissistic supply" to describe the needs of narcissists. The phrase originally referred to the essential needs of babies and young children in normal mental and emotional development. Loss of necessary supplies in childhood can lead to depression and later attempts to get those needs through addiction and other means. Freud identified aggression or ingratiation as the main methods to find fulfillment. Whereas these two paths are practiced by young children before maturing, narcissists go on using them in adulthood to fuel their narcissistic supply. Freud later named these strategies sadistic and submissive. To get their needs met, narcissists may be sadistic, while their partners may be submissive. Examples of "narcissistic supplies" (distinguished from *essential* supplies) include the following:

1. Praise and compliments
2. Achievements and professional success even if by unethical means
3. Financial gain
4. Status symbols, such as a big home, expensive car, and frequenting five-star restaurants and hotels
5. Acquaintances with celebrities and other public figures
6. Wearing designer labels and expensive accessories and jewelry
7. Winning
8. Using alcohol, drugs, or other addictive substances or behaviors
9. Sex
10. Provoking arguments, emotional reactions, and chaos
11. Receiving awards
12. Attention in the news or social media
13. Being admired and loved by romantic partners
14. A desirable or powerful mate, such as a trophy wife or successful husband

Because narcissists' sense of self is determined by what others think of them, they use relationships for self-enhancement and use other people as objects to provide their supply. Getting their emotional needs met is life-or-death; everyone must feed them. They manipulate to control what others think to feel better about themselves, which only makes their dependency worse.

Yet because inside they're empty and disconnected from themselves, nothing sticks and their relentless hunger is never satisfied. They require continuous reassurance, but like parasites, whatever or however much you give is never enough to fill their emptiness. They resemble vampires who exploit and drain those around them. (Like many devouring narcissistic mothers, in Anne Rice's *The Vampire Chronicles*, vampire Lestat had a cold, emotionally empty mother, who devotedly bonded with him and used him to survive.)

They find fault with your efforts and give backhanded compliments that feel like putdowns. If they're momentarily pleased, they're soon disparaging you and demanding more. If you fail to see what you're dealing with, you could continue to sacrifice yourself for them, leaving you to also feel devalued, empty, and dead. But by seeing clearly who they are, you can not only change your behavior and reactions, but also appreciate what it was like to have an invasive, cold, or unavailable (i.e., narcissistic) parent.

For narcissists, their early losses, emptiness, and needs are so great that, if not fulfilled, they disintegrate mentally. Thus, their need for admiration is insatiable and infinite. Heinz Kohut observed this in his narcissistic clients, who suffered from profound alienation, emptiness, and powerlessness. Beneath the surface, they lacked sufficient internal structures to maintain cohesiveness, stability, and a positive self-image to support a stable identity.

> The characteristic subjective experience of narcissistic individuals is a sense of inner emptiness and meaninglessness that requires recurrent infusions of external confirmation of their importance and value. When the environment fails to provide such evidence, narcissistic individuals feel depressed, shamed, and envious of those who succeed in attaining the supplies that they lack.[29]

Perfectionism

Freud defined narcissism as the quality of "perfection" in the early developmental stage when a toddler feels as though the world is his oyster. In adults, this is considered a distortion of our limitations and vulnerability. Narcissists love feeling powerful and "the best" in every way — the first and one and only; this experience is referred to as *narcissistic gratification*.

A healthy ego enables you to establish reality-based relationships with yourself and others. You can accept your disappointments and limitations. But due to splitting, narcissists see themselves as all good or all bad, vacillating between states of self-inflation and inferiority. Narcissism and perfectionism go hand in hand because narcissists cannot admit to failures, shortcomings, limitations, or dependency. Being ordinary isn't good enough for them, as anything less than perfect feels inferior. They're caught between trying to appear perfect and feeling utterly powerless and ashamed. When their sense of perfection is questioned, they experience a *narcissistic injury*. This often triggers abusive anger, known as *narcissistic rage*. Narcissistic rage is a secondary strategy when the defensive illusion of perfection fails.

When ego development is impaired, a compulsive pursuit and expectation of perfection in yourself or someone you love may result. Referring to the blissful feeling of oneness between infant and mother in his book, *The Narcissistic Pursuit of Perfection*, psychoanalyst Arnold Rothstein considers narcissistic perfection to be "a defensive distortion of reality — an affectively laden fantasy based on the original perfection of the...symbiotic phase."[30]

Perfectionistic narcissists (more often male than female) are generally "other-oriented perfectionists," meaning that they tend to focus on other people's shortcomings. People who fall into this subgroup of perfectionists have traits of NPD, including admiration-seeking and a sense of entitlement. They tend to value dominance, authoritarianism, and control and are exploitative, manipulative, callous, and insensitive to other people. They aggressively or arrogantly put others down to uplift and sustain their illusion of perfection. Someone with a secure ego admires and learns from a successful competitor, but a perfectionistic narcissist might seek to undermine and destroy a rival.

Research on other-oriented perfectionist traits reveals that these perfectionists don't value nurturance, intimacy, or pro-social norms, such as showing interest in and understanding others, building friendships, helping, being supportive, and making others comfortable or happy.[31] Instead, they have exceedingly high internal standards and demand that other people do the "right thing" according to their standards, and they obsessively strive for perfection as well. They may prefer to do things themselves rather than rely on someone else to do a less-than-perfect job. This adds stress and conflict to relationships. When you don't measure up to their standards, they can become impatient, hostile, blaming, and highly critical. An example might be Steve Jobs, who was notorious for his "demotivational" tirades.[32]

Attachment Style

Attachment style describes how we behave in intimate relationships, starting with our earliest relationships with caregivers. Self and object constancy materially impact our style, which is termed secure or insecure. People with a secure style (about half of couples in the U.S.) see themselves and others in a positive light and anticipate that they will be reliable, available, and trustworthy.[33] They feel autonomous and believe that it's easy for them to be in close relationships and depend upon other people.

People with an insecure attachment style lack self-esteem and feel basic insecurity. They doubt the reliability of other people to satisfy their emotional needs, yet base their behavior on the others' responses. These are the pursuers and distancers who find relationships so difficult. Psychologists have developed two models of insecure attachment styles, described below:

Anxious or Preoccupied: About 20 percent of the U.S. population has an anxious attachment style. They view others positively and themselves as unworthy and unlovable. They seek relationships to validate their self-esteem, because they feel less valued being on their own and believe relationships hold the promise of acceptance. Their unconscious belief is, "If I'm loved, then I must be lovable." Hence, they're preoccupied with their relationship and are highly attuned to their partner with whom they want greater intimacy but worry that their partner wants less. Their insecurity sensitizes them to any sign of withdrawal or abandonment, leading them to question their partner's feelings and commitment. They please and accommodate and may behave desperately to gain attention and reassurance of love and acceptance. But, because they cannot accept themselves, they become dependent on partners who can never give them the psychological self-nurturing that they require and end up feeling unhappy and emotionally abandoned.

Avoidant: People with an avoidant attachment style make up about 30 percent of the U.S. population. Independence and self-sufficiency feel more important than intimacy. Although they lack connection with others, they can enjoy closeness — to a point. In relationships, they act self-sufficient and rarely share personal information and feelings. Their partners complain that they don't seem to need companionship or that they're not open enough. In one study of partners saying goodbye at an airport, avoiders didn't display much contact, anxiety, or sadness in comparison to others.[34]

Opposite of anxious attachers, avoiders are hypervigilant of attempts to control them or limit their autonomy and freedom. They engage in distancing behaviors, such as flirting with others, making unilateral decisions, ignoring their partner, or dismissing their partner's feelings and needs. They protect their freedom and delay commitment. If they do commit, they create mental distance with ongoing dissatisfaction about the relationship, focusing on their partner's minor flaws or reminiscing about their single days or another idealized relationship. They see their partner as needy, and this makes them feel strong and self-sufficient by comparison. They don't worry about a relationship ending. But if the relationship is threatened, they tell themselves that they don't have attachment needs and bury their feelings of distress. It's not that these needs don't exist; they're repressed. Alternatively, they may act like anxious attachers, because the possibility of closeness no longer threatens them and the threat of abandonment awakens their attachment needs.

There are two subtypes of avoidant attachers:

1. **Dismissive-avoidant:** Dismissives represent about 5 percent of the U.S. population. They can achieve autonomy and a positive

view of themselves, but they're disdainful of other people and close relationships. This protects them from rejection and disappointment. They treasure their independence and don't want to depend on others or have others depend on them.

2. **Fearful-avoidant:** People with a fearful style, also known as disorganized, make up the balance of avoidant attachers. Like anxious attachers, they feel unworthy and unlovable and view other people as unavailable, untrustworthy, and rejecting. Although they want a close relationship, they avoid them to feel safe. They fear becoming dependent and getting hurt given their negative view of others.

Narcissists' Attachment Style

Narcissists have insecure attachment styles that are generally either avoidant, anxious, or a combination,[35] but research on the attachment styles of exhibitionist narcissists is inconclusive. The attachment style of grandiose narcissists in some cases differs from their experience of early parenting styles and childhood trauma.[36] Surprisingly, high grandiose narcissism correlates with a secure attachment in their romantic relationships; those with less grandiosity report an avoidant or dismissive/avoidant attachment style. They feel independent and self-sufficient, denying interpersonal distress.[37] They're indifferent to what you think and need unless it threatens them.

Vulnerable narcissists have a more anxious or anxious/fearful attachment style,[38] are capable of romantic love, and are more willing to compromise for the relationship.[39] Vulnerable narcissists still focus on themselves and their needs, while also being hypersensitive to other people's feelings and evaluations. Their moods, need for attention, and varying love styles can be confusing. It may seem they want you, but what they're really seeking is reassurance and attention to soothe their insecurity and unstable emotions.

Pursuers and Distancers in Relationships

Anxious and avoidant attachment styles look like codependency in relationships.[40] They characterize the feelings and behavior of pursuers and distancers. Each partner is unconscious of their own needs, which the other partner expresses. This is one reason for their mutual attraction. Pursuers with an anxious style usually seek avoiders. Someone with a secure style seems boring. Although uncomfortable, the anxiety of an insecure attachment is exciting and familiar and winds up making them even more anxious. It validates their fears about relationships and beliefs about being abandoned and unlovable.

Anxious types tend to bond quickly and don't take time to assess whether their partner wants to or even can meet their needs. They tend to see only the things they share with each new, idealized partner while overlooking potential problems. In trying to make the relationship work, they suppress their needs, sending the wrong signals to their partner in the long run. All this behavior makes attaching to an avoider more probable. When they withdraw, pursuers' anxiety is aroused and they confuse their longing and anxiety for love rather than realizing it's their partner's unavailability that's the problem. They hang in and try harder instead of facing the truth and cutting their losses.

➤ *Innercises: Understanding the Narcissist*

Underlying beliefs develop from childhood experiences. For instance, if you experienced abuse, you'll form beliefs based on distrust and shame. To better understand your partner, link your knowledge of their childhood with your observations of current behavior. See if you can identify any of the following underlying beliefs, *of which they may be unaware.* Feel free to modify the list or add beliefs that apply.

- "I must never need anyone because no one will meet my needs."
- "I must always perform or produce; otherwise, I feel inferior and worthless."
- "Who I am is unlovable. I can't be me, because no one will ever love me for who I really am."
- "I can't trust people. They're out for themselves and want to exploit me."
- "Because I'm unlovable, people are nice to me only to use me; so I'll use them, too." ("It's a dog-eat-dog world.")
- "Relationships are based on power. I must control people, or they will control me."
- "I'm not good enough, and whatever I do isn't good enough. Less than perfect is inferior."
- "Rules are for other people."
- "I'm better than others and am entitled to special treatment."
- "I can't tolerate disappointment and the frustration of not immediately getting what I want. It sends me into a rage."
- "I can't tolerate feeling ordinary; therefore I need to associate with important or successful people."
- "I doubt myself and need the approval and validation of others."

Reviewing these beliefs can help you gain insight into what drives your partner. You'll come to realize that it's not a reflection of you, but of your partner's internal world. With greater empathy and understanding, you react less and respond in productive ways that de-escalate conflicts.

THE NARCISSISTIC PARENT

Like all narcissists, a narcissistic parent behaves as they imagine themselves to be, like the king or queen of the family, or someone whose activities are more important than being part of the family. As a vulnerable child, your parents are your world and your survival and self-concept depend on them. A narcissistic parent can harm healthy child development, which requires love and acceptance from both parents. Children of narcissists typically grow up codependent with insecurity, shame, and low self-esteem. Parenting by a narcissistic mother or father may impact male and female children in unique ways.[41]

Lack of Empathy

Because narcissists lack empathy, they're not nurturing and can't mirror or understand a child, which is necessary for the development of self-worth. Some are neglectful to varying degrees and outsource parenting if they're able, while others might be abusive. Even a narcissistic mother who holds and cares for her baby can't accurately empathize with and respond to her infant's cues and emotions, limiting normal child development. As adults, these children neglect their emotional needs and can't nurture themselves.

Selfish Control — It's All About Them

Mature parents sacrifice their individual needs and wants for the good of the child. In contrast, narcissistic parents put their feelings and needs, particularly emotional needs, ahead of those of their children. Children generally become codependent and gradually deny their needs and feelings to adapt to their parent and later other people. Narcissistic parents personalize their child's failures and natural impulses toward autonomy and either ignore their child or become more controlling and abusive. Their child's independence is a threat that can compete with and encroach on them. Watching her 20-month-old grandchild explore her living room, my narcissistic mother remarked, "He thinks he owns the place!"

A negligent, controlling, or mixed parenting style is emotionally abandoning. This is to be expected because, like all narcissists, these parents don't see their children as separate human beings. The child's needs, wants, and emotions become inconveniences, personal affronts, or burdens, like the father who coldly told his young son that he had no value because he had no net worth. Many such parents behave like children, reversing roles and confiding in their children inappropriately about the other parent (especially after a divorce), about sexual experiences, or about personal sorrows and distress.

Don't expect narcissistic parents to be involved with their children's hobbies, goals, or interests unless it's also *their* goal or interest. They won't take pleasure in their children's accomplishments or attractiveness except to the extent that it reflects well upon them. Similarly, they don't share in their children's pride or excitement about something unless it was their idea or of interest to them. They often insist that their children dress, think, and behave according to their wishes. This extends to their choice of school, spouse, and career. They may force their aspirations on their children to live vicariously through them. As a result, their children are often driven to try to win their teachers', employers', and partners' approval or find little incentive to pursue their wants and goals when not externally supported.

These parents sometimes expect their children to listen to their rants and rages; meet their social, sexual, or financial needs; or clean the house or yard immaculately while they relax. One cruel father demanded that his son dig a swimming pool, while another ordered his son to cut the grass with a razor blade or face physical abuse. Some narcissistic parents threaten to physically harm their children or cut them off emotionally and/or financially if they fail to measure up to their parents' desires and expectations. As adults, children of narcissists are afraid of making waves, making mistakes, and being authentic, and they learn to subjugate their needs and feelings to others.

Competition, Envy, and Jealousy

Narcissistic parents envy and compete with their children's attractiveness, athletic or intellectual abilities, and other sorts of favorable attention that their children attract. For example, they may flirt with their children's romantic partners; they often envy their children's connection with the other parent and may interfere with that relationship; narcissistic parents may even envy the advantages they provided to their children that they didn't have growing up, sometimes following up with accusations of ingratitude.

Narcissistic parents make negative comparisons to put their children down. They might compare a child to a sibling, friend, cousin, or even to themselves — going on about how spoiled, inferior, or lucky their child is compared to them when they were young. Such behavior stems from the same jealousy and envy that motivates competition. Sadly, many children of narcissists struggle for years or a lifetime with shame and low self-worth.

You're Never Good Enough

Like all narcissists, narcissistic parents are prone to brag about themselves, their achievements, their family, and their children. No one is equal to them or good enough for them. Arrogantly, they judge and expect excellence of their spouses and children. Although narcissistic parents may sometimes appear attentive and caring, their behavior can easily switch to controlling and shaming. Their children try to win acceptance, but their love is conditional, and the conditions are always changing. Trying to please any narcissist is a fruitless endeavor. Growing up according to "should's" further alienates children from their true self and leaves them feeling sad and hopeless.

Abuse and Manipulation

Children are suggestible and easy to manipulate, and narcissistic parents control their children with guilt, threats, and belittling. They shame their children with name-calling, criticism, undermining, blame, and withholding love. Frequently, they project onto their children their feelings of unworthiness and negative traits, such as attention-seeking or selfishness; characteristics which they disown. At the same time, they ignore, deny, and criticize their children's feelings and needs, sometimes punishing them for expressing normal emotions, claiming they're too sensitive or weak. Parents often punish by withholding love, creating constant insecurity, and teaching children that love is conditional. Such abuse damages any child's sense of self and self-esteem and can be as traumatizing as physical and sexual abuse.

The lack of unconditional love, acceptance, and emotional connection in childhood leaves a void and unfulfilled yearning. Lack of emotional support for their feelings, needs, and desires creates a pervasive feeling of deprivation. This is emotional abandonment, when you feel undesired, left behind, insecure, or discarded by a trusted loved one.[42] Often adult children of narcissistic parents become depressed, have unacknowledged anger, and feelings of emptiness. To varying degrees, they lack motivation and the ability to express their rights and feelings, fulfill their own needs and wants, and set boundaries, further limiting their development and self-esteem.

Until children of narcissists accept their narcissistic parents' limitations and begin to love themselves, they're never free of suffering. They relive the emotional abandonment of their childhood and seek self-worth, validation, and lovability in relationships with abusive and/or emotionally unavailable partners, including addicts and narcissists. They may contribute to the problem by reacting as they did as a child to their parent. They continually find fault with themselves because conditional love is all they've ever known. This can lead to lifelong misery because external validation never heals internal shame and emptiness. Healing requires recovery from the codependency and shame acquired in childhood to feel entitled to love and appreciation. (See *Codependency for Dummies* to assess your symptoms and begin recovery.)

Chapter 3

IDENTIFYING NARCISSISTIC BEHAVIOR

Narcissists vigilantly crave power over and control of their surroundings, the people in their lives, and their feelings and those of others. Control is all-important because without it they feel powerless and humiliated. Command of their environment helps them get their needs met and protects them from feeling insecure, unworthy, guilty, and self-contempt. Due to their extreme vulnerability, psychiatrists consider them to be "fragile." Their defense systems, which are discussed below, protect them but inevitably hurt their partners. The more insecure they feel, the more malicious they become, regardless of the impact of their actions.

Nothing is more important to a narcissist than managing their esteem, image, appearance, and social rank. They see the world and themselves in a hierarchy where they're superior and others are inferior. In their mind, their superiority entitles them to special privileges. Their needs, opinions, and feelings always matter more than those of others.

To bolster their weak ego, they accumulate symbols of power, success, and strength, such as a title, property, prestige, and social status. They have grandiose fantasies in which they're the most attractive, talented, powerful, smartest, strongest, and wealthiest.

DEFENSIVE BEHAVIOR

Narcissists aggressively protect and preserve their false front because they fear criticism and humiliation. Typically, they defend against feelings of insecurity and inferiority by moving against people and pushing them away. Compelled to maintain this self-deception, they do what it takes to prop up their image and block negative feedback. Facing the truth about themselves would be devastating. In fact, their entire personality is a defense of their fragile self. Their reactions betray how frail their ego really is.

Despite saying or doing things that feel cruel, most narcissists aren't inherently evil (as distinguished from socio- and psychopaths in chapter 2). Their antagonistic and sometimes heartless behaviors that make them so unpleasant and difficult are merely designed to protect a vulnerable and lonely core, of which they're ashamed. Those behaviors are the glue that holds their fragile personality together.

Narcissistic Defense Mechanisms

To cope with negative emotions and pain, we all use defense mechanisms, especially the ones learned in childhood. Our defenses against feeling shame are often what challenge our ability to develop healthy relationships and intimacy. This is especially true for narcissists. Their most offensive behaviors stem from the aggressive defenses they developed to protect their fragile self. The ones most used are described below:

Denial and Repression: Narcissists deny reality and live inside a fantasy world that protects their fragile egos. They distort, rationalize, twist facts, and delude themselves to avoid anything that may chip their armor, which can be so thick that no amount of evidence or argument can get through. Their memories are often faulty, and self-deception can convince them that their altered reality is true.

Arrogance and Contempt: To compensate for shame, narcissists maintain an attitude of superiority. This defense inflates a narcissist's ego with an air of superiority to shield them against unconscious feelings of inadequacy. They're often disdainful of others, especially groups such as immigrants, racial and ethnic minorities, the poor, or the less-educated.

Projection and Blame: Abusers, addicts, and narcissists typically use these defense mechanisms to disown their unacceptable feelings, thoughts, or qualities and assign them to others, either mentally or verbally. The projector says, "It's not me, it's you!" In doing so, you become the target of a narcissist's projection; you're the one who is "selfish," "weak," and "worthless."

Coping strategies reflect emotional maturity, and projection is considered a primitive defense because it distorts or ignores reality in an attempt to preserve a weak ego. It's reactive without forethought and used by children. When employed by adults, it indicates arrested emotional development. Low self-esteem and shame impair narcissists' ability to accept responsibility for mistakes and negative feelings. Projecting allows narcissists to accuse others of being the source of the pain and shame they bear and make someone else feel the way they do inside. Rather than suffer self-judgment, projection provides a temporary respite from their negative impulses and traits, which they find too uncomfortable to acknowledge. It preserves feelings of innocence and esteem rather than guilt and shame, or at the very least it preserves a narcissist's sense of security in maintaining their façade of infallibility.

Externalization is like projection in that it is blaming others for your problems rather than taking appropriate responsibility for them, like addicts who blame their drinking or drug use on their partners or job supervisors. Thus, externalizing also makes you feel like a victim.

But narcissists aren't the only people who project and blame. You might think to yourself, "He hates me," when you hate him or think he's being controlling or judgmental; in other words, you remain blind to your similar shortcomings or uncomfortable feelings because you're projecting them onto someone else.

To illustrate how projection works, it's essential to understand that shame has two faces: one with an inflated ego and one that is depressed. This diagram illustrates how a self is divided by shame is comprised of a superior-acting, grandiose self and an inferior, devalued self.[43]

The Paradox of Shame

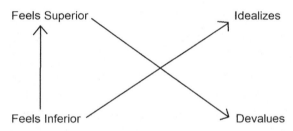

When the devalued self is feeling inferior, shame manifests by idealizing others. This is what partners do when they're attracted to and idealize a narcissist. When a person is feeling superior and defending against shame, the grandiose self devalues others by projecting its disowned flaws and negative self-concept. Both devaluation and idealization are commensurate with the severity of shame and associated depression. Shame can make people fluctuate between the superior and inferior positions, but grandiose and vulnerable narcissists are more-or-less static in their respective positions, regardless of reality.

Projection can be crazy-making, especially if you experience it for a long time. When you're vulnerable or have impaired self-esteem and weak boundaries or are sensitive about a specific issue, such as your looks, parenting, or intelligence, there's no filter. You *introject* the projection. Because internally you agree, it sticks like a magnet. Then you react to the shaming and compound your relationship problems. Doing so validates and augments the abuser's authority, control, and ideas about you. You're sending the message that your partner has power over your self-esteem and the right to approve you.

Aggression: Although not listed in the DSM, antagonism is a core trait of narcissists who see the world as hostile and threatening and therefore move against people; grandiose narcissists are more aggressive than vulnerable narcissists.[44] This temporarily relieves feelings of shame, which are usually unconscious and transferred to someone else. They may express their aggression through machismo, bullying, or other forms of emotional and physical abuse. Narcissists may respond to confrontation or criticism with rage, which they perceive as an assault on their wounded self. Vindictive narcissists retaliate to reverse feelings of humiliation and restore their pride.

Perfectionism and Envy: Striving for perfection also defends against feeling inferior or inadequate. Narcissists must believe they're the best to avoid feeling that they're the worst. Competitive narcissists are not only envious of people who have what they want, but they may react vengefully to bring others down, especially if they feel threatened (see chapter 2 – Perfectionism).

Self-Pity — Playing the Victim: Sometimes, we aren't responsible for bad things happening and we truly are victims, but feeling victimized can also be used as a defense against self-hatred, shame, and guilt. It's usually equal to the "victim's" inner feelings of unworthiness. It may seem strange to think of this attitude as a defense, but similar to blame, it externalizes the cause of bad feelings about the self. The victim thinks, "Poor me," and hence is blameless, even superior and self-righteous. When narcissists don't get their way or they're cornered with accusations of abuse, they twist the facts so they become the victim.

▶ *Innercises: Understanding Defenses*

As Yogi Berra said: "You can observe a lot just by watching." So watch for the defense mechanisms that you and your partner use when your egos are challenged. (Of course, your own defenses may be harder to identify.) You can begin to depersonalize attacks when you realize they're untrue or merely a projection. To help you, below is a list of questions. If answering a question is difficult, watch your daily interactions. Write about them to identify what's going on (see chapter 9 – Stop Reacting).

- Does your partner use any of the defense mechanisms described above?
- Can you see through their façade?
- What are your defenses? Do you use some of the same ones as your partner?
- What defenses did your mother use with your father, and vice versa?

- What defenses did you use with your mother? With your father?
- Did you learn and adopt the defenses that your mother or father modeled?
- Do you react to your partner's defenses with your own?
- Do you continually try to please or appease your partner to avoid conflict? (i.e., apologize, act extra nice, go along with it, etc.)
- When your partner becomes defensive, do you react angrily and accuse or blame? (If not verbally, do you do so internally, which is also a defense?)
- Are you passive-aggressive, or do you express your anger indirectly? (i.e., by being late, by "forgetting" things that are important to your partner, etc.)
- Do you deny, rationalize, or minimize your pain to make the relationship work?
- Do you share or stuff your feelings? What reaction would you expect if you shared them?
- Do you silence your opinions? What reaction would you expect if you shared them?
- Do you know your wants? Do you ask for it? If not, what reaction would you expect if you did?
- Do you accept blame from your partner and feel guilty or apologize?
- Do you compliment or bolster your partner when you don't want to? How does this make you feel?
- Do you withdraw rather than confront problems or avoid conversations out of fear of being belittled?
- Do you usually give in to your partner?
- Do you withhold affection or sex? If so, is it out of resentment?

CONTROLLING THE ENVIRONMENT

Narcissists' constant concern is to improve their status and self-esteem.[45] It's a compulsion. Their hidden shame and insecurity drive their hypervigilance and behavior regarding their self-image, self-esteem, appearance, and power. They can be extremely sensitive to cues that hold the potential to threaten their self-image. They expend continuous effort employing a variety of tactics, such as the three discussed below:

1. **Scanning for Status:** They scan other people and their surroundings constantly to calculate their rank, evaluate their influence, and assess the attention and praise they're receiving relative to how others are doing. They attempt to elevate their status at any opportunity and watch for impediments to regulating their self-esteem.

2. **Selective Environments and Relationships:** They select situations that are likely to raise rather than lower their esteem. Thus, they seek public, high-status, competitive, and hierarchical environments that reward competition over intimate and egalitarian settings. They prefer acquiring many contacts, friends, and partners rather than spending time on developing and deepening their existing relationships.

3. **Impression Management:** Once narcissists have assessed the environment and whom they're dealing with, they determine the best way to achieve superior status is by either raising theirs or lowering that of others. To regulate their self-esteem, they primarily utilize internal self-inflation and their interpersonal skills. Narcissists use impression management to gain self-esteem and external status, such as money, power, and desirable romantic partners. They employ charm, wit, talent, conversational skills, and self-promotion through boasting, embellishing, and lying to manage the impression they intend to give. This is also why narcissists gravitate toward celebrities and high-status people, schools, businesses, and other institutions. When self-promotion doesn't work, grandiose narcissists resort to dominance. They're excellent manipulators and do whatever it takes to achieve their ends, as discussed in the below section on Abusive Behavior.

These tactics work best in the initial stages of a relationship or during short-term interactions. One main difference between vulnerable and grandiose narcissists is that vulnerable narcissists employ threat-oriented defenses and negative self-talk that don't satisfy their needs for esteem and validation. In contrast, grandiose narcissists use more mature reward-seeking strategies to achieve acceptance and admiration.

ENTITLED BEHAVIOR

Like aggression, a sense of entitlement is also a core trait of most narcissists. It reveals how they believe they're the center of the universe. Rules don't apply to them. They feel entitled to get what they want from others regardless of their behavior. They expect you to listen to them but have no interest in your affairs. They don't recognize their behavior as hypocritical, because they feel superior and special. However, those feelings mask their inner shame and insecurity.

Norms of courtesy don't pertain to them except when they want to make a good impression. For example, their time is more valuable than others, and they shouldn't have to wait in line like the masses. They might expect planes or cruise ships to delay their departures for them. If they're accused or convicted of wrongdoing, it's everyone else's fault or the law was wrong. A relationship with this person is painfully one-sided, not a two-way street. They believe that your purpose is to serve their needs and wants.

EXPLOITATIVE BEHAVIOR

You may not spot this trait until you get to know a narcissist better, but if you start to feel used, it could be because you're being exploited. For example, a narcissist may take credit for your work. Romantic partners often feel used because narcissists show no genuine interest in them. Partners who give money or provide other types of help to a narcissist can also feel used because their own needs are never considered.

As skilled manipulators, narcissists are always "gaming the system" or the relationship to gain whatever advantage is available to them. This leaves their partners feeling exploited. The way to prevent this from happening is to notice the behavior, tell the narcissist you won't tolerate it, and follow through on your promise. Examples of serious exploitation are lying (including gas-lighting), cheating, and financial or business fraud. Narcissists typically brag about how they put one over on someone, so if you think your partner may be a narcissist, take note when they behave in these ways. Don't imagine you're exempt.

CALLOUS BEHAVIOR AND LACK OF EMPATHY

According to the DSM, narcissists are "unwilling to recognize or identify with the feelings and needs of others."[46] Although some people who aren't narcissists also lack empathy, this trait is a crucial and determining symptom when combined with a sense of entitlement and a tendency to exploit others. Research shows that narcissists have structural abnormalities in brain regions associated with *emotional empathy*.[47] Lacking normal emotional empathy, narcissists inflate the little they have.[48] They do, however, possess *cognitive empathy*, which is an ability to take someone else's perspective, but they're motivated to do so only when it serves their narcissistic needs.[49]

Without empathy, narcissists can be selfish, hurtful, and cold when it doesn't serve them to be charming or cooperative. Unable to genuinely respond to others' feelings, they become inured to the pain that they cause, while their cognitive and emotional intelligence gives them an edge in manipulating and exploiting others. Behaviors that typify empathy deficits include rudeness, not listening, disregard for your feelings and limitations, ignoring your needs, and so on. Notice their expression when describing or hearing about sad events. Do they lack empathy for your hardships and those of others? I once told a narcissist I wouldn't be able to travel abroad due to a back injury. I was shocked by his insensitive reply: "You wouldn't let a little back pain stop you, would you?" All these issues impair narcissists' capacity to accurately take in another person's reality, including a person's love for them.

ABUSIVE BEHAVIOR

Many of the narcissist's coping mechanisms are abusive, hence the term, "narcissistic abuse." Remember, however, that not all abusers are narcissists — NPD and abuse exist on a continuum, ranging from silence to violence. But ultimately, abuse is abuse. The most important thing to remember about intentional abuse is that it's meant to dominate you. Aggression is typical of narcissism. When self-promotion and charm don't work, narcissists maintain their control and authority by increasing feelings of doubt, shame, and dependency in their victims. They create conflict and put down others to dominate and feel superior.

Despite their defenses of rage, arrogance, and self-inflation, they always suffer from shame. Appearing weak, wrong, or humiliated is their biggest fear. Thus, rarely do narcissists take responsibility for their behavior; understanding that can empower you. Generally, narcissists deny their actions and augment the abuse by blaming you. It's essential not to take personally the words and actions of an abuser. This enables you to confront narcissistic abuse.

Myths and Facts about Abuse

Victims of abuse often live in denial, and people who haven't experienced it are quick to judge and don't understand, so getting accurate information about abuse is essential if you're going to deal with it effectively. Here are some *myths* about abuse:

1. Abuse is physical violence.
2. Abusers are easy to identify.
3. Partners who stay with abusers are weak, poor, or uneducated.
4. Enough love can change an abuser.
5. Verbal abuse can't hurt you.
6. It's easy to leave an abusive relationship.
7. Abusers can't control themselves.
8. The abuse is your fault.

Anyone can be abusive when they're frustrated or hurt. In such situations, you may react by judging, criticizing, withholding, and controlling, but narcissists take abuse to another level. To recover from abuse, the first step is to identify it. Then get support and learn to protect yourself. Here are some *facts*:

1. Abuse usually takes place out of sight. Your partner may be publicly charming and privately abusive.
2. Abusers deny their actions.
3. Abusers blame the victim.
4. Verbal abuse usually precedes physical violence.
5. Even if you don't believe it, abuse can damage your self-esteem.
6. About one-third of abuse victims and about two-thirds of perpetrators have been drinking or using drugs (and the presence of a gun in the home increases homicide rates by 500 percent).

Profile of an Abuser

You may not realize that abusers typically feel powerless, regardless of whatever worldly success they have attained. To them, communication is a zero-sum game. Often, their abuse mimics the way they were treated growing up. They're usually impatient, unreasonable, unforgiving, and are often withholding. Isolation, shaming, and fear are tactics abusers use to make you more malleable to their control.

Their moods can shift in a heartbeat from fun-loving and romantic to sullen and angry and back again. Partners of such abusers typically love Dr. Jekyll while making excuses for Mr. Hyde. Due to splitting, they fail to see that the abuse springs from the whole person. Here are typical traits of an abuser:

1. Insecure
2. Needy with unrealistic expectations of relationships
3. Distrustful
4. Self-centered and insensitive to others' feelings and needs
5. Suspicious and jealous
6. Verbally abusive
7. Needs to be in control ("It's my way or the highway.")
8. Possessive and may try to isolate their partners from friends and family
9. Hypersensitive and aggressively reactive
10. Has a history of aggression
11. Cruel to animals or children
12. Blames others (especially their partners) for their behavior

13. Had abusive and/or traumatic childhood
14. Suffers from untreated mental health problems (including depression or suicidal behavior)

Types of Abuse

Regardless of whether your partner is a narcissist, abuse can take practically any form you might imagine, including physical, sexual, financial, psychological, and emotional. Some types of emotional abuse can be disguised, such as manipulation by withholding, but abuse is always about power and domination over you. Narcissists don't need to be violent to exert their power. They can easily achieve the same ends with emotional abuse. *If you suspect that you're in an abusive relationship, you probably are.*

Physical Abuse: Physical abuse and violence involve any intentional use of force. The types of physical abuse are practically endless (hitting, burning, biting, hair-pulling, shoving, arm-twisting, choking, spitting, restraining, etc.) and can also include destruction of your property (such as ruining your clothing, throwing your phone, smashing sentimental objects, or killing a pet). Although violence correlates more strongly to psychopathy than narcissism per se, research shows that people who strongly exhibit more narcissistic traits, especially entitlement and a lack of empathy, and who are deficient in affect regulation and self-control are more prone to violence.

Sexual Abuse: This includes any type of deliberate and unwanted sexual act or exposure. In the bedroom, narcissists may be as controlling, cold, and selfish as they are in other aspects of the relationship. You might experience unrelenting pressure to have sex, to carry out certain sexual acts, or to be filmed or photographed naked or performing such acts. Coercion and manipulation can result in marital rape, threesomes, polygamy, or prostitution.

Financial Abuse: Financial abuse might include dominating you through economic means by withholding money or draining your finances through manipulation, gambling, accruing debt in your name, extortion, selling your property, and outright theft. Financial abusers sometimes interrogate their partners about every dime they spend. But not every money issues imply abuse; it's one thing to say, "If you buy the dining room set, we can't afford the vacation," but another thing if your partner cuts up your credit cards.

Spiritual Abuse: Spiritual abuse is an attempt to control you by undermining your faith, misusing religious texts, or invoking a divine rationale for behavior. It goes beyond mere disagreement of beliefs because it's motivated by domination. The premise is that the narcissist knows "God's will" better than you, which you must accept, or be damned or punished. This is particularly damaging to children who have an undeveloped understanding of God.

Psychological and Emotional Abuse: This is the willful infliction of mental or emotional distress. It includes speech and other behaviors that are degrading, controlling, punishing, or manipulative. Spotting this type of abuse can be difficult because it can be subtle and has become more common in the media. It may also be hard to recognize if you've been emotionally abused in the past because it feels familiar and you may have not experienced healthier relationships. Abusers often act as though they have no idea why you would be upset, blame you, and believe that you deserved it. Moreover, when you're abused in private, there are no witnesses who can validate your experience.

Being subjected to emotional abuse over time can lead to anxiety, post-traumatic stress disorder, depression, inhibited sexual desire, chronic pain, or other physical symptoms. The following are some behaviors that indicate psychological and emotional abuse: (Verbal abuse and manipulation are discussed in more detail below.)

- **Controlling:** Narcissists typically exercise control by giving orders and making demands and unilateral decisions. They may try to control what you wear, what you eat, where you go, to whom you talk, what you can say or think, or even what brand of shampoo to use. They expect you to comply or suffer punitive consequences. Control may be carried out with financial or verbal abuse, spying or electronic monitoring, threats, or using your children to punish or pressure you.
- **Withholding:** Abusers withhold love, communication (stonewalling), sex, affection, support, or money (financial abuse) as methods of control.
- **Ignoring:** This is indifference to your pain or need to communicate by behavior such as looking away or texting while you're talking, waving you off, or changing the subject. Like all forms of abuse, ignoring is meant to shame and dehumanize you.
- **Sabotage:** This form of abuse disrupts or otherwise interferes with your endeavors or relationships.
- **Privacy Invasion:** Privacy invasion is emotional abuse that ignores your boundaries. It includes spying, stalking, secretly going through your communications (cell phone, email, etc.) and possessions, and

persistently interrupting your time or space, such as in the bathroom or while you're having a private phone conversation.

- **Isolation:** Narcissists may try to limit other people's influence to increase their control and your dependence so that their domination goes unchallenged. They attempt to isolate you by slandering your character or spreading malicious gossip or lies about you to other people, often making themselves appear to be the victim. To limit your access to professional services and relationships with friends and family, they may belittle them, refuse to attend family gatherings, and forbid you to attend them or talk to someone your partner objects to, or else you're befriending the enemy.

- **Exploitation:** Exploitation is abuse that takes unfair advantage of you for personal ends without regard for your feelings or needs. The symptoms of narcissism, such as entitlement, lack of empathy, and arrogance make it natural for narcissists to exploit others. You're there to serve the narcissist's needs. You may feel objectified or like you don't exist as an individual. Exploitation may be sexual, financial, or using your time, resources, contacts, or work. If your partner shows specific interest in something, they may plan to use you for their selfish agenda. See chapter 2 – Exploitative Behavior.

- **Verbal Abuse:** Narcissists are masters of verbal abuse, the most common form of emotional abuse. Direct verbal abuse, such as threats, blame, abusive criticism, orders, judging, criticizing, blaming, shouting, and raging, is easy to recognize. When experienced over time, verbal abuse has a harmful, insidious effect, because you begin to doubt and distrust yourself. Beware that abusers may speak in a loving, quiet voice, or may be indirect, even concealing putdowns disguised as playful teasing or jokes; however, sarcasm or teasing that is hurtful is abusive. Below are less obvious forms of verbal abuse that are just as damaging as overt attacks, particularly because they're harder to detect.

  - ✓ **Opposing:** The abuser argues against anything you say, challenging your perceptions, opinions, feelings, and thoughts. The abuser doesn't listen or volunteer thoughts or feelings but treats you as an adversary, in effect, saying "no" to everything, so a constructive conversation is impossible.
  - ✓ **Name-Calling:** This includes not only demeaning epithets and labels, such as "slut" or "retard" and "bastard" or "loser," but also derogatory pet names, like "flabby fanny" or "chunky Chuck."

✓ **Tirades:** Tirades include raging at you, outbursts, and shouting, but also lecturing or unleashing grievances about you and other people. You don't have to be an audience for a narcissist's belligerence, rants, or speeches.

✓ **Blocking:** This is another tactic used to abort conversation. The abuser may switch topics, accuse you, or use words that in effect say, "Shut up."

✓ **Discounting & Belittling:** This category includes a wide range of behavior that makes you feel "little," such as patronizing, criticizing, dismissive remarks, or non-verbal conduct that imply you're inferior. Examples are eye-rolling, head-shaking, sighing, and yawning when you're speaking. It also includes verbal abuse that minimizes or trivializes your feelings, thoughts, achievements, or experiences. It's saying that your feelings don't matter or that you're wrong.

✓ **Undermining:** These words and put-downs are meant to undermine your self-esteem and confidence, such as, "You're out of your league," "You don't know what you're talking about," or "Your artwork is a joke."

✓ **Interrupting:** Persistent interrupting, finishing your sentences, or speaking on your behalf without your permission is abusive.

✓ **Competition:** Competing and one-upping to always be on top, sometimes through unethical means; e.g. cheating in a game.

✓ **Negative Contrasting:** Unnecessarily making comparisons to negatively contrast you with him or herself or other people.

✓ **Lying:** Persistent deception to avoid responsibility or to achieve the narcissist's ends.

Manipulation: Manipulation is intended to covertly influence someone with indirect, deceptive, or dehumanizing tactics. On the surface, manipulation may seem benign, friendly or flattering, or even show interest and concern for your needs and problems. But in the end, all these ploys serve an ulterior motive.

Most narcissists develop exceptional skills at manipulation, which they use to maintain their grandiose illusions and to impress and seduce others, but when used to dominate and control, it's abusive. You might feel demeaned or sense veiled hostility. You might feel off-balance and unsure of how to behave.

Narcissists do almost anything to avoid responsibility and being confronted. They lie, twist your words and reality, make pretenses of compassion, appear shocked or hurt, and put you on the defensive to deflect criticism of their unacceptable behavior. They make you unsure of yourself and doubt your perceptions while concealing their aggressive intent.

If your parents, siblings, or other influencers manipulated you when you were a child, you might have difficulty identifying manipulative behavior, ironically because it feels familiar. A narcissistic manipulator may apologize, make displays of apparent generosity, speak in a pleasant or ingratiating way, or play on your guilt or sympathy so you disregard your instincts and go along. You may not even comprehend that the narcissist is trying to control and confuse you. Encouraging you to doubt your perceptions is a special type of manipulation, known as gaslighting, which is discussed in detail in chapter 7.

Manipulation will likely continue and over time can traumatize you and severely damage your self-worth. A full list of manipulative tactics could fill a book, but here are a few of the most common:

- ✓ **Denial:** Manipulative narcissists willfully and deceitfully deny their behavior, promises, agreements, conversations, motives, and your perceptions. They may feign ignorance or innocence ("Who me!?"). Denial also includes minimization, rationalization, and excuses. Manipulators act as if you're making a big deal over nothing or they rationalize and excuse their actions to make you doubt yourself or even to gain your sympathy.
- ✓ **Foot-in-the-Door:** This starts with small requests that are easy to agree to. The manipulator makes increasingly painful requests that become harder to deny because you already said yes so many times.
- ✓ **Reversal:** This is when manipulators reverse the meaning of what you said to make it serve their agenda. When you object, they act like the injured party and put you on the defensive. For example, narcissists might claim you're the one who is abusing them or is having an affair, or they might accuse you of oversensitivity or selfishness, that "You think only of yourself." See DARVO, below.
- ✓ **Fake Concern:** They pretend they're concerned for you when their real object is to undermine your confidence and increase your dependency on them.
- ✓ **Lying:** Narcissists don't lie out of guilt. They lie to confuse you and get you to see things their way. Unlike sociopaths, many narcissists won't lie in response to a direct question, but practice avoidance or tell the truth in part while omitting material facts. Lies are often combined with reversals.

✓ **Guilt-Tripping:** This shifts the responsibility onto you, which weakens you and makes the abuser feel superior. Narcissists may falsely claim to have allies or that others are judging you, too; it's all a ruse to make you feel that you're the one at fault. They may play the victim by acting needy or helpless and say, "I can't manage without your help," or "You don't care about me." They may act like a martyr and complain, "Why do you treat me like this after all that I've done for you?"

✓ **DARVO:** Narcissists are experts at DARVO, which involves not just "playing the victim" but also victim-blaming. The acronym stands for "Deny, Attack, and Reverse Victim and Offender." Manipulators deny the abuse ever took place, attack you when you try to hold them accountable, and then claim that they're the victim, thus reversing the reality of the abuser and victim. For example, if you uncover your partner's flirtatious text, they might deny its significance, act outraged, and attack you for looking at their phone. By "blaming the victim" a narcissist avoids being held accountable and is free to carry on; while you, the real victim, feel guilty for spying, thus undercutting your justified anger. I once remarked to a violent spouse who blamed his wife for his behavior: "I'm surprised to hear your wife has that much power over you." He was dumbfounded since his whole agenda was to gain power over her.

✓ **Shaming:** Shaming goes beyond guilt to make you feel inadequate and unworthy. Narcissists shame their partner's appearance, personality, interests, abilities, and any shortcomings you could imagine. It can even be couched in a compliment: "I'm surprised that of all people you'd stoop to that!" Disclosing private facts about you in public is designed to mock and humiliate you. Negative comparisons are a potent form of shaming, especially comparisons to an ex or an abusive parent. Even if the qualities being shamed are true, shaming demeans and subjugates you as a person.

✓ **Avoidance:** Manipulators desperately avoid responsibility and confrontations about their behavior. Avoidance tactics include refusal to talk, vagueness, glossing over, whitewashing, and evasiveness that blur the facts, confuse you, and plant doubt. They might combine their avoidance with boasting, compliments, or statements you want to hear, such as, "You know how much I love you," or guilt-tripping and reactive complaints that you're too precise, nagging, or questioning. Don't be dissuaded. When you have doubts, trust them!

✓ **Inventing Sentiments:** Narcissists may voice assumptions about your intentions or beliefs and then behave as if they were true to justify their actions. Similarly, they may act as if something had been agreed upon when it hasn't and refuse to hear your objections.

✓ **Intimidation:** Intimidation is behavior intended to make you overestimate both your weaknesses and your intimidator's strengths. It can be as overt as a threat of physical violence or veiled, such as "No one's irreplaceable." Other examples are, "I always win," "I have methods and friends in high places," "Think twice about leaving if you want to see your children," or "Have you considered the repercussions of that decision?" Another strategy is telling a story meant to provoke fear, such as: "She left her husband and lost her kids, her house, everything"; or "I fight to win. I once almost killed a guy." Intimidation also includes behavior intended to instill fear. Examples are destroying property, lurking, staring, or hovering over you while you're on the phone or working. A narcissist might get in your face and refuse to move away to frighten and dominate you.

✓ **Emotional Blackmail:** Emotional blackmail overlaps with guilt-tripping and shaming. Abusers might threaten to withhold affection or otherwise cause you emotional harm unless you acquiesce. It can range from threatening suicide to making statements like, "Do you want the children to know about your past?" Victims often feel FOG, which stands for Fear, Obligation, and Guilt, an acronym created by psychotherapist and author Susan Forward. If you *fear* your partner, feel *obligated* to comply, and feel *guilty* if you don't, you're probably being emotionally blackmailed.

✓ **Passive-Aggression:** Narcissists can also exercise their power and avoid responsibility through passive-aggression. It's a hostile refusal that's often done "silently." Manipulators refuse to do what they don't want to do by forgetting, doing it too late, or doing it half-heartedly. For example, they may refuse to participate in family responsibilities, take care of the children, or sabotage your efforts, such as offering you dessert when you're dieting. See my article, "Dealing with a Passive-Aggressive Partner."[50]

> ▸ *Innercises: Identifying Narcissistic Behaviors*

Perhaps aspects of the foregoing description of abusers and abuse are familiar.

• What did you feel reading about it?

- Which types of abuse have you experienced presently and in the past?
- What did you feel in your body at the time? What posture or action did your body want to take?
- In the days ahead journal about abuse you're currently experiencing, including your thoughts, feelings, and physical reactions.
- The following is a checklist of narcissistic behaviors. It's not for scoring, but to heighten your awareness about your relationship and comfort level. Assess whether your partner does many or some of these behaviors. The more you recognize, the more likely it is your partner is a narcissist. You may need help from someone objective. Write down conversations and identify abusive tactics.

✓ Treats people rudely
✓ Takes things without asking or offering to return them
✓ Criticizes you, your opinion, interests, work, family, or friends
✓ Judges and criticizes others
✓ Must get their way or else becomes angry
✓ Manipulates you and others to get their way
✓ Values appearances above friendship or integrity
✓ Expects special treatment, such as not waiting in line or getting the best seats, often tipping to get it
✓ Tells you what to do
✓ Blames you unjustly
✓ Lies
✓ Only wants to hire "the best" in any field
✓ Befriends people of high-status or
✓ based on what they can provide

✓ Thinks they're superior to or more important than others
✓ Needs a lot of attention, validation, and compliments
✓ Never forgives or forgets
✓ Dismisses or minimizes your opinion, feelings, needs, or wants
✓ Seeks retribution or revenge
✓ Is charming in public, but different at home
✓ Is addicted to drugs, alcohol, gambling, sex, work, or something else
✓ Violates moral or ethical values to get their needs met
✓ Rages
✓ Imagines success or fame
✓ Is very defensive
✓ Makes time available on their terms
✓ Works less than you on the relationship

- ✓ Pressures you to say or do things against your values
- ✓ Takes center stage (sometimes after others lose interest)
- ✓ Often interrupts or stops you from speaking
- ✓ Lacks concern for your safety, needs, or feelings
- ✓ Takes credit for your or other people's effort or work
- ✓ Never apologizes
- ✓ Abuses you physically, financially, emotionally, or sexually
- ✓ Expects you to read their mind without making requests
- ✓ Imagines others envy them
- ✓ Unremorsefully exploits you or your resources or those of others
- ✓ Avoids responsibility for their behavior
- ✓ Betrays you or feels entitled to flirt in front of you or with your friends
- ✓ Misrepresents stories to look good or to make you or others look bad
- ✓ Makes hurtful jokes about you in public
- ✓ Emphasizes appearances
- ✓ Needs to be the best, the first, or have the most expensive or prestigious things
- ✓ Envies perceived competitors
- ✓ Slanders your and other people's character
- ✓ Is unpredictable and may explode abruptly
- ✓ Is hypersensitive to criticism or humiliation
- ✓ Harms perceived competitors
- ✓ Disrespects rules and boundaries; e.g., inappropriately asks people favors or misappropriates their property
- ✓ Brags

Chapter 4

ECHO: UNDERSTANDING YOURSELF

Not everyone romantically involved with a narcissist is like Echo, but those who stay for more than a few years come to resemble her: someone who sacrifices their own life to accommodate others. Unconscious yearning to magically heal your wounded self can drive you to find an ideal partner — someone who instantly captivates you with their attractive appearance or charisma. For a while, your partner may have indeed fulfilled certain unmet childhood needs or longings that perhaps one of your parents never gave you, but these wounds blind you from recognizing the narcissist's charm as seduction.

ECHO, AN ACCOMMODATOR

Like Narcissus, narcissists are overly self-absorbed, and like Echo, accommodators are overly other-absorbed. In contrast to narcissists, accommodators move toward people, believing that loving and being loved will protect them from being hurt. They yearn for happiness, validation, and unity — a feeling of oneness with a romantic partner with whom they can finally achieve wholeness and the solution to inner emptiness and insecurity stemming from childhood. Their longing often leads to an insecure, anxious attachment style.

Accommodators react to and worry about their partner's and other people's expectations. They try harder than their partners to make relationships work by accommodating and pleasing them — an ideal fit for a narcissist. However, inner shame often drives them to love people who don't sufficiently reciprocate their love. In this way, their belief in their unlovability becomes a self-fulfilling prophecy operating beneath conscious awareness.

In contrast to the audacious air of the narcissist, accommodators shun power and have less personal agency. Their personality is generally passive, compliant, and self-effacing. They're quick to believe what others tell them. They idealize connectedness and being loving and unselfish. They're attentive and want to be desired, accepted, supported, understood, needed, and loved. Thus, being accused of selfishness or self-centeredness deeply wounds them. Above all, they want their love received and to feel needed. To that end, they please, try to understand, and take care of others, whose needs and feelings they prioritize to ensure that they're approved of, needed, and not abandoned. Like Echo, this makes them prone to dependency on a relationship although their own needs go unmet.

Preferring a subordinate role, accommodators repress their pride, ambition, anger, power, independence, and competitive impulses. Many avoid recognition and positions of authority, as they're uncomfortable winning or being in charge. Rather than develop their expansive needs, they prefer to live vicariously through the self-assured narcissist. It boosts their inferior self-image and allows them to feel taken care of.

To feel safe and accepted, at an early age accommodators learned to adapt to their parents' needs and suppress their own. Then as adults, they hide their true feelings behind what they imagine are their likable traits. They often feel flawed, guilty, not enough, and unworthy of respect. Whereas narcissists feel entitled, many accommodators don't believe they have any rights and feel selfish and guilty expressing their needs (if they're aware of them). They not only ignore their needs but also their wants. Narcissists agree and treat them accordingly.

They go along to get along, putting others' needs and feelings first and sometimes self-sacrificing at great lengths to please. When something bothers them, to their peril, they try to forget it and overlook feelings of discomfort that signal trouble. In doing so, they deny, minimize, or rationalize abuse or hurt, and find fault in themselves, apologize, and try to be more understanding. The abuse they endure may be intertwined with affection, a pattern so familiar from their past that it goes unrecognized, or they see it but deny its impact. Little by little they tolerate increasingly self-centered and abusive behavior to prevent their greatest fear, rejection. That would dash their hope of finding lasting love and confirm their belief of being unlovable. However, their behavior only enables narcissistic abuse and compounds their suffering.

Emotionally trapped in their youth, accommodators deny or hold back their anger and are unable to assert and protect themselves. Like Echo, they've lost their independent voice. Denial of self-interest and fear of conflict and abandonment limit their ability to effectively set boundaries and get their needs met. They often confuse healthy assertiveness with aggression. To their ears, being assertive sounds harsh and unkind, setting limits appears rude, and making requests feels selfish. Saying "No," or "I don't like that," both to those who abuse them and to those who need them, causes them guilt and anxiety at the idea of potentially jeopardizing the relationship. They feel selfish putting themselves ahead of others and can feel rejected if someone doesn't want their help. After years of dysfunctional parenting and narcissistic abuse, they fear that their views, feelings, needs, and wants will be met with indifference, abuse, or rejection. In sum, narcissists sacrifice peace for power, and accommodators sacrifice themselves for peace.

When you hesitate to disagree or express disappointment, irritation, or hurt feelings and only echo what narcissists believe and want to hear, your integrity gradually disappears, as did Echo's. Failing to speak up and defend your feelings and boundaries gives a narcissist greater power and no incentive to change. Meanwhile, you feel increasingly helpless and unentitled to be happy, loved, successful, or worthy of pursuing your dreams. Eventually, accommodators withdraw and turn their denied aggression inward as guilt and self-judgment.

➤ *Innercises: Are You an Accommodator?*

Write about the motives and ideals that drive your behavior. If you think you might be an accommodator, evaluate yourself with this list. Do you:

- Look up to your partner with admiration?
- Placate your partner to deescalate conflict?
- Have trouble speaking your opinions?
- Give in to your partner's decisions or requests?
- Allow your partner's moods to affect your feelings and behavior?
- Spend time analyzing your partner's feelings, behavior, and motives?
- Try hard to win your partner's approval?
- Empathize with and give more to your partner than yourself?
- Violate your values or do things you're uncomfortable with to please your partner?
- Give up friends to be with your partner?
- Change plans to accommodate your partner?
- Avoid asking for what you want or need?
- Remain loyal even though you're not treated well?
- Care more about your partner's feelings than they care about yours?
- Participate in sex you don't want in the hope of receiving love?
- Practice self-care and meet your needs?
- Ask for support?
- Have difficulty saying no and setting clear boundaries?
- Express your authentic feelings with your partner, including anger?

- Criticize yourself or think you should try harder?
- Do extra work and feel resentful or unappreciated?
- Absorb blame or criticism from your partner?
- Feel trapped or powerless?
- Pursue your personal and professional goals?
- Maintain hobbies and interests separate from your partner?

Chapter 5

CODEPENDENCY

Codependency originates in childhood and is passed on generationally through role modeling and dysfunctional parenting. Codependents have a "lost self" — they've lost the ability to respond to their internal cues and have difficulty accessing their feelings, wants, and needs. Instead, their thinking and behavior revolve around someone or something external that they react to and try to control rather than respond to their innate self.[51] Codependency underlies all addictions, including romance, relationship, and love addiction. Thus, addicts are codependent on the object of their addiction.

Echo's self-sacrificing personality resembles the stereotypical codependent (see chapter 4). Narcissists and codependents are usually considered opposites. Although their outward behaviors may contrast, they share the core symptoms of codependency and many psychological traits.[52] While generally narcissists and accommodators are codependent, the reverse isn't true. Not all codependents are accommodators, nor are they narcissists. The DSM criteria to diagnose narcissism aren't related to codependency.

Although both narcissists and accommodators focus on other people, they have different agendas. Whereas Narcissus was transfixed by a reflection, Echo was transfixed on Narcissus. She sacrificed her life waiting for his glance or kind word that never came. Narcissists obsess over wanting people to admire and revere them, while accommodators obsess over wanting people to accept and love them. Sadly, their codependent habit of looking outside themselves doesn't help, but only alienates them further from their lost, true self.

CORE SYMPTOMS OF CODEPENDENCY

The core symptoms of codependency are shame, low self-esteem, dependency, denial, control, and dysfunctional boundaries and communication, all of which lead to intimacy problems and painful emotions. These symptoms are expressed differently by narcissists and their partners, as explained below:

Shame

Shame is at the core of codependency and accounts for most codependent symptoms, such as people-pleasing or bragging in order to be liked. It manifests as feelings and beliefs, which may be unconscious, of inadequacy, inferiority, and of not being enough, likable, or lovable. Shame breeds irrational guilt, fear, anxiety, depression, and impaired self-esteem. Codependents don't believe they truly deserve to be loved simply for who they are, but that they must earn love. Love is always conditional. This creates fear of abandonment and sensitivity to criticism and rejection. They grow up feeling insecure and cope by withdrawing, seeking power, or accommodating. Whereas narcissists choose the path of power, accommodators choose compliance, each based on their unique personality and environmental influences, such as role models and culture. Beneath shame is emptiness, which codependents don't often experience unless they feel lonely or abandoned.

Narcissists: As explained in chapter 2 – Underlying Features, narcissists' impression management, bragging, and need for constant affirmation and attention are all driven by deep shame. Same goes for their arrogance and need to be the best, wear the best, associate with the best, and be treated better than anyone else. They're ashamed of vulnerable feelings and hide any signs of weakness, insecurity, or fear. Narcissists' impaired self-esteem is inflated to compensate for shame, which triggers aggression when their superiority or power is challenged in any way. They guard against their inner emptiness by demanding constant nourishment of their narcissistic supplies.

Accommodators: Instead of feeling superior and entitled, shame makes them feel inferior and unentitled. Their impaired self-esteem is unrealistically low. They're hard on themselves and tyrannize themselves with "should's" that mirror the attacks they receive from narcissistic partners. Shame inhibits their authenticity and ability to take risks and share their thoughts and feelings, predominantly "negative" or aggressive ones that might displease people.

Dependency

Codependents are dependent on others, particularly in romantic relationships. They're afraid of being rejected or abandoned and need people to like them to feel okay about themselves. They lack autonomy and have difficulty making decisions and taking action independently. Many codependents feel lonely by themselves for too long and prefer to be in a relationship. Yet, they often feel trapped because dependency makes it hard for them to leave even if it's a painful or abusive relationship.

Narcissists: Although they might act as if they're needless and push people away, narcissists are dependent on others for affirmation. Their self-image, thinking, and behavior are other-oriented in a futile effort to stabilize and validate their self-esteem and fragile self. More than most codependents, they depend on people to assuage their inner emptiness and feed their insatiable needs for attention and admiration (see chapter 2 – Underlying Features). Although they like to take charge, they can become quite dependent on their partner but use their power over them to avoid the humiliation of feeling dependent. Only the threat of abandonment reveals how dependent they truly are.

Accommodators: They yearn for a close relationship, which becomes the center of their lives. They give up friendships and hobbies to be with their partner and may even adopt the narcissist's view of their interests, friends, and family. They prefer to do things with someone else and have difficulty acting autonomously. Thus, they're comfortable following a leader. When alone, they risk becoming depressed without a support system or a structure, such as work or school, to motivate them. Losing a relationship can devastate them. More than other people, it affects their sense of worth. They can feel like they're losing themselves since they invest so much in their relationship. It triggers their biggest fear — ending up alone.

Denial

One of the obstacles to getting help for codependency is that codependents are in denial about it. Usually, they believe the problem is someone else, or they attribute it to other factors. They try to fix their partner or go from one relationship or job to another, never realizing that they have a problem. They also may deny their addiction, pain, past trauma, or problems in a relationship. Often, they don't know what they're feeling and instead focus on what others are feeling. The same goes for their wants and needs. Although some codependents seem needy, others act like they're self-sufficient. They won't reach out for help and deny their vulnerability and needs for love and intimacy (see chapter 8 – Come Out of Denial).

Narcissists: They tend to deny many of their feelings and emotional needs and hide behind a façade of self-possession and aloofness, despite their neediness. Having needs makes them feel dependent and weak, so they won't admit that they're being demanding and needy. They mainly feel humiliation and anger when their inflated pride isn't supported and deny feelings of hurt, loneliness, emptiness, fear, and any need for connection.

Accommodators: Accommodators deny their pain and problems in the relationship for the sake of maintaining it. They're sympathetic and adapt to the narcissist's feelings, wants, and needs, which they attend to, while they deny their own. Similarly, they also deny their wants and needs, particularly needs for safety, autonomy, power, and many emotional needs. Instead, they accept the narcissist's version of reality, condemn themselves, and try to be more understanding and loving. Some accommodators expect people to satisfy their needs, but most act self-sufficient and deny their need for support, nurturing, and tenderness.

Control

It's normal to want control over our environment. Childhood trauma and insecurity cause codependents to need a greater degree of control. Their dependency makes what people think, say, and do paramount to their sense of well-being and safety. Hence, they need to control them directly or indirectly with people-pleasing, lies, or passive manipulation. Some codependents are bossy and tell others what they should or shouldn't do, even when it's clear that the other person isn't taking their advice. An addiction, like alcoholism, can loosen them up, or help them hold their feelings down, like overeating and workaholism, so they don't feel out of control in close relationships.

Narcissists: Narcissists control others indirectly and directly to feel safe, powerful, and superior. They use seduction, impression management, and all forms of abuse. Driven by their shame, narcissists control their vulnerable feelings, such as fear, hurt, and sadness, to not appear weak or dependent.

Accommodators: Accommodators often feel morally superior to their partner narcissist or other people and exercise indirect control with advice, criticism, caretaking, and people-pleasing. Helping and being needed bolster their self-worth and assure them they won't be abandoned. They can become resentful when their advice is ignored, yet usually hide aggressive feelings to avoid abandonment and conflict.

Dysfunctional Boundaries

Boundaries are an imaginary line between people. They divide up what's yours and somebody else's. Boundaries apply not only to your body, money, and belongings, but also to your feelings, thoughts, and needs. Codependents get into trouble because generally they have blurry or weak boundaries. Because there's no boundary, they get easily triggered and react to other people. They absorb their words and feel responsible for other people's feelings, opinions, and problems or blame their own on someone else.

With boundaries, they'd realize people's words are just their opinion and they wouldn't feel threatened by criticism and disagreements. On the other hand, some codependents have rigid boundaries. They're closed off and withdrawn, making it hard for other people to get close to them. Sometimes, people flip back and forth between having weak and rigid boundaries (see chapter 7 – Lack of Boundaries).

Narcissists: They're uncertain of their boundaries and *don't see other people as separate* from themselves. They disregard and violate other people's boundaries by controlling and abusing them. As discussed in chapter 3 – Projection and Blame, they project their thoughts and feelings onto others and blame them for their own shortcomings and mistakes, all of which they cannot tolerate in themselves. Lack of boundaries makes them thin-skinned, highly reactive, and defensive; so they take everything personally.

Accommodators: Accommodators *don't see themselves as separate* from others; so they disregard themselves. Due to their weak boundaries, like narcissists, they're reactive, defensive, and take things personally. They have weak filters between themselves and others, are suggestible, and feel responsible for other people's feelings and problems. They absorb shaming and blaming and feel powerless to stop abuse.

Dysfunctional Communication

Healthy communication is clear and assertive (see chapter 9), but codependents' communication is passive, aggressive, or both. When codependents can't identify or fear being direct about their feelings and need, their denial, shame, and insecurities create dysfunctional communication, which becomes dishonest and confusing. They communicate through control, judgment, criticism, and complaints. As a result, problems are never talked about or resolved but fuel repetitive fights. Some boil with resentment until they blow up.

Narcissists: Their communication is predominantly aggressive and abusive or passive-aggressive. Some narcissists intellectualize, obfuscate, and are indirect. Aside from anger, they find it challenging to identify and clearly state their feelings. They express opinions and take positions, but they frequently don't listen and are dogmatic and inflexible.

Accommodators: Their communication is primarily passive or passive-aggressive. Sometimes, they're aggressive, too. They avoid discussing problems, taking positions, confronting others, and being direct. They edit themselves in anticipation of the other person's reaction. They prefer to listen rather than reveal their true thoughts and feelings and go along or give advice. This suits a narcissist who wants attention. Without boundaries, accommodators feel trapped to listen.

OTHER SYMPTOMS

Relationships can't thrive without self-esteem, autonomy, assertiveness, and clear boundaries that afford partners freedom and respect. The combination of codependent patterns makes intimacy virtually impossible for narcissists and codependents and leads to painful emotions.

Problems with Intimacy

The openness required by emotional intimacy is a problem for narcissists and many accommodators. They fear that they'll be judged, rejected, or left. Codependents who are emotionally unavailable fear being smothered and losing their autonomy. Their attention is on an addiction or distraction, such as work or preoccupation with a child. They deny their need for closeness, while their partners deny their need for autonomy and separateness (see chapter 7 – Intimacy Problems and my blog, "The Dance of Intimacy").[53]

Painful Emotions

Codependency leads to stress and painful emotions, often caused by shame and low self-esteem, which create anxiety and fear about being judged, rejected, or abandoned. Codependents fear making mistakes, being a failure, being close, being alone, and feeling smothered. All of the symptoms lead to anger and resentment, depression, hopelessness, and despair. When the feelings are too much, they can become numb and develop physical symptoms.

Obsessions

Codependents spend time thinking about other people or relationships. Often, they try to decipher what someone else is thinking or feeling and why. They can obsess about a "mistake" they believe they made. Narcissists become obsessed with anyone who has humiliated them or whom they envy or perceive to be more powerful. Accommodators obsess over loved ones and their problems and people they believe judged or reject them and how to rectify the situation.

Perfectionism

Perfectionism is a compulsion to achieve unrealistic standards. It negatively impacts the perfectionist's self-esteem when they fail to do so. It's more than doing their best. It's a defense to shame based on black and white thinking. "If I'm not perfect, then I'm a failure (or unlikeable, unattractive, etc.)" (See Underlying Features – Perfectionism and *"I'm Not Perfect - I'm Only Human" - How to Beat Perfectionism*).[54]

Chapter 6

DATING A NARCISSIST

It may seem self-evident, but when you begin dating someone, you don't know who they are. Even if you've been casual friends or colleagues, you don't know how this person acts in an intimate relationship. So dating is a time to gather information, not to make commitments. Your first commitment must be to yourself – to protect yourself and hold onto your heart.

Narcissists are drawn to a partner who can support their pride. They may seek someone of exceptional beauty, talent, or influence who admires them. They also look for someone to fill their emptiness — someone emotionally expressive and nurturing, qualities that they lack. They need partners they can control, who won't challenge them or make them feel weak.[55] Accommodators meet those needs. They in turn typically seek partners who appear bold, self-assured, spontaneous, or eager to take charge. It's a perfect, albeit painful, match.

I once went to dinner with a narcissist who was chillingly rude to the hostess. When I expressed my displeasure, he proudly claimed, "Some women like it. They feel protected." Sometimes, two narcissists get involved, but they blame and push each other away, fight over whose needs come first, and end up miserable with their need for each other. This is why two accommodating codependents rarely are more than good friends and not romantic partners. Usually, they would be repelled by the accommodator's weakness or deference.

Generally, people who date narcissists fail to recognize their personality disorder. Narcissists are engaging, charming, and energetic, and research reveals that they possess emotional intelligence that helps them perceive, express, understand, and manage emotions.[56] They frequently but not always consciously, use their well-developed social skills and manipulative and deceptive tactics to make a good first impression.

Most narcissists show great interest in their romantic prospects and employ their charm and powers of persuasion to achieve their aims. Their strategy can include appearing generous, flirty, boastful, subtle, loving, flattering, sexy, romantic, or eager to commit. Male narcissists often seduce with lavish gifts, fine dining, and a classy or opulent lifestyle. Females are typically flirtatious and charm men with their beauty and sex appeal. Once they've attracted a potential partner, however, they play cat and mouse, encourage jealousy, or act nonchalant to keep those prospects primed to give them what they want.

Don't judge yourself for succumbing. Narcissists' alluring performance is designed to win trust and love, implicitly promising that their attentiveness will continue. Research revealed that most people like them initially.[57] Narcissists don't hide their true colors for long. In the study, it took seven meetings for participants to perceive a narcissist's darker side. When dating, narcissists are even more motivated to win you over – sadly, sometimes all the way to the altar. So it's important to pay attention.

THE END IS IN THE BEGINNING

A wise woman once advised me about relationships: "The ending is in the beginning." What she meant was that early on people communicate in words or actions that they're not interested in commitment, that they don't do well in relationships, that they have an addiction, or that they have a selfish, angry, or controlling nature. Your feelings and intuition know what those signals mean. Believe them.

Finding Your Blind Spots

Clients who thought that their spouses completely changed only after they were married, upon reflection, admitted there were telltale signs early on that they'd overlooked. Spotting a narcissist may be difficult. Narcissists are never boring. They're often physically attractive, charismatic, and sexually appealing. It's easy to be drawn to their intelligence, entertaining personality, special talents, or professional success. But you don't want to fall in love with one. Over time, you can end up feeling ignored, uncared for, and unimportant as the narcissist's criticism, demands, and emotional unavailability increase, while your confidence and self-esteem decrease. So be alert to these blind spots when dating:

Idealization: It's natural to idealize a partner in the romantic phase of a relationship. On first impression, you might be awed by a narcissist's self-direction and "strength," then idealize those qualities you hope to absorb, unaware of the narcissist's fragile persona and hidden shame.[58] Of course, it's the positive, not negative, qualities that make you fall in love. This makes them easy for you to idealize as you listen, transfixed and fascinated, to their achievements, interesting stories, and entertaining banter. For insecure individuals, such a display can be very impressive. You may be attracted to traits or a lifestyle you wish you had, and narcissists will soak up your admiration. The downside is that idealization blinds you to contrary information and can turn red flags into green ones.

Loneliness: If you're lonely, depressed, or codependent, you're even more likely to idealize someone you admire (see chapter 3 – Projection and Blame). When you lack a support system or are unhappy, you might rush into a relationship and become quickly attached before really knowing someone. Following a breakup or divorce, you may find "love on the rebound" or enter into a "transitional relationship." It's far better, however, to recover fully from a breakup before dating again.

Sexual attraction: The greater the physical attraction and sexual intensity, the easier it is to ignore red flags. You might mistake anxiety as excitement or even "love," particularly if you were abused or had an angry, judgmental, or controlling parent. The aura of a person's sexual energy obfuscates mental and emotional energy that impairs your reason and possibly self-control.

Seduction: When your self-esteem is low or you doubt your lovability or attractiveness, you can easily be seduced by sweet talk. As master manipulators, some narcissists can be quite seductive, and not just sexually. They may be adept listeners and communicators or allure you with generosity, flattery, self-disclosure, and vulnerability – just the opposite of what you might expect from a narcissist. They may even believe they're sincere in their behavior, but they're still emotionally unavailable and acting in self-interest.

Familiarity: If you had a narcissistic parent, being with a narcissist feels familiar – like family. This attraction is often unconscious and may feel like "chemistry." With help from a good therapist, you can learn to understand this attraction for what it is, enabling you to spot and even feel repelled by someone self-centered or potentially abusive.

Codependency and Low Self-Esteem: Codependency and low self-esteem make you vulnerable to idealization, seduction, and confusing romance with real love, especially if you've lost touch with your feelings and natural aliveness. The drama of a close relationship with a narcissist can feel energizing. The attention and romance make you feel desired and lovable. They promise an antidote to being alone and your search for ideal love that offers you protection, affection, sympathy, and understanding. In addition, the neurochemicals of sex can lift a depressed mood but can also fuel codependency and love addiction if a relationship is used to alleviate loneliness or discontent.

Codependents give themselves freely to friends and are eager to share activities in new relationships. They're used to accommodating to get along and don't protect themselves. The tendency to accommodate is stronger in early dating when you try to make a good impression. Your desire for a partner further induces you to sacrifice your needs. When something bothers you, instead of mentioning it, you try to forget it. This can be particularly perilous if you overlook or rationalize feelings of discomfort that signal trouble.

Signs You're Dating a Narcissist

While under the romantic spell of a narcissist's charm, you will likely overlook the symptoms of NPD described earlier. Note the behaviors that you should be concerned about when you're getting involved with another person outlined in chapter 3 – Identifying Narcissistic Behavior. Don't get hung up on a diagnosis; any narcissistic behavior that occurs repeatedly should give you pause to reconsider. However, if enough of them add up and you still want to remain in the relationship, seek counseling to help you discern what's going on and protect yourself.

Self-Centeredness: When you talk to your date, ask yourself whether this person is interested in getting to know you or do they always center the conversation on themselves. Even though it can make first dates easier and being a good listener is an asset, someone who talks mainly about numero uno is a tell-tale sign that you will feel less valued and be a minor partner in the relationship. If you felt invisible in your family while growing up, this might feel familiar. You could feel validated by the attention you receive as a good listener, but beware that this pattern will likely continue.

Some narcissists, however, can appear to be fascinated by you and even mirror your interests to make you like them. In the short term, this might enhance intimacy and make you feel special, but no narcissist can keep this act going for long. Sooner or later, you realize that they're not truly interested in you or your life, but that their attention is a set-up for getting what they want, such as sex or financial help.

Lack of Empathy: True narcissists lack empathy. When you share something sad or important to you, if your partner doesn't seem interested or show an appropriate emotional response, it may signal a lack of empathy. Pay attention if you feel ignored, invisible, annoyed, patronized, or drained by conversations. Other signs to be aware of include walking ahead of you, making you track them down for return phone calls, arriving late, disregarding your boundaries and needs, and interrupting conversations to text or take calls from other people. Admittedly, these are minor things — any one of them alone may not be significant — but together they paint a picture of someone who doesn't care about you and who will behave similarly on bigger issues.

Arrogance: Narcissists feel superior to other people and can be rude or abusive when they don't get what they want. They must always be right, and they won't listen to differing opinions. Pay attention to how your date treats cashiers, waitresses, car valets, and others providing services. Does your date show people respect or act superior to them?

Because of their insecurity, narcissists gravitate toward high-status people, material things, and institutions (the best schools, best cars, the best table at the best restaurants, designer labels, etc.) A simple, intimate restaurant won't meet their standards or provide them the public visibility they seek. Their style may impress you now but will later depress you when you're told you're second class or when you feel ignored or like a prop in their life.

Bragging and Need for Admiration: Because narcissists are deeply insecure, they need constant validation, appreciation, and recognition. Most successful grandiose narcissists developed their attractive qualities to mask their unresolved feelings of insecurity. Although not all braggarts are narcissists, many narcissists are given to boasting to convince themselves and you of their greatness. If they haven't yet achieved their goals, they may brag about how they will or how they should have more recognition or success than they do. Don't be dazzled by a narcissist's grandiose plans, bragging, or name-dropping. It might be a pack of lies, and even if it's not, it reveals insecurity. See chapter 3 – Impression Management.

Entitlement: This trait is a real give-away. To narcissists, their needs come first, not only before yours, but before all. Take note of whether your date refuses to turn off their cell phone in a theater, expects special treatment from others (such as parking attendants, maitre d's, stewardesses, and other service providers), cuts in line, steals things like tableware, airline blankets, hotel ashtrays, and so on. One narcissist shamelessly admitted to me that she had no curiosity in her husband's work or interests but fully expected him to attentively give her his undivided attention.

Don't lose sight of your needs and desires. Notice how your partner responds to your requests. A narcissist may be gracious with your wishes for a while but is unlikely to continue over the long term. A narcissist is unlikely to value your choices and insist that theirs are best. See chapter 3 – Entitled Behavior.

Aggression: A small disagreement can quickly erupt into a major conflict, and narcissists never take responsibility for the escalation. Difficulties and frustrations are always someone else's fault. Early in a relationship, many narcissists mask boorish behavior with charm and flattery, but observe how your date speaks about past romantic partners, co-workers, the opposite sex, or groups of people. Eventually, narcissists speak disparagingly of anyone who has impeded their agenda or disappointed or confronted them. Expect that one day you, too, will be the target of such attacks. See chapter 3 – Aggression.

Criticism and Blame: When narcissists can no longer feel superior through charm and boasting, or should you complain, they devalue you to maintain their illusion of superiority. They typically criticize and tell you how you should act or change in some way. Perfectionistic narcissists are the most difficult and might obsess over your behavior and appearance. If you object, narcissists usually respond with even more criticism, explaining that they're only trying to be helpful or that you're too sensitive.

At first, you might overlook their comments, especially if they're delivered in a teasing or calm manner, but demeaning remarks will become more frequent, overt, and callous. People who blame others for their feelings or circumstances aren't taking responsibility for themselves. They're invested in their victimhood, and they often color their blame with contempt. Beware of your empathy getting the better of you and getting sucked into taking care of them. They have no interest in caring for your needs and feelings. See chapter 3 – Verbal Abuse and Manipulation.

Control and Manipulation: When planning activities, observe your date's use of control and manipulation to get their needs met and to avoid compromising to meet yours. You might have difficulty agreeing on a place and time to meet. Narcissists often insist on their choices, especially if they suspect that they've already won you over. You may not notice that the relationship is developing on the narcissist's terms. In the beginning, your date might appear to consider your point of view, but to narcissists, compromise is always a painful loss of power. If you complain, they may act offended, accuse you of ingratitude or distrust, or protest that they're doing everything for you, yet never bother to ask what you want. Eventually, they insist that you behave in certain ways, try to limit your contacts and activities, and may even interrogate you about your other relationships and conversations with family, your therapist, or friends. Failure to object early on only ensures that their encroachments will get worse.

The signs of dating a narcissist are usually insidious at first. When falling in love, you're eager to please your partner and spend as much time as possible together. But you should be careful, especially when you notice that you're accommodating out of fear of rocking the boat and losing your partner.

THE UNAVAILABLE LOVER

Loving someone emotionally unavailable hurts; you can never enjoy deep intimacy with such a person. Narcissists are emotionally unavailable and uncomfortable with their vulnerability or yours. They make excuses, are evasive, or are inept when it comes to talking about feelings or the relationship. After a wonderful, intimate evening, they pull away, shut down, or become abusive. In time, they keep you at a distance because they're afraid if you get too close, you won't like what you see. They also use anger, criticism, or various distractions to create distance. You start to feel undesired and insecure. They may have an avoidant-dismissive attachment style. In most cases, they're afraid of intimacy and their avoidant behavior is unconscious. Nevertheless, when you don't hear from them, you become anxious and keep seeking closeness. You confuse your pain and longing with love and you wind up feeling alone, depressed, unimportant, or discarded.

Narcissists lack the motivation and skills to engage in true intimacy. No relationship will ever be as important to them as defending their hollow egos. Real intimacy would require them to be authentic, vulnerable, and to share their feelings honestly with you, which they're loath to do. When it comes to a new romance, the exciting sex and promises that come with it might feel like intimacy, but they're not. Establishing deep intimacy takes time, and although some narcissists may seem emotionally available at first, eventually they reveal their inability to connect emotionally and/or make a commitment.

Signs of Emotional Unavailability

When you're looking for an intimate, committed relationship, potential partners who live at a significant distance, are married, or are still in love with someone else raise bright red flags. Similarly, addicts (including workaholics) are unavailable because their addiction is their priority and it controls them. Recently divorced individuals, too, may be unable to commit to someone new. Here's a list of more subtle red flags that may signal unavailability, especially when several are present:

Flirting with Flattery: Like snake charmers, flattering flirters may woo you with their attentiveness and communication skills. They may be able to maintain short-term intimacy and some can add self-disclosure and vulnerability to the mix, but they prefer the chase to the catch.

Control Issues: Some people simply won't be inconvenienced or modify their routines. Typically, these commitment-phobes are inflexible and resist compromising. Relationships revolve around them.

Admitting Shortcomings: In the early days of a dating relationship, pay attention if your date admits or even hints that they aren't good at relationships, have had affairs or addiction issues, or aren't ready for marriage. Chances are that these admissions are true, unlike their bragging or gratuitous compliments and displays of vulnerability.

Clues from the Past: Ask your dates about any long-term relationships they've had and why they ended. If a pattern emerges that the relationships ended when intimacy normally develops, you may have uncovered how this relationship will probably end.

Perfection Seekers: Perfectionists look for and inevitably find fatal flaws in their romantic partners. The real issue, however, is that intimacy frightens them. When they can't find a flaw, they become anxious and eventually come up with an excuse to end the relationship. Don't be tempted to believe that you're better than their past partners.

Anger: Rudeness to waiters and other service providers is a red flag that indicates pent-up rage. People who are demanding and readily display anger are usually also emotionally abusive.

Arrogance: Avoid people who brag and act cocky, as these are signs of low self-esteem. It takes confidence to be vulnerable and commit to intimacy where flaws are inevitably revealed.

Lateness: Chronic lateness is a form of self-centeredness and may also indicate this person is avoiding the relationship (but don't assume that punctuality proves your date is a catch).

Invasiveness or Evasiveness: Secrecy, evasiveness, or inappropriate questions about money or sex may indicate hidden agendas and an unwillingness to allow relationships to unfold organically. People who conceal their past may feel ashamed, which may create an obstacle to intimacy.

Seduction: Beware of sexual cues given too early. Seducers avoid authenticity because they don't believe they're good enough for the partners they attract. Once the relationship becomes too real, they'll sabotage it. Seduction is a power-play about conquest.

What You Can Do

Most people reveal their emotional availability early on. Pay attention to the facts, especially if there's mutual attraction. Offering yourself to someone who appears to be "Mr. or Ms. Right," but who is emotionally unavailable, will leave you with nothing but pain. If you overlook, deny, or rationalize to avoid short-term disappointment, you risk long-term misery, and pressuring a partner to become more intimate is usually counterproductive. Practice these dating tips:

1. Listen to what your dates say about themselves and past relationships.
2. Notice whether your date takes responsibility or blames other people.
3. Pay attention if your date admits to serious shortcomings, commitment issues, infidelity, criminality, addiction, or abuse.
4. Be mindful of your feelings, especially if you feel anxious or uncomfortable, pressured, controlled, ignored, or belittled when you're with your date.
5. Try to discern whether your date is interested in you for yourself or only for what you can offer them.
6. Be authentic. Speak up about your needs, wants, and feelings, and watch your date's response.
7. Evaluate whether your date is willing to compromise and satisfy your needs, too.
8. Take things slowly. Notice if your date pressures you to change your boundaries.

➤ *Innercises: Are You Unavailable?*

If you've been in relationships with emotionally unavailable people, you may be unaware that you also are emotionally unavailable. Getting hooked on someone unavailable, like a narcissist, might mask your own problems and keep you in denial of your own unavailability.

- Are you angry at the opposite sex? Do you make or enjoy jokes at their expense? If so, your past wounds may need to heal before you're comfortable getting close to someone.
- Do you make excuses to avoid getting together?
- Do you think you're so independent you don't need anyone?
- Do you fear falling in love because you may get hurt?

- Are you always waiting for the other shoe to drop? Although people complain about their problems, many have even more difficulty accepting the good.
- Are you distrustful? Were you betrayed or lied to in the past and now look for deceit in everyone?
- Do you avoid intimacy by filling quiet times with distractions?
- Are you uncomfortable talking about yourself and your feelings? Do you have secrets you're ashamed of that make you feel undesirable or unlovable?
- Do you usually like to keep your options open in case someone better comes along?
- Do you fear a relationship may place too many expectations on you, that you'd give up your independence or lose your autonomy?

DATING AS A GAME

When you understand how the narcissistic mind works, you realize that narcissists see relationships as means to get what they want without sacrificing for you, except to the extent they can manipulate you to get what they want. They use relationships to enhance their egos and give them what they value, such as status, power, positive attention, esteem, and sex and get their narcissistic supply. You must have something to offer them, but don't expect to receive much in return. To them, relationships are like buying and selling, and their goal is to get what they want at the lowest price. It's a self-centered, business mindset. Emotions don't intrude.

In dating, narcissists focus on achieving their goals. For a male narcissist, that's usually sex or at least a beautiful woman at his side. A female narcissist may be looking for material gifts, sex, acts of service, and/or an extravagant courtship. The things most of us seek in relationships — exclusive commitment, care, support, and intimacy — are drawbacks to narcissists, who like to keep their options open. They don't see the connection between sex and intimacy. A relationship with a narcissist will never develop into an I-Thou relationship or even one based on love.

Some narcissists act like honeybees, chasing one partner after another, and sometimes continue to do that in a committed relationship. Amorous narcissists are adept and persuasive lovers with many conquests. Narcissists who play the field use relationships for self-enhancement. They have a style of love the Greeks called "Ludus," which is to seek uncommitted pleasure.[59] They're expert game-players and they aim to win, but for them, the thrill comes with the chase, not in enjoying the catch. Their objective is to receive admiration and have their sexual needs met with as little emotional investment as possible. Such game-playing thus strikes the perfect balance, and they keep their options open to flirt or date multiple partners to meet their endless need for supply.[60] Consequently, they typically lose interest in recent "conquests" and move on to the next before emotional intimacy has a chance to blossom. (Note that the research supporting this involved college students, who may outgrow those tendencies as they mature.Some narcissists check out other prospects and flirt right in front of you! While they may not blatantly lie when confronted, they're very skilled at deception. For example, a narcissist might tell you that you're her boyfriend, but later you discover she has another "boyfriend," and she'll deny she ever lied. Or, a narcissist might say he was working late at the office but omit that he had a romantic dinner with his co-worker. Narcissists who also have psychopathic traits are more nefarious and dangerous.

Examples of this sort of game-playing include the following:

1. Being hard to reach or ghosting (disappearing)
2. Making promises they can't or don't keep
3. Lying or being slippery and hard to pin down
4. Being very seductive and moving fast in the beginning
5. Refusing to discuss the relationship
6. Flirting with others in front of their romantic partner
7. Keeping your relationship secret from friends and family
8. Expecting their romantic partner to read their minds
9. Withholding emotional communication or sex
10. Blaming others and playing the victim
11. Not being the one to call or text first
12. Going hot and cold, such as coming on strong but then being slow to return calls or texts, or responding with only short, impersonal notes

ROMANCE

Most everyone wants to fall in love, as relationships are enlivening and motivating. This is especially true for codependents, for whom love is perhaps the highest ideal and relationships give life meaning and purpose. Sadly, however, a beautiful romance can turn sour or abruptly evaporate. With a narcissist, you wake from a wonderful dream to a painful nightmare.

Many forces come into play when you're attracted to a potential romantic partner. Most of those influences are unconscious and often lead to painful relationships if they stem from childhood trauma. When you heal your wounds, the veils of the past disappear, and you're able to more clearly perceive reality and your feelings and respond to them mindfully.

Forces of Attraction

Our brains are wired to fall in love, to feel the bliss and euphoria of romance, to enjoy pleasure, and to bond and procreate. Feel-good neurochemicals flood the brain at each stage of lust, attraction, and attachment. Dopamine provides a natural high and ecstatic feeling that can be as addictive as cocaine. Oxytocin (also known as the "cuddle hormone") engenders deeper feelings and is released during orgasm. To a large degree, it's responsible for bonding and increasing trust and loyalty in romantic attachments. What this means is that having sex early can contribute to bonding, regardless of whether the relationship is durable and healthy.

Psychology plays a role, too. Your self-esteem, mental and emotional health, life experiences, and family relations all influence how you feel and whom you find attractive. The unconscious is a mighty force. Reason may not stop you from falling in love, even when you're aware of the flaws in a potential romantic partner. You may be attracted to subtle attributes, usually unconsciously, that remind you of a family member. What's even more mysterious is that you can be attracted to someone who shares emotional and behavioral patterns with a member of your family even before they become apparent.

The Stages of Romance

Romantic relationships go through stages: the ideal, the ordeal, and the real deal. Most narcissistic relationships don't get to the third stage, which requires real love, mutuality, and acceptance.

The Ideal Stage

Indeed, love is blind. Healthy idealization is normal and helps you fall in love. You admire your beloved, are willing to explore your partner's interests, and accept their idiosyncrasies. Love also brings out parts of your personality that were dormant. You might feel manlier or more womanly, more empathic, generous, hopeful, and more willing to take risks and try new things. In this way, you feel more alive, because you have access to other aspects of your ordinary or constricted personality. Additionally, in early dating, you may feel freer to be more honest than down the road when you're invested in the relationship and fear that speaking truthfully could precipitate a breakup.

Although *healthy* idealization wouldn't blind you to serious warning signs of problems, unhealthy idealization both stems from and causes feelings of inferiority. Idealizing a prospective partner motivates you to sacrifice your needs and wants, and overlook warning signs, such as your partner's unreliability, interpersonal problems, addiction, disrespect, or abuse. Intrigue or a partner's unpredictability or unavailability may heighten excitement and desire. Such troubling behaviors may be denied, ignored, minimized, or rationalized because seeing the whole person would raise your fears of emptiness and loneliness that you're trying to avoid. Basing "love" on how your partner makes you feel or how they feel about you, puts the emphasis on your self-centered, codependent need...similar to that of a narcissist.

Codependent and Healthy Love Compared

Codependent Relationships	Healthy Relationships
Intense attraction	Attraction and friendship begin
Feel anxious	Feel comfortable
Idealize one another, ignoring differences	Attraction grows as you know one another
Fall "in love" and make commitments	Acknowledge differences (or leave)
Get to know one another	Grow to love one another
Become disappointed	Make commitments
Cling to a fantasy of love	Compromise needs
Try to change your partner into your ideal	Love and acceptance of one another grows
Repeat conflicts and disappointment	Feel supported and loved

The Ordeal Stage

About six to nine months after the ideal stage, couples enter the ordeal stage. As the high of idealization wears off, you revert to your ordinary personality, as does your partner. This is when you learn more things about your partner that displease you. You don't feel as expansive, loving, and unselfish. In the beginning, you may have gone out of your way to accommodate him or her, but now you feel, and perhaps even complain, that your needs aren't being met. You discover habits and flaws you dislike and attitudes you believe to be ignorant or distasteful. Sometimes, even traits that once attracted you are now annoying. For example, you may have been charmed by your mate's warmth and affability, but now feel ignored at social gatherings. Or you may have been captivated by their unfettered expressions of love and a promised future, but now see that they're prone to exaggerate and embellish.

You've changed and don't feel as wonderful, but you want those blissful feelings back. At this point, two things can damage relationships. First, now that you're attached and fear losing or upsetting your partner, you may hold back feelings, wants, and needs. This hampers intimacy, the secret sauce that keeps love alive. It also encourages narcissists to believe they can always get their way. The second fatal mistake, especially typical of narcissists, is to expect you to embody their ideal and then blame you whenever their expectations are unmet. Narcissists who do commit often lack the motivation to romance you once you're hooked. They drop their charismatic façade having won their prize. They begin taking you for granted, fault-finding, and making less effort to accommodate your needs. You may be disappointed, too, and less enthralled with their bragging and less tolerant of entitled behavior.

You may remain attached and devoted and hang on to embers of that romantic glow, even though your discomfort and unhappiness increase. Despite mounting troublesome facts or character traits, your desire to be with your partner takes center stage. You may feel controlled or neglected, unsafe or disrespected, as you discover that your partner is unreliable, tells lies, manipulates you, rages, keeps secrets, or has a major problem such as drug addiction or serious legal or financial troubles.

You hide your worries and doubts while relying on sex, romance, and fantasy to sustain the relationship. Out of sympathy, you might even be drawn to "rescue" your partner and/or try to change him or her back into the ideal person you "fell" for. These are signs of codependency or relationship addiction. Nonetheless, your denial grows as you disregard your own better judgment and/or the advice of friends.

This is the ordeal stage of romance because one or both of you can feel cheated and disillusioned in that the other is now behaving differently than when the relationship began. This stage is often fraught with conflict and power struggles as partners vie to get their needs met and their ideals fulfilled. They must cope with their disappointment, and decide whether to stay or leave the relationship. Feelings can also come out sideways through sarcasm, passive aggression, withdrawal, and betrayal. Many romantic partnerships never survive this stage. Those that do move on toward the real deal are discussed in the next chapter.

Signs of Relationship Addiction

You may wonder whether your relationship is based on lust, love, or addiction and codependency. The following are some things to think about if you suspect you're addicted to relationships:

1. It takes time to love someone. "Love at first sight" may be triggered by many things, but not real love.
2. Having sex with strangers or multiple partners is a sign of sexual addiction.
3. Compulsive activity that feels out of control, such as compulsive sex, stalking, spying, calling, or texting, is a sign of addiction.
4. Ignoring your partner's boundaries and abusing, controlling, or manipulating him or her (regardless of whether your motivation is well-intentioned, suspicious, or malicious) are signs of addiction.
5. Using sex or a relationship to cope with emptiness, depression, anger, shame, or anxiety is a sign of addiction.
6. Using sex or romance as a substitute for vulnerable, authentic intimacy is a symptom of addiction.
7. Staying in a painful relationship out of fear of abandonment or loneliness is a sign of codependency and addiction, not love.
8. Inability to commit to a relationship or staying involved with someone emotionally unavailable shows a fear of intimacy, another symptom of addiction.
9. Trusting too much or too little are signs of codependency.
10. Sacrificing your values or standards to be with someone is a sign of addiction.

LOVE BOMBING

Being bombarded with lavish attention and affection at the beginning of a romantic relationship seems to answer your prayers. Such a love bomb from someone you're attracted to feels glorious! You imagine that you've found your soul mate, unsuspecting that you've been targeted by a narcissist.

Love Bombing and Narcissistic Supply

Love bombing is typical of individuals with low self-esteem and an insecure attachment style.[61] Some love bombers are narcissists, but not all narcissists are love bombers. However, like all narcissists, love bombers want to control what others think in order to feel better about themselves.

So they shower you with love and behave in ways to convince you that they're the best at everything and your perfect partner. That is, they love-bomb you to gain attention, boost their ego, and fulfill their needs for sex, power, and control.

Dating a love bomber is intense and moves quickly. Their attention can be dizzyingly exciting and lift your self-esteem. You're hopeful you've found the "one" and feel seen and appreciated unlike ever before. Many targets of love bombers imagine a future free of sadness and loneliness with this ideal mate who will always love them. But the abundant amorous and/or frequent communications (phone calls, texts, and social media messages) indicate neediness for affirmation, usually at a distance so they can exercise more control. It's all about securing more narcissistic supplies, not establishing a sustainable relationship.

Idealization and Devaluation

For a narcissist, it's not enough to be liked or appreciated; it only counts when it comes from people with highly valued status or qualities such as wealth, beauty, or special talents. Narcissists idealize prospective partners to augment their lack of self-esteem, thinking, "If I can win the admiration of this attractive person, then I must be worthy." Their desperation intensifies and motivates their love bombing.

As reality inevitably colors the relationship, love bombers discover that their partners aren't the ideal, perfect person they'd imagined, and/or the love bomber fears that their flawed, empty self will be revealed when expectations for emotional intimacy increase. Any slights or imagined shortcomings in their idealized partner are painfully disappointing, and as their vision of their perfect partner deteriorates, their hidden shame increasingly causes discomfort. They in turn blame, criticize, and devalue their partner. Frequently, perfectionistic narcissists very fit this profile. Their campaign of disparagement makes their partner both unworthy of love and incapable of being a satisfactory object to boost their self-esteem. Unaware of their role in this drama, they discard that partner and look for a new source of narcissistic supply.

What You Can Do

Here are a few steps you can take to protect yourself from becoming a victim of a narcissist's seductive games. If your relationship doesn't improve after trying these, you may have to end it. This can take a terrific amount of courage, but it's ultimately less painful than being left.

1. Know yourself, your needs, wants, and limits. (Do the exercises in *Codependency for Dummies.*)
2. Knowledge is power. Learn more about narcissism and your date before you start fantasizing about a romantic future and give away your heart. Pay attention to words and actions over time, not just flattery and words of endearment.
3. Stay connected to your body and your feelings. If you're uneasy or suspicious, trust your gut. Notice inconsistent stories and explanations that don't compute.
4. Are you walking on eggshells? Evaluate whether you feel free to be open and honest and set limits.
5. Are you complying to please your partner? If so, analyze why. Has this been a pattern in past romantic relationships and with friends and family?
6. Be yourself from the start. Don't hide who you are, including your needs. Strive to be authentic, to be able to say no, and to express negative feelings. Speak up when you dislike something.
7. Talk honestly about what you want and expect in a relationship. If your partner doesn't want the same things, don't drift into denial or expect him or her to change. End the relationship. This may not be easy, but the relationship wouldn't have satisfied you.
8. Walk away from a date who doesn't respond, seems too busy, is preoccupied, or uninterested in you.
9. Talk about distancing behavior. Share your feelings, and find out what's going on. You may learn that your date is seeing other people, just wants to have "fun," or doesn't want a commitment.
10. Take control and confront bad behavior, such as unreliability, criticism, and rudeness. This requires you to trust your feelings and assert yourself. Confrontations aren't ultimatums. Learn to be assertive and do it strategically.
11. Don't be available 24/7. If you're a man, restrain yourself. Don't call or text multiple times a day at the beginning of a relationship. If you're a woman, stop calling or texting him first. Don't chase a man, or you'll be chasing him the entire relationship.
12. Go slow in terms of the frequency of dates and the degree of emotional and physical intimacy. Take time to build trust and to feel physically and emotionally safe with each other, not just excited.
13. Question whether the intensity you feel might also be anxiety about rejection and uncertain hope for a rosy future.
14. If your partner disappears, ask him or her about it. But the bottom line is that ghosting behavior speaks volumes. Just move on.

15. Remember, there are other fish in the sea, and it's never too late to throw this one back.

END GAME

Not all relationships with narcissists end abruptly. Some marry or break off an engagement, others dangle you along for years, cohabiting or not, without a proposal. But for narcissists who are solely interested in the chase, landing the catch is the end of the game. They lose interest once you stop distancing and start to depend on them. After you're attached and express your needs and/or expectations, the novelty wears off for them, and they're on to chasing the next shiny object.

The Discard

Narcissists can break up without warning, which of course is a shock devastating when you can't understand what happened and are still in love. What lingers is the confusion over their unexpected change of heart, proposing one minute and then exiting the next. Breakups are hard during the romantic phase when passions are strong, especially after love bombing. Discarded partners are in shock, especially if the news was delivered by text, email, or a call. But even if a narcissist shows up in person and says, "It's over," you're still bewildered by such coldness from someone who just recently expressed their love and promised an amazing future together. Trauma almost inevitably results when someone you care about suddenly cuts you off without any explanation.

Partners feel duped, crushed, and abandoned as they try to make sense of suddenly being dropped. You may discover that you were deserted for a new prospect or that you were two-timed all along. All the empty promises come crashing down in a sea of confusion and betrayal. What you thought was real was in fact a mirage. You search for answers and doubt and unjustifiably blame yourself.

It takes time to accept the reality of who the bomber was. Denial can protect you somewhat from the painful truth that the relationship was not what you imagined, but it perpetuates longing. You would have seen through the narcissist's seductive veneer eventually anyway. Still, when all you have are positive memories, letting go is especially difficult.

Being Ghosted

When a spouse disappears after years of marriage, it's like a sudden death of a partner and the marriage all at once. But even the unexpected and unexplained end to a brief romantic relationship can shatter trust in yourself, in love, and in others. You might ask for answers only to receive vague or uninformative responses like, "I just don't feel it anymore" or "You deserve someone better." And you're still left wanting to know *why?* Our brains are wired to wonder and search for solutions to problems. This is compounded by the fact that we're also wired to attach and to experience rejection as painful. So you might try to reconnect. This is why babies cry fiercely when they need their mother. Rejection can also cause obsessive thinking and compulsive behavior, like stalking your ex's social media, which fuels more anxiety and pain.

Ghosted in a Romance

Ghosting usually occurs during the romantic phase of relationships. You don't know your partner that well and are still in a blissful haze of idealization, only to have your hopes for the future abruptly and inexplicably dashed. Normally, a relationship progresses from the romantic ideal stage into the realistic ordeal period, when couples struggle with ambivalence and conflicts. When a relationship fails during the ordeal stage, at least you have an idea of why it didn't work, and sometimes you realize that ending the relationship was for the best.

Why You Were Ghosted

Dating relationships typically involve less accountability than committed ones. This could be because of the way you two met (e.g., a chat room or hookup app — technology makes it easy to maintain emotional distance), your psychological maturity and values, the length of the relationship, or the frequency of face-to-face contact. Meeting through mutual friends usually provides more incentive to be on good behavior because people you care about will find out.

Ghosting almost always starts with an unanswered text or call; then come long silences between replies until there are none. Here are eight reasons why a person might ghost instead of communicating.

1. **They're Game-Players:** Narcissists aren't interested in a commitment or concerned with others' feelings, though they may show passion when they're in seduction mode because the chase excites them. They're not emotionally involved and can act callously once they're no longer absorbed.
2. **They're Conflict Avoidant:** Many narcissists fear confrontation because they imagine it will lead to criticism, drama, and ultimately a breakup. They may tell themselves that they're sparing your feelings by not admitting that they no longer want to continue the relationship, but leaving without a word, let alone closure, is more cruel and painful.

79

3. **They're Attachment Avoidant:** Ghosters are likely to have intimacy problems, which explain why they leave a relationship when it's becoming more intimate.

4. **They're Ashamed:** People with low self-esteem want to avoid criticism and the shame they anticipate if you get to know them better and see their flaws. They also expect to feel shame for hurting you. Their lack of boundaries makes them feel responsible for your feelings, although the reverse is true (they're responsible for how they communicate, but not for your reaction.) Thus, in trying to avoid false responsibility, they err by not taking appropriate responsibility for their behavior, causing you the unnecessary pain they were hoping to avoid.

5. **They're Busy:** If you're not exclusive and have acknowledged that dating someone else is okay, your partner may assume the relationship is more casual than you may have imagined and neglect to tell you when their interest begins to wane.

6. **They're Depressed or Overwhelmed:** Some people can hide depression for a while. The ghoster might be too depressed to continue and may not want to reveal what's going on in their life. There may be other life events you don't know about that take precedence, like a job loss or personal or family illness or emergency.

7. **They're Seeking Safety:** If you've raged in the past or are violent or verbally abusive, you may be ghosted out of self-protection.

8. **They're Setting a Boundary:** If you smother your dates with frequent texts or calls, especially when you've been asked not to, their silence can be a message that you've ignored their boundaries.

What You Can Do

If you've been discarded, the main thing to realize is that that behavior reveals the other person's character, not yours. It's time to let go. Here are some do's and don'ts:

1. **Face Reality:** The person has decided to move on for whatever reason. Accepting that is more important than knowing why. The ghost is also demonstrating that they don't respect your feelings and lacks essential communication and conflict resolution skills that make relationships work. Would you want a relationship with someone like that?

2. **Accept Your Feelings:** Recognize that you can't always figure out someone else's motives. Let go of obsessive thoughts and allow yourself to feel both sadness and anger without shame. You need

time to grieve, so take it. Open your heart to yourself with extra doses of self-love — all you wanted from the other person.

3. **Avoid Self-Blame:** Rejection hurts, but you don't have to pile on unnecessary suffering. Don't blame yourself or allow someone else's bad behavior to diminish your self-esteem. Even if you weren't what the ghoster wanted, that doesn't mean you're undesirable! You cannot make anyone love you. You simply might not have been a good match. No one is your last hope for finding love.

4. **Do Not Contact:** If you're tempted to write or call, think first about how the conversation will go, how you will feel, and whether you would even get truthful answers. Often the person ending a relationship won't be honest about the reasons or may not even be able to articulate them because they're just going with their gut feelings. Men tend to do this more than women, who analyze and ruminate more. In addition, the odds are you'll be rejected a second time. Would that hurt more? Experts advise no contact after a breakup, including all social media, as this leads to quicker healing.

   If the temptation to communicate is just too strong, however, tell the ghoster only that their behavior was hurtful and unacceptable. In other words, be resolved that you're now rejecting them. Then, move on. If you don't feel strong, such a conversation may not help you let go. But also remember that anger isn't always a sign of strength. It may be a temporary stage of grief, followed by more feelings of missing the person.

5. **Evaluate Your Boundaries:** It's always possible to give your heart to someone untrustworthy. So it's wise to evaluate your boundaries when dating. Were you easily seduced? Were you too anxious to fall in love with someone you didn't know well?

6. **Don't Isolate:** Get back into life and plan activities with friends. You may need a break from dating for a while, but always continue to socialize and do other things that you enjoy. Don't allow yourself to fall into depression, which is different from mourning.

7. **Remember Yourself:** Remember who you were and your life before this relationship. Invest in your goals and interests.

8. **Mindfulness:** Regulate your emotions by practicing mindfulness. Try not to ruminate about the past or fantasize about an illusory future. There are many meditation techniques, such as Mindfulness-Based Stress Reduction (MBSR), which can calm and help you stay in the present.

9. **Cognitive Reframing:** Be mindful of how you interpret the relationship. Rather than think your ex was a wonderful partner who rejected you, reinterpret the relationship in light of all their behavior. Were they deceitful, withholding, and self-centered, or were they forgiving of your mistakes, attentive to your needs and boundaries, open and communicative, and considerate of your feelings? Even if your ex showed good qualities during a romantic phase, their discarding behavior reveals the truth of who they are. They wouldn't be able to keep up that façade and spared you a longer unhappy relationship.

10. **Change Your Dating Style:** This experience might be a wake-up call to reconsider your dating pattern. See Chapter 7 – Healthy Relationships: The Real Deal.

Chapter 7

LOVING A NARCISSIST

Most people involved with narcissists grew up in dysfunctional families and have never had healthy intimate relationships. Your family may have appeared normal and happy to others and you may believe it was. Even if your parents were involved in your life and your material needs were met, you may have felt lonely or inadequate. Shame and low self-esteem can derive from many things, including sibling abuse, over-control, or insufficient nurturing by one or both parents. Some children receive help and nurturing from a grandparent or older sibling, but that doesn't replace the needed unconditional love from a parent.

Children who grow up in healthy family environments feel secure in knowing that they're accepted and respected for who they are. They feel consistently safe and expect to be nurtured, helped, protected, and treated fairly. Their feelings and needs are taken seriously. They witness affection, respect, and caring between their parents, who behave maturely and don't use their children to fulfill their emotional needs. Such parents collaborate and solve problems without drama and fights. Anger is unavoidable but also acceptable; when it's expressed appropriately, it can be resolved quickly.

This security, respect, and acceptance form the basis for self-worth and interdependent adult relationships. Interdependency requires autonomy and the ability to express your feelings, thoughts, and needs. When you're capable of living independently, you're not afraid to say no or assert your wants, feelings, and needs.

HEALTHY RELATIONSHIPS: THE REAL DEAL

Lasting relationships move past the ideal and ordeal stages to the real deal — a real relationship based on mutual understanding and acceptance. These couples communicate freely and accommodate each other's needs and personalities. It takes two compatible and committed people to make a relationship work. They must also have enough self-esteem and autonomy to give without feeling robbed or unappreciated and to receive without feeling unworthy or smothered.

True love requires that you recognize each other's separateness and love your mate for whom they truly are. This requires acceptance and authenticity that goes beyond romance. There's always some idealization in a new relationship, but true love endures when that fades and the real deal emerges. As your relationship grows, you develop trust and greater closeness; you want to share more of your time and life, including your problems, friends, and family.

Your mutual needs, feelings, and happiness become more and more important, and you think about planning a future together. Instead of feeling anxious about failing to please your partner, you feel safe and secure to be yourself, and instead of trying to change your partner, you grow to accept him or her (that doesn't include unacceptable behavior). Gaining true intimacy requires effort and a commitment by both partners to get through the ordeal stage with mutual respect and a desire to make the relationship work. When the passion is still there, you're lucky to have both love and lust.

Interdependency means that you value and respect your needs, feelings, and wants and those of your partner equitably. To do this, you need the courage and assertiveness skills to speak up honestly about your needs and wants, to share your feelings, to compromise, and to resolve conflicts peacefully. Wanting to please your partner is a healthy attitude, but feeling compelled to self-sacrifice is not. You should be happy to receive as well as to give. One way to think about it is to forget the idea of a giver and receiver; instead, think in terms of a circular flow of goodwill and helping one another.

In healthy relationships, authenticity is a priority, not keeping the peace. The consistency and security in the relationship and your self-esteem allow you the freedom to be yourself. Partners in the real deal don't try to control or feel responsible for one another's behavior or feelings. They're not reactive. They take responsibility for their own independent feelings and actions and, at the same time, are both still mindful of their need for each other. They can give, negotiate, and compromise without feeling robbed or exploited. They can say no, allowing them to accept no from their partner, too.

RELATIONSHIPS WITH NARCISSISTS

As relationships progress over time, problems inevitably arise, but the difficulties in relationships with narcissists are far different from those in healthy relationships. It's not an equal, two-way arrangement, but a one-way transaction: their way. When you feel undeserving of receiving love, you don't expect to be loved for who you are, only for how you look or what you give or do. Hence, your partner puts him or herself first, and so do you. This makes the relationship work…in the beginning. Eventually, however, you feel drained, hurt, angry, disrespected, and lonely.

After a romantic prelude, they can act completely different. Once narcissists stop trying to win you, they begin to examine you. They become less attentive and spend less time with you. It may not start until after an engagement, marriage, or pregnancy. Although you were idealized at first, now you're devalued. If you weren't alert to the warning signs when dating a narcissist, you may not realize whom you're dealing with until you've already committed, and changing course becomes so much more difficult.

Friends may envy your new relationship, but in private, narcissists denigrate people they were just entertaining, including you. Their empathic deficits compromise their ability to understand, appreciate, and see you as separate from themselves. They don't care about your needs unless it somehow benefits them. Although you feel loved by occasional expensive gifts, caring words, gestures, or displays of jealousy or protectiveness, you may doubt your partner's sincerity and question whether it's manipulation, pretense, or a manufactured "as if" personality. Meanwhile, you're expected to appreciate the narcissist's specialness, meet their demands for admiration, service, love, and purchases as needed, and are dismissed when you don't. No wonder partners of narcissists feel drained, hurt, resentful, disrespected, and lonely.

Escalating Abuse

Emotional abuse may start innocuously, but grows as the narcissist becomes more assured that you won't leave the relationship. Anger and distance replace love and romance. And as mentioned earlier, narcissists subject their partners to their gratuitous flirting with other people, inconsiderate behavior, demands, judgments, and self-centeredness, all to protect their fragile egos against humiliation and shame. Because they see your insecurity and emotional needs as character flaws, abuse escalates as you express a normal need for connection and intimacy. And when they're angry or you dissatisfy them, their defenses kick in, which usually lead to abuse. Due to splitting, they forget about their need for connection, and you become all bad. They make you responsible for their behavior and negative feelings, which they can't accept.

Compliments and positive rewards may have stopped altogether. Their attacks become more frequent and less civil. They begin to make unreasonable and insulting demands. Perfectionists can go to extremes. They make suggestions about your body, grooming, behavior, and just about anything that could be criticized. Instead of normal disappointment and acceptance of who you are, which would lead to a healthy relationship, they're personally affronted that you don't follow their advice and change *for them.*

With some narcissists, any act toward autonomy, such as setting a boundary, threatens their authority and control, which they will attempt to maintain by any means. To this end, your partner may isolate you from family, friends, and professional help. In a worried effort to save the relationship, you gradually comply with the new normal, not unlike many Jews during the early years of Nazi rule in 1930s Germany.

An extroverted narcissist generally acts needless and can be remote and emotionally cold, but their constant demands reveal just how needy they are. Although not all narcissists are verbally abusive and some may show friendliness toward their partners, others are continually critical and contemptuous. Many engage in all forms of emotional abuse, including false accusations, the silent treatment, and gaslighting. They can be vindictive, fly into rages, or act dismissive and withhold when you don't comply with their demands. Look out for subtle manipulation, distortions of reality, blaming, and guilt-tripping. They may become unpredictably aggressive, throw tantrums, and express unjustified indignation about small or imaginary slights.

If addiction is involved, life can become an unpredictable emotional rollercoaster. Similarly, a vulnerable narcissist, like a person with borderline personality disorder, can vacillate between idealizing/caring behavior and devaluing/rejecting behavior for no apparent reason.

When you try to communicate your hurt or disappointment, it gets twisted and met with defensive blame or further put-downs. Your partner can dish it, but can't take it. You try to appease, reason, and accommodate your partner, believing that if you do, things will improve and your love will be returned. But the relationship does not improve. Appeasement doesn't help and fighting increases the abuse, which may become crueler and more contemptuous.

You absorb the blame, guilt, and shame directed at you and try to be more understanding. You have to fit into the narcissist's cold world and get used to living in an emotional desert. Meanwhile, the narcissist maintains control to keep you subordinate, dependent, and feeling inadequate. Your declining self-esteem and independence allow the narcissist to abuse and exploit you further. In the process, you sacrifice your needs because you're fearful of displeasing your partner. You worry about what they will think or do and become as preoccupied with your partner as your partner is with him or herself. Over time, you feel drained, hurt, angry, disrespected, and lonely. When abuse is interspersed with affection, it creates an addictive emotional bond that is especially difficult to change. Without outside support, you feel trapped.

Your Role in the Relationship

Whereas narcissists freely express their needs and anger, you may feel needless or guilty asserting your needs and wants. You may not believe you have any rights. Naturally, to avoid conflict, you go along to get along and put your partner's needs and feelings first, sometimes self-denying at great lengths to please. Caretaking and pleasing give you a sense of purpose. The role of helper/nurturer is more pronounced if your partner is an addict or vulnerable narcissist. Being needed feels like love. It boosts your self-esteem and assures you that you won't be abandoned, even though despite your efforts to be helpful, the person you care for and try to please takes your efforts for granted and projects their inner shame on you.

Most partners of narcissists are insecure and have weak boundaries. They're neither able to stop the abuse, nor stop the derogatory words from planting seeds of self-doubt, which are often accepted as the truth. Even one episode of explosive rage or intimidation can make you avoid disagreements or confrontations. All you want is peace. You make vain attempts to win approval and stay connected but feel powerless to satisfy the narcissist, guilty for "mistakes," diminished by the "shortcomings" you're accused of, and resentful that your efforts are unappreciated.

Each time your partner insists on getting their way, you're confronted with the untenable choice of losing yourself or losing the relationship. You must give up yourself to keep it. To please your partner and not make waves, you collude in foregoing your needs, wants, and yourself. Thus, whereas narcissists try to maintain their power and forget about the relationship, you try to maintain it and forget about yourself.

You slowly sacrifice yourself over and over in small and big ways, from insignificant concessions to giving up a career, cutting off a relative, or condoning or participating in behavior that before would have seemed unimaginable. You try to control the uncontrollable, forgo yourself, and try harder to please and be accepted. "Trying harder" may be a virtue, but narcissists never appreciate your effort and your reactive, accommodating role amplifies your focus on your partner, further distancing you from your true self and effecting discernible change.

As your tension and anxiety grow, you deny, minimize, or rationalize the abuse and your pain. Your coping mechanisms mask your fear of abandonment and rejection. Your fears and longing to find lasting love may be unconscious. They conceal a hidden belief of being unlovable. But the more you concede, the more permission you give and power you surrender, a pattern that may have been established in childhood.

Narcissists are keenly aware of your triggers and sensitivities, which they manipulate to gain power and make you crave their attention. The more love is withheld or inconsistent, the more you try to win it, falling into the trap of turning over your self-esteem, power, and sense of well-being to your partner. You join the narcissist in heaping more blame on yourself, building up more shame and resentment that you may rarely express directly. You never feel good enough, reinforcing feelings of inadequacy.

The dynamics in abusive relationships heighten your stress and escalate your attempts to appease your partner. The reality of the narcissist starts to infect both your self-concept and your perceptions of reality. You're drained trying to abate a crisis, avoid abuse, and hold the relationship together. As your self-esteem and self-respect are whittled away, you feel guilty, doubt yourself, and distrust your perceptions. You may become obsessive and/or compulsive or develop an addiction or physical symptoms. If you look back, you may recall early signs of control or jealousy. Eventually, you and the entire family "walk on eggshells" and adapt so as not to upset the narcissist.

You slowly give up your autonomy until you feel trapped and hopeless. You may come to feel invisible, no longer a separate person with independent needs and wants, assuming you knew what they were. Over time, you have changed from a trusting, loving, and confident person into a shell of your former self, feeling anxious, confused, unhappy, insecure, and resentful.

Defining Love

Narcissists may claim they love you, but you must determine whether you feel loved by the way they treat you. Real love requires empathy, compassion, and deep knowledge of people you care for. You show active concern for their lives and growth. You try to understand their experiences and world views, though they may differ from your own. If you haven't experienced such genuine love or it was mixed with abuse, then you may not appreciate real love, nor expect to be treated any better.

Real love isn't romance, and it's not codependency. Love is difficult to measure, but research[62] shows that people feel loved when their partner:

1. Expresses words of affirmation
2. Spends quality time with them
3. Gives gifts
4. Performs acts of service
5. Touches them affectionately
6. Shows interest in their affairs
7. Provides emotional and moral support
8. Discloses intimate facts

9. Expresses feelings for them, such as, "I'm happier when I'm near you."
10. Tolerates their demands and flaws to maintain the relationship

For Aristotle and St. Thomas Aquinas, love is "to will the good of another." In *The Psychology of Romantic Love*, Nathaniel Branden states, "To love a human being is to know and love his or her person."[63] It's a union of two individuals, which requires that you see another person as separate from yourself. Further, in *The Art of Loving*, Erich Fromm emphasizes that love entails an effort to develop knowledge, commitment, and responsibility.[64] You must be motivated to know your partner's wants, needs, and feelings and provide encouragement and support. You show active concern for your beloved's life and growth and take pleasure in their happiness and try not to hurt them. Caring involves offering attention, respect, compassion, support, and acceptance. You must devote the necessary time and discipline.

How a Narcissist Loves

Anyone who's loved a narcissist wonders, "Does he really love me?" or "Does she appreciate me?" You're torn between your love and your pain, between staying and leaving, but can't seem to do either. Some partners swear they're loved; others are convinced they're not. It's confusing because sometimes you experience the caring person you love, whose company is a pleasure, only to be followed by behavior that makes you feel unimportant or inadequate. Narcissists claim to love their family and partners, but do they?

For most narcissists, their relationships are transactional.[65] They're playing a game, and winning is the goal. They may show passion in the early stages of dating, but the highs and lows of romance aren't love but rather based on their own needs and projections. As described in chapter 6 – Game-Playing and Love, many narcissists have trouble sustaining a relationship for more than six months to a few years. They prioritize power over intimacy and loathe vulnerability, which they consider weak.[66] To maintain control, they avoid closeness and prefer dominance and superiority over others.

Some narcissists are practical in their approach to relationships based on friendship and shared interests. They may develop positive feelings for their partner and seek a long-term relationship. They develop "Pragma" or pragmatic love for their partner. They focus on long-term goals and having their needs met and may develop "Agape" or spiritual love.[67] Many even marry, but that may not stop some from thrill-seeking and continuing to play games with new conquests. Once married, they lack the energy to maintain their romantic façade and employ defenses to avoid closeness. They become cold, critical, and angry, especially when they're challenged or don't get their way. They're likely to support their spouse's needs and wants only when it's convenient and their ego is satisfied. After devaluing their partner, they need to look elsewhere to prop up their inflated ego.

Loving a narcissist can leave you starved for many expressions of love. It's not that narcissists are incapable of feeling or even intellectually understanding someone's feelings. A narcissist might feel "I love you, but...," what they say after "but" sounds pretty cold: "I'm too busy to come to the hospital." Although their words don't express love for the person hospitalized, when the importance of a visit and necessity for reciprocity is explained to them as outlined in chapter 9 they might make the trip.

Romantic love can evolve into love, but narcissists aren't motivated to know and understand others.[68] The issue is rooted in childhood trauma and physiological deficits that impact emotional mirroring, assessment, and appropriate empathetic expression. They have many hurdles to loving, such as:

1. First, they lack emotional empathy and the ability to respond to your needs and feelings.
2. Second, they see neither themselves nor others clearly, and they don't appreciate that you have needs, desires, and feelings distinct from their own. This also means that they don't accurately perceive and receive love extended to them.
3. They lack object constancy and can't hold a consistent image of people close to them. When they're angry, you're seen as a threat, an enemy, and of no value to them.
4. They overestimate their emotional empathy.[69]
5. Fifth, their defenses distort their perceptions and interactions with others. They brag and withdraw to control closeness and vulnerability; they project onto others unwanted, negative aspects of themselves; and they use denial, entitlement, and narcissistic abuse, including blame, contempt, criticism, and aggression, to ward off shame.[70]

All these issues impair narcissists' capacity to accurately take in another person's reality, including that person's love for them. Narcissists' emotional intelligence helps them manipulate and exploit others to get what they want, while their impaired emotional empathy desensitizes them to the pain they inflict.

When they're motivated, they may show love, but it's conditional. Their behavior depends on how it affects them. Because narcissism exists on a continuum from mild to malignant, when it's severe, a narcissist's selfishness and the inability to express love become more apparent. Dating or long-distance relationships that have fewer expectations are easier for them and conceal their inadequacies.

> *Innercises: A Relationship Inventory*

Wondering whether a narcissist loves you is the wrong question. Although it's wise to understand a narcissist's mind, like Echo in the myth of Narcissus, partners who overly focus on the narcissist do so to their detriment. Instead, ask yourself whether you feel valued, respected, and cared for. If not, how is that affecting you and your self-esteem, and what can you do about that? Reflect on the following questions:

- Were you "swept off your feet" by romance in the early stage of your relationship?
- Does your partner have traits you lack? What stops you from developing them?
- Do you feel insecure or inferior?
- Do you feel anxious about expressing yourself?
- Do you feel intimidated?
- Do you feel unsafe?
- Do you feel used, exploited, or taken advantage of, like an object?
- Do you feel invisible or like an audience?
- Do you feel that you're unimportant?
- Do you feel that your opinions, needs, and feelings don't matter?
- Do you feel manipulated?
- Do you feel that they can dish it out, but not take it?
- Do you feel you're treated unfairly or that there's a double standard?
- Do you feel abused or mistreated?
- Do you feel lonely or abandoned?
- Do you feel left out of their life, work, family, or plans?
- Do you feel you and your relationship revolve around what they want?
- Do you feel that you can't please your partner; nothing you do is good enough?
- Do you feel criticized?
- Do you feel sexually seduced or deprived?
- Do you feel empty?
- Are you getting your needs met? If not, do you feel resentful or angry about it?
- Do you feel the relationship isn't reciprocal or that your love isn't returned?

- Do you feel embarrassed by their public behavior?
- Do you feel drained by their demands or need for attention?
- Do you feel ignored?
- Do you feel hopeless about getting what you want from him or her?
- Do you feel blamed, guilty, and often apologize?
- Do you feel dominated or controlled?
- Do you feel as though you've lost yourself in your relationship?
- Do you monitor and adapt to your partner's needs, wants, and feelings?
- If asked what's on your mind, is it usually about your partner or the relationship?

LOVING AN ABUSER

Don't judge yourself for loving someone who doesn't treat you with care and respect. You're at the mercy of unconscious forces. Falling in love can happen before you really even know your partner. By the time the relationship turns abusive, you're attached and want to maintain your connection and love. There may have been hints of abuse that you initially overlooked because abusers are good at seduction. They wait until they know you're hooked before showing their true colors. By then, your love is cemented and doesn't die easily.

It's difficult to leave an abuser. It's possible and even probable to realize that you're unsafe and yet still love an abuser. (See chapter 10 – Why Leaving Is Hard.) Undoubtedly, the abuser and the relationship have positive aspects that you enjoy, recall, or look forward to recurring. Often abusers are also good providers, offer a social life, or have special talents. Narcissists can be exceedingly interesting and charming. Many spouses claim that they enjoy their narcissistic partner's company and lifestyle despite the abuse. People with a borderline personality disorder can light up your life with excitement — when they're in a good mood. Sociopaths can pretend to be whatever you want (but only for their own purposes).

Research shows that even domestic violence victims try to leave seven times on average before leaving permanently and often experience as many as 50 incidents of abuse before getting help.[71] Even so, staying in an abusive relationship can feel humiliating. Those who don't understand ask why you love an abuser and why you stay. You may not have good answers. But there are valid reasons. Your motivations are outside your awareness and control. Your instincts to attach for survival control your feelings and behavior.

Denial of Abuse to Survive

If you weren't treated with respect in your family, you probably tend to deny the abuse. You don't expect to be treated better than how you were controlled, demeaned, or punished by a parent. Denial doesn't mean you don't know what's happening, but you may not realize that you've been abused. Instead, you minimize or rationalize it or its impact.

Research shows we deny to stay attached and procreate for the survival of the species. You might minimize or twist the facts and feelings that would normally undermine love in order to keep on loving. You blame yourself or imagine if only your partner would control their anger, or agree to get help, or just change one thing, everything would be better. This is denial. By doing this and appeasing your partner to connect to your love again, you stop hurting. Your love reignites and you feel safe again. However, unless your partner wants to create a more equitable and respectful relationship, you're clinging to an unrealistic hope that reinforces the status quo. See chapter 8 – Denial.

Projection, Idealization, and Repetition Compulsion

If you haven't worked through trauma from your childhood, you're more susceptible to idealizing your partner when you fall in love. You likely seek out someone who reminds you of a parent with whom you have unfinished business (not necessarily your opposite-sex parent). You might be attracted to someone who has aspects of both parents. Your unconscious is trying to mend your past by reliving it, hoping that you'll master the situation and receive the love you didn't get as a child. But it doesn't work. Instead, you keep reliving the same pain unless you get help.

The relationship is also familiar. If you were manipulated as a child, you might not notice it as an adult. If love was withheld as punishment, this, too, would feel justifiable and normal. Similarly, if your needs were shamed, ignored, or inconsistently met, you might not feel entitled to having them met and feel shame when asserting them. Interestingly, both abusive or neglectful patterns and the longing for what you didn't get make it easy to overlook signs that might indicate trouble.

Low Self-Esteem

If you have low self-esteem, you tend to believe the abuser's belittling, blame, and criticisms, which only further damages your self-esteem and confidence. You might be brainwashed into thinking that you must change to make the relationship work and then blame yourself and try harder to meet the abuser's demands. You might interpret sexual overtures, crumbs of kindness, or just the absence of abuse as signs of love or hope that the relationship will improve. Thus, as your trust in yourself declines, your idealization and love for the abuser remain intact. You may even doubt that you could find anything better.

Empathy for the Abuser

You may have empathy for your partner, but not for yourself. You may make light of or be unaware of your needs and/or feel ashamed about asking for them. If this sounds like your situation, you're especially susceptible to manipulation if your partner plays the victim, exaggerates guilt, shows remorse, blames you, or talks about a troubled past (they usually have one). Your empathy feeds your denial system with justification, rationalization, and minimization of the pain you endure. Most victims hide the abuse from friends and relatives to protect the abuser, both out of empathy and shame about being abused, but secrecy is a mistake and gives an abuser more power.

Intermittent Reinforcement and Trauma Bonding

Behavioral psychologists use the term "intermittent reinforcement" to describe the conditioning (or "training") behavior by giving only intermittent rewards. When you receive occasional and unpredictable positive, intermittent reinforcement, you keep looking for the positive. Surprisingly, research confirmed that this is true even after the rewards stop coming! Seeking rewards can become addictive, like constantly checking your phone or email. In studies, rats neglected their grooming and other self-care habits but kept pushing the reward lever like a slot machine. It's like gamblers who keep chasing an elusive win to get back their losses, even as they go into debt.

In relationships, you can get addicted to emotionally unavailable partners because they may periodically want closeness. Narcissists might intentionally withhold communication and affection to manipulate and control you with rejection or withholding, only to randomly fulfill your needs later. You become anxious and try even harder to decipher the narcissist and how to please him or her to get what you previously had but to no avail. Like the experimental rats, you get accustomed to long periods of not getting your needs met. This is how you become increasingly childlike and dependent on the narcissist — watching and accommodating to avoid abuse and to receive the occasional reward.

Such intermittent reinforcement creates "trauma bonding" that's resistant to change. You can become addicted to any sign of approval or bits of kindness or closeness that feel all the more poignant (like make-up sex) because you've been starved and are relieved to feel loved. You might give up hobbies, interests, and friends and completely lose yourself trying to please and not displease your partner. This pattern may have developed in childhood and is now activated and exacerbated in your current relationship.

If you end up completely under the narcissist's control and can't escape, you might develop "Stockholm syndrome," a term applied to captives who sympathize with their abuser. Any act of kindness or even the absence of abuse feels like a sign of friendship and being cared for. The abuser seems less threatening. You imagine that you're friends and share common values and goals, believing you're in it together and may view helpers or the police as the enemy.

Because of the powers of attraction and emotional and physiological bonding, this occurs in intimate relationships that are less perilous than hostage situations. Codependents are loyal to a fault. You want to protect the abuser rather than yourself. You feel guilty talking to outsiders, thinking about leaving the relationship, or calling the police. Outsiders who try to help feel threatening. For example, you might see counselors and twelve-step programs as interlopers who want to brainwash and separate you and your partner. This reinforces the toxic bond and isolates you from help, which is *exactly* what the abuser wants!

The Cycle of Abuse

Some abusers feel remorse after an abusive episode, but most narcissists will only further justify their actions. The stages are as follows.

1. Your partner feels threatened or insecure. It might be due to jealousy, insufficient attention, or real or imagined disapproval or rejection. You sense your partner's tension and feel apprehensive.
2. Your partner engages in some form of abuse, perhaps only a verbal retort. The more you listen and engage, the more abuse the narcissist piles on.
3. Eventually, and especially if you fight back, your partner takes the role of victim and blames *you* for neglect or being abusive in some way. You accept the blame, argue, or placate to keep the peace, but it doesn't help. You may even apologize for your partner's abuse just to stop it.
4. Your partner feels justified and self-righteous about their behavior and free to continue it unless you detach and calmly confront it in the manner suggested in the next chapter.

Sometimes after an abusive episode, there's a honeymoon period when an abuser seeks connection and acts romantic, apologetic, complimentary, or at minimum acts like nothing has happened. You're relieved that there's peace for now. If there are promises that the abuse won't be repeated, you believe your partner because you want to, because you're wired to attach, and because you've become addicted to intermittent reinforcement. You yearn to feel connected again, and the breach of the emotional bond feels worse than the abuse. Your partner may desire sex or express love. To feel reassured about the relationship, hopeful, safe, and lovable, you once again cling to signs of approval.

HOW A NARCISSIST CONTROLS YOUR MIND

Healthy relationships are balanced and allow both individuals an equal say in decision-making and in getting their needs met. They each can assert themselves and negotiate on their behalf. There is the give and take of compromise in an interdependent relationship, which requires autonomy, self-esteem, mutual respect, and assertive communication skills.

On the other hand, imbalance characterizes abusive relationships; one person leads and the other follows, one dominates and the other accommodates. One level up relationships are characterized by constant conflict and power struggles, where both partners struggle to get their needs met.

My book, *Conquering Shame and Codependency,* describes the traits and motivations of "master" and "accommodator" personalities.[72] The master is aggressive and motivated to maintain power and control, while the accommodator is passive and motivated to maintain love and connection. Most of us have aspects of both types in our personality, although some people predominantly fall into one category. For example, most codependents are accommodators like Echo, and most narcissists are masters.

Research on mice, whose brains are remarkably similar to those of humans, reveals that our brain is affected by those around us. The key factor is dominance. The brains of subordinate mice "synchronize" to those of dominant mice.[73] This likely applies to human relationships. Typically, people with stronger personalities make the decisions and get their needs met more often than their partners do. Other factors play a part as well. The more the mice interacted with each other, the more their brains' activity was synched. Hence, the longevity and intensity of a relationship affect the degree of influence.

A further twist on the correlation of brain activity turns on two types of brain cells. One set is important for your behavior (self neurons), and the second focuses on the behavior of others (other neurons). These cells indicate how you think and where you place your attention in relationships.

Brain synchronization enables a subordinate animal to read the cues and follow a dominant animal who leads. The synchronization process happens automatically and outside of conscious control. In healthy relationships, this is helpful and allows partners to be "in sync" and read each other's cues and even minds. You know what your partner feels and needs and when mutual, love deepens, and happiness multiplies.

On the other hand, if this process enables one partner to control the other, the relationship becomes toxic. Love and happiness wither and die. In unequal relationships, the dominant partner's brain entrains that of the subordinate partner, whose brain synchronizes with it. In longer relationships, this pattern becomes more established. Like Echo, because accommodators focus on others more than themselves, it's probable that their personalities prime their other neurons to light up more consistently than self neurons.

Perhaps you were assertive and behaved independently before being in your relationship. But once attached to a narcissist, you increasingly accommodated your dominant partner. (Take the above Relationship Inventory.) Many variables are at work, but presumably, brain synchronization makes it harder for you, the subordinate person in the relationship, to think and act autonomously and challenge the power imbalance.

The dominant partner has no incentive to give up control. It's up to you to change the dynamics of the relationship. In doing so, the balance of power may realign. Regardless, you will gain the autonomy and mental strength to enjoy a better life and perhaps leave the relationship.

LACK OF BOUNDARIES

Because narcissists experience you as an extension of themselves, they lack boundaries. Some narcissists expect you to read their mind and know their needs without having to ask. Even when you try, nothing you do is right or appreciated. You might go out of your way to fill their requests and endless needs, only to have your efforts devalued because you didn't get it right. You end up in a double bind — damned if you please them and damned if you don't. That you're ill or in pain is inconsequential.

A horrendous example involved a wealthy man who became infuriated at his daughter's request for a small loan. At the time, she had terminal cancer and was a single, unemployed mother. He replied, yelling that she was insensitive to ask him for money "at a time like this" when *he* was stressed about her illness.

Narcissists don't like to hear "no" or to have others set boundaries. They can act like children who believe they're the center of the universe and throw tantrums when others don't comply. Not getting their way threatens their facade of being all-powerful and in control. Your limits can trigger their childhood wounds and make them feel powerless like they did as small children, which is very frightening. So they manipulate you to get what they want and may punish you or make you feel guilty for turning them down.

Should their illusions of authority crumble, they react with rage. You fear that if you don't please them, you'll face an onslaught of blame and punishment, withheld love, and a rupture in the relationship. You just have to fit in. The weak boundaries and reactivity of narcissists and codependents make intimacy difficult. Not only do narcissists hate hearing "no," when boundaries are weak, you have trouble saying "No" and take your partner's feelings, words, and actions personally. If you and your partner continually react to one another's behavior and feelings with attacks and withdrawal, it's impossible to feel safe and be vulnerable.

Ultimately, you stay because you love your partner or because being alone would be worse. You may feel helpless or unworthy of being happy, loved, successful, or able to pursue your dreams. You don't realize that self-sacrificing behavior fuels your anger and compounds your suffering. If the abuse continues for a long time, denial of your needs and anger leads to bitterness, resentment, and depression that can result in psychosomatic symptoms and despair.

Someone in your past installed those buttons that your partner knows exactly how to push. In most cases, it was one or both of your parents or an abusive sibling. By removing those buttons from your neural circuitry, you become empowered, less fearful, and begin to not take things so personally. Al-Anon Family Groups recommend Q-TIP, or "Quit Taking It Personally."

INTIMACY PROBLEMS

Intimacy is a challenge for most people because they're afraid of being judged, abandoned, or smothered. For narcissists, however, intimacy is a monumental hurdle. The thought of letting down their guard to be authentic and emotionally close threatens their illusion of independence. Being dependent is abhorrent to them. It not only limits their options and makes them feel weak but also exposes them to rejection and feelings of shame, which they strive to keep from consciousness. Narcissistic defenses, which they adopt to keep them safe and pain-free, almost ensure that they won't feel love or experience real intimacy beyond companionship or "romantic encounters." Rather than relinquish their position of power and control that risks exposure of their false persona, they substitute sex for intimacy without much emotional investment.

Real intimacy[74] requires two autonomous individuals who want to know and understand each other, particularly emotionally. Narcissists aren't connected to their inner emotional world, to the extent they have one.

Intimacy also involves an empathetic understanding of what is shared. With little or no ability to empathize or see others as separate from themselves, many narcissists have little capacity to listen and care about the needs of others. Some narcissists don't bother with any pretense. Oscar Wilde aptly described a narcissistic attitude: "I'm the only person in the world I should like to know thoroughly."

Because of these and other obstacles to intimacy, narcissists are usually the distancers in close relationships when their partners expect more than sex. They distance themselves physically or wall off their emotions to buffer their weak boundaries. They also create distance by talking about themselves or someone who isn't present or by devaluing you. One woman recounted her loneliness and anger when, immediately after lovemaking, her husband spent 15 minutes bragging about himself.

Studies reveal that narcissists show less commitment to an ongoing romantic relationship.[75] Because of their lack of feeling, sometimes even their sexual responsiveness is limited. But they can't fully let go of their need for control, so they rely more on charm and technique.[76] Their partners feel their coldness and miss having an intimate connection. Yet, they anxiously pursue them, unconsciously replaying the emotional abandonment from their past. In the end, narcissists and their partners alike feel unloved and unlovable. Nevertheless, narcissists cannot see that their partner is giving them the love that they desire, while their partner cannot see that the narcissist is incapable of giving the love they, too, desire. They're both stuck playing out a drama from their childhoods.

GASLIGHTING

Gaslighting is a malicious and surreptitious form of mental and emotional abuse that is designed to plant seeds of self-doubt and alter your perceptions of reality. Like all abuse, it's based on the need for power, control, or concealment. Some people occasionally lie or use denial to avoid taking responsibility. They may forget or remember conversations and events differently than you, or they may have no recollection, sometimes due to a blackout if they were drinking. These situations are occasionally called gaslighting, but the term refers strictly to a deliberate pattern of manipulation calculated to make the victim trust the perpetrator and doubt their perceptions or sanity.

The term derives from the play and later film *Gaslight* with Ingrid Bergman and Charles Boyer. Bergman plays a sensitive, trusting wife struggling to preserve her identity in an abusive marriage to Boyer, who tries to convince her that she's ill to keep her from learning the truth.

As in the movie, a gaslighter progresses gradually with intermittent lies, denials, and undermining remarks so that you continue to trust them. The perpetrator often mixes in kind acts and displays of concern to dispel any suspicions. Someone capable of persistent lying and manipulation is also quite capable of being charming and seductive. Often the relationship begins that way. When gaslighting starts, you might even feel guilty for doubting the person whom you've come to trust.

Gaslighting can occur with anyone, but especially in close relationships. A typical scenario is when your partner lies to hide a relationship with someone else. In other cases, it may be to conceal gambling debts or investment losses. This treacherous behavior is usually perpetrated by a narcissist, addict, or sociopath, particularly when it's premeditated or used to cover up a crime.

In one case, a sociopath was stealing from his girlfriend with whom he shared an apartment. She gave him money each month to pay the landlord, but he kept it instead. He hacked into her credit cards and bank accounts and was so devious that to induce her trust, he bought her gifts with her money and pretended to help her find the hacker. Only when the landlord eventually informed her that she was way behind in the rent did she discover her boyfriend's treachery.

Signs of Gaslighting

To secure control, sometimes a narcissist attempts to divide and conquer by separating you from any outside influence. Undermining your relationships with friends and relatives can be achieved by attacking both you and them. A common strategy to isolate you is to accuse you of disloyalty and insist that you side with your partner. Your partner might interrogate you about conversations with other people, attack you for listening to them, or disparage them to erode your trust in anyone else. A typical tactic is to claim other people agree with your partner's negative statements. Your partner might spread lies about you to your friends and relatives or suggest to them that you're unbalanced and losing touch with reality. This is also done so that they won't believe you if you tell them you're being abused.

When the motive is purely for control, your partner might use guilt and shame to undermine your confidence, loyalty, or intelligence. A wife might attack her husband's manhood and manipulate him by calling him weak or spineless. A husband might undermine his wife's self-esteem by criticizing her looks or her professional or domestic competence.

To further play with your mind, an abuser might offer evidence to show that you're wrong or question your memory or senses. More justifications and explanations, including praise and expressions of love and flattery, eventually come into play to confuse you. You get temporary reassurance, and increasingly, you doubt your senses, ignore your gut feelings, and become more confused.

The gaslighter might act hurt and indignant or play the victim when questioned or challenged. Covert manipulation can easily turn into overt abuse with accusations that you're distrustful, ungrateful, unkind, overly sensitive, dishonest, stupid, insecure, crazy, or abusive. Abuse might escalate to anger and intimidation with punishment, threats, or bullying if you don't accept their false version of reality.

Here are a few examples of gaslighting tactics:

- **Shaming:** The perpetrator may shame what's integral to your self-worth: "You're unfit to be a mother. What kind of mother lets her children talk back to their father?"; "A real man would tell off his boss"; "You're a cry-baby. What kind of man are you?"; "If you were a man, you wouldn't be late for work"; or "You're looking old. You're lucky to have me."

- **Discounting Your Feelings:** Your partner shows disdain and blames you for your feelings. "You're always exaggerating"; "You're such a drama queen"; "You're hypersensitive"; "What's wrong with you? No one would react like you do"; or "Oh yeah, now you're feeling really sorry for yourself."

- **Claiming Allies:** Your partner says people agree with him or her and talk behind your back: "Your own children complain to me about you"; "Don't you know everybody talks about you? They think you're crazy"; "Your siblings agree with me, but they wouldn't tell you to your face"; "Your friend warned me about you"; or "No one believes you. They know you always over-react."

- **Disparaging Confidants:** This tactic is used to isolate and control you: "Your friend isn't trustworthy. He's envious and spreads lies about you"; "Your so-called friend was flirting with me at that party"; or "Your therapist is trying to control you and distort what's going on."

- **Denying Facts and Events:** A gaslighter may deny statements, events, or previously made promises: "You're imagining things"; "I never said that"; "You're making it up"; "You're losing your memory. What are you talking about?"; "You're very mixed up. We never ate there"; "That never happened"; or "How dare you accuse me of that!"

- **Hiding things:** A gaslighter might hide things to make you doubt your mind. "You lost that expensive necklace I gave you!"; "I thought you got my jacket from the cleaners"; or "I'm concerned that you keep losing your keys. Maybe you should talk to a doctor."

Symptoms of Being Gaslighted

Gaslighting becomes more insidious the longer it occurs. Initially, you won't realize you're being affected by it, but gradually you lose trust in your instincts and perceptions. It destroys trust and love in a relationship.

Gaslighting hurts your self-confidence and self-esteem, trust in yourself and reality, and your openness to love again. If it involves verbal abuse, you may believe the truth of the abuser's criticisms and continue to blame and judge yourself even after the relationship is over. Love and attachment are strong incentives to believe lies and manipulation. We use denial because we would rather believe the lie than the truth, which might precipitate a painful breakup. Answer the questions on denial in chapter 8. In the meantime, think about whether you often do or feel the following things:

- Wonder if you're too sensitive.
- Doubt your reality.
- Feel confused.
- Feel crazy in the relationship.
- Accept the blame and apologize to your partner.
- Don't know why you're unhappy.
- Question your partner's statements.
- Distrust friends or relatives because of your partner's statements.
- Feel isolated from friends and family.
- Have difficulty making simple decisions.
- Wonder if you're good enough to keep your partner.
- Don't feel like the person you used to be.
- Are more insecure or anxious than you used to be.
- Feel like everything you do is wrong.
- Feel apathetic or hopeless.

Recovery from Gaslighting

A gaslighter's words are meant to confuse and manipulate you. Disregard them and pay attention to your partner's *actions* instead. Learn to identify their behavior patterns and your own. Realize that they're due to their insecurity and shame, not yours. It's critical to have a strong support system and counseling to combat gaslighting. See chapter 8 – Your Support System.

Once you acknowledge what's going on, you'll be better able to detach and not believe or react to falsehoods, even though you may want to. You'll also realize that the gaslighting comes from your partner's serious character flaws. It does not reflect on you, nor can you change someone else. For a narcissist to change, it takes willingness and effort.

Chapter 8

MAKING CHANGE

You're likely looking for information and answers because you've been in pain or are just fed up with not getting your needs met in your relationship. You may feel hopeless and powerless to make changes, but you're not ready to leave for any number of reasons, such as financial, the needs of your children, or simply love. You may be looking for help in changing your partner, but people make changes only when they're ready to do so. Change won't begin until you focus on your own behavior and recovery, not on changing your partner, over whom you're essentially powerless. That doesn't mean that you don't have any power or choices, but your power reigns only over your own actions and life.

You're likely the one who wants change. A narcissist who has the power in a relationship has no incentive to change and will most certainly resist either individual therapy or your attempts to change the status quo. Both threaten the narcissist's security. Narcissists are more likely to change their behavior not out of concern for you, but when changing benefits them. Though when sufficiently motivated, people with only some narcissistic traits can learn to empathize. In either case, expect resistance.

If you're motivated to make some changes, doing so can have a positive effect on you and your relationship. Focusing on your partner only degrades your ability to effect change and achieve happiness. Even if you're being emotionally abused, you have the power to effect change once the locus of control shifts from the perpetrator to yourself. Eldridge Cleaver famously said, "If you are not part of the solution, then you are part of the problem." The endeavor won't be easy. It takes time, consistent effort, and courage. You might slip back into old habits, but this is part of the process of change. Here are some facts to think about:

- Changing beliefs and habits requires motivation, self-awareness, practice, and considerable patience. Consider your underlying beliefs discussed in chapter 4 and the difficulty you'll experience in changing them. It's even harder for a narcissist who has little insight and resists accepting responsibility for their beliefs and behavior.

- With a diagnosis of full-blown NPD, it's less likely that your partner will want to change. But if they're capable of insight, are motivated to change, and have fewer narcissistic traits, there is a much better prognosis.
- Making change is a learning process. Expect to slip back into old habits and reactions. Recognizing that slippage is a sign that you're growing.
- It's much easier if you have a therapist, coach, or twelve-step program to guide and support you in maintaining your resolve and establishing new thinking and behavior patterns, particularly in the face of inevitable resistance.

You may be asking yourself why you should bother to change if your partner won't. First, even though you're the one *initiating change*, that doesn't mean your partner won't also make changes. Once you begin changing and are consistent, you're altering the status quo, and they will probably shift as a result. You'll also feel better about yourself. Your relationship may improve. Even if it doesn't, you will be more empowered to enjoy your life whether you stay or leave. Finally, any changes you make will serve you in all your relationships. They will raise your self-esteem and make you a better partner should you leave.

> ### Innercises: Uncovering Your Motivation

If you're ready to work on yourself, consider the following questions:

- What motivates you (e.g., financial security, intimacy, your work, your children's welfare)?
- Why do you want to change (e.g., fear of worse pain, greater peace, or mental and physical health)?
- What motivates your partner (e.g., power, reputation, money, respect, sex)?
- What would incentivize your partner to change (e.g., risk of divorce, loss of sex/affection/attention)?

CHANGE THE IMBALANCE OF POWER

In an abusive relationship, it's easy to blame the abuser. When you take an accommodating, supportive role to avoid conflict, you allow your partner to define the relationship. What you may not realize, however, is that your behavior is likely facilitating the unhealthy dynamics, which in turn worsen abuse and the toxic environment. All the traits of accommodators and codependents contribute to the dysfunctional relationship, which if untreated, worsen over time.

This unspoken contract works for a while depending on the degree of your autonomy and your partner's narcissism. The status quo can be sustained for years, as long as you provide enough warmth and attention to a narcissist and you get sufficient needs met. However, the longer you self-sacrifice, the more your sense of self deteriorates. *The very patterns that made the relationship work become its undoing.*

While trying to adapt to and control someone else to feel better, you move away from real solutions. You hold the misguided belief that you're responsible for the narcissist's feelings and needs and ignore your own. Your behavior reinforces the narcissist's false belief that you're at fault and responsible for their discontent. And things continue to get the worse. You both deny your pain and prevent your partner from taking responsibility for their behavior, needs, and feelings. Denial blinds you to the possibility of change and fact that your beliefs and behavior contribute to your unhappiness. Getting informed and taking action can prevent you from entering the later stages of trauma and codependency.

Changing the relationship dynamics requires you to do the opposite of what comes naturally and what you likely have been doing. That isn't easy and takes time. The first step is developing a new perspective on your relationship because you've become isolated and confused by the attacks, threats, and skewed reality of a narcissist. It's important to learn all you can about narcissism, abuse, and codependency.

Awareness and acceptance of these truths at a deep level enable you to detach and not react to what a narcissist may throw at you just because they're uncomfortable in their own skin. You begin to realize that although abusive words may hurt, they're not true. Detaching doesn't require leaving or being aloof. It's like having an invisible, protective force field.

Instead of reacting, you honor what you need, feel, and want. You look to meet those needs from people who are safe and supportive. As your self-worth grows, you're more assertive. You ask for what you want and set limits on what you don't. You may have tried this, but with a narcissist, there are specific techniques to follow outlined in chapter 9.

Eventually, what happens is that your role and that of the narcissist reverse! As your self-esteem and autonomy increase, the self-esteem, independence, and power of your partner decrease. You will be amazed that the person you once feared is now fearful of you. The one you looked to for approval and attention now seeks that from you. The codependency and insecurity of the narcissist become apparent. You may have been afraid of leaving or being left, but now it's your partner who is afraid that you will leave.

Changing the power imbalance isn't easy, but your courage and self-respect will grow. You might get strong enough to leave or insist that your partner get treatment. Even if you don't, your life will be happier, because you're taking charge of your self-esteem and sense of well-being. Often, a narcissist will make changes in reaction to you.

COME OUT OF DENIAL

We're all more-or-less in denial. Denial is a refusal to acknowledge truth or reality. Life is unpredictable, and you'd barely get through the day if all you did was worry that you might die today. A healthy amount of denial keeps your mind clear to focus on what you must do to survive. An unhealthy amount of denial is serious if it causes you to ignore parts of yourself and problems that you might be able to solve. It impairs your ability to express your rights and hinders your power, self-esteem, and capacity to pursue your goals.

If you're under the spell of an abuser, your perceptions and autonomy are compromised. To become empowered, you need to come out of denial to see reality for what it is. One of the most pernicious aspects of denial is that it's invisible—when you're in denial, you don't even know it. Denial deadens your senses. When you deny negative feelings and memories, it deadens all your feelings, including joy and love. You become increasingly numb as your heart closes. Similarly, when you deny your wants and needs, your enjoyment of life diminishes. You sacrifice your desires and live in quiet desperation. Denial of your worth prevents you from receiving love and achieving your goals or gaining any satisfaction from your successes.

You may deny problems, abuse, or that you're not getting your needs met, or you might feel guilty and/or lack the courage to speak up. When you repeatedly tune out narcissistic behavior, your partner feels empowered. Left unchecked, abuse escalates and is harder to correct later. *Denial of needs is a major reason people remain in unhappy relationships.* Learning to identify and express your feelings and needs is a major part of recovery and is essential to well-being and enjoying satisfying relationships.

Your discomfort might manifest as passive-aggressive or addictive behavior, displaced anger (yelling at your children instead of your spouse), or a physical or mental health problem. Research shows that denial of stress and negative emotions has serious health risks that can lead to heart attacks, surgery, and death. You can become numb, develop a sense of futility, and a downward spiral ensues.

Denial is a Defense Mechanism

Denial is the first and simplest psychological defense mechanism. Children typically deny wrongdoings to avoid reprimands. I fondly recall my four-year-old shaking his head and denying that he'd been eating ice cream in the wee morning hours despite the chocolaty evidence smeared all over his cheeks. Of course, adults deny wrongdoing too, particularly the criminals, abusers, addicts, dishonest politicians, and adulterers. Conscious lies usually arise out of a self-preservation instinct and fear of punishment.

Denial isn't an all-or-nothing phenomenon; it's a matter of degree. It can include anything from consciously lying to repressing painful memories. You not only deceive yourself, but you also forget, excuse, rationalize, and minimize. You might be aware of the facts, yet still deny or minimize the consequences, or even acknowledge them, but still refuse to change or get help.

Denial serves a survival function. There are many motives for denial, including avoidance of physical or emotional pain. Here are a few reasons why denial is so persistent:

Social Cohesion: Denial can build cohesion, especially between loved ones. It's a unifying force between spouses and among families and groups that motivates us to overlook things that might cause arguments, hurt, or separation.[77] We defend the untruths and blatant lies of the people we want to believe and ignore truths that would disillusion us and/or require us to struggle with uncomfortable feelings or possibly leave our partner.

Difficult Emotions: We deny reality to allay fears of change and the unknown. Denial is adaptive when it helps us cope with a sudden trauma or difficult emotions, as in the initial stages of grief after the death of a loved one. It isn't adaptive when you deny a problem out of fear of possible pain, loss, or shame.

Inner Conflict: You might deny the truth if it would require you to act when you don't want to. For example, you might not look at how much debt you've accumulated because that would require you to lower your spending or standard of living, creating inner conflict. A deceived spouse might prefer to rationalize facts and believe lies rather than confront a situation that triggers the pain of betrayal, humiliation, loss, and the possibility of divorce, as well (see my blog, "Secrets and Lies: The Damage of Deception").[78]

Partners of addicts or abusers can spend a lot of time on the so-called "merry-go-round of denial" that happens in alcoholic relationships after a bout of drinking followed by promises of sobriety. Similarly, narcissists can be loving and even responsible at times and promise to stop their abuse, but soon return to breaking trust and promises. Then the apologies and promises come pouring out again, and their partners believe them out of love, denying their own needs and worth to prevent the relationship from ending.

Familiarity: We also deny problems and behavior that we grew up amidst. When they regularly recur, we assume that they're normal and deserved, even if they're painful, such as abuse and conflict. If you were emotionally abused as a child, you might not consider mistreatment by your spouse to be abusive. You might acknowledge that your spouse is verbally abusive but excuse, minimize or rationalize it: "It's enough that she loves me"; "My husband doesn't mean it"; "My wife just has a temper"; or "At least he doesn't cheat." Having empathy for narcissists because of their abusive childhood is a common excuse. Most abuse victims deny the detrimental impact that it's having on them; this often leads to post-traumatic stress disorder (PTSD) long after leaving the abuser. Once you face the truth, you're more likely to seek help.

Shame and Trauma: Most people, including myself for many years, don't realize the extent to which shame drives their lives, even if they think their self-esteem is pretty good. Shame is an extremely painful emotion that breeds denial in victims of abuse as well as liars. It's usually why victims minimize, deny, or don't disclose their abuse; and it's a big reason why abusers often don't seek help.

➤ Innercises: Are You in Denial?

You might be wondering whether you're in denial. It's tricky to uncover something unconscious. Look for the signs of denial in yourself and your partner.

About Yourself

You may be in denial about the abuse and pain you're experiencing if you:

- Wish about how things should be in your relationship
- Wonder: "If only he (or she) would ..."
- Doubt or dismiss your feelings
- Believe repeated broken assurances
- Conceal embarrassing aspects of your relationship
- Hope things will improve after some event occurs (e.g., a vacation, moving, or marriage)

- Make concessions and placate, hoping it will change your partner
- Feel resentful or used by your partner
- Spend years waiting for your relationship to improve or someone to change
- Walk on eggshells, worry about your partner's whereabouts, or dread talking about problems

What You Can Do

Here are some tips for recognizing and dealing with denial:

1. Become more mindful through meditation and journaling.
2. Don't be defensive if friends or relatives are worried about you or your relationship. Ask why and listen to alternative opinions and interpretations of facts.
3. Challenge your underlying assumptions. Where do your beliefs come from? Are they helpful? Might reasonable people disagree? Are you dealing with a problem through wishful thinking when the facts prove otherwise?
4. If you find yourself excusing, rationalizing, or minimizing your partner's behavior or concealing it from others, analyze why you do this and how it makes you feel.
5. Don't bury problems or assume no one notices. They do. Instead, get information. Be willing to initiate difficult conversations about uncomfortable subjects.
6. Don't procrastinate. Talk to a professional about your concerns.

About Your Partner

You may be in denial about your partner's ability to change. Consider whether your partner:

- Has insight into their motives and behavior
- Acknowledges responsibility for their behavior
- Is motivated to seek therapy and change
- Cares about the impact of their behavior on you and others
- Is dishonest and won't admit it
- Disregards your boundaries and those of others
- Feels entitled and above social norms and rules
- Violates the law or ethical standards without remorse
- Is emotionally abusive without remorse
- Is grossly irresponsible
- Abuses alcohol or drugs

- Has ever been violent, including with property, animals, or people, including you (remember that greater aggressiveness is a sign of more severe narcissism)

When You're Trained to Deny

Unbelievably, many parents train their children to deny their perceptions. Parents do this to manipulate them, to protect another family member, or to hide a family secret such as addiction. Parents also deny children's needs and feelings when they tell them they shouldn't feel a certain way or need or want something. Children idealize their parents and must adapt to survive. They blame themselves and learn to doubt or deny perceptions, feelings, wants, and needs. This can lead to toxic shame that unconsciously colors their entire adult life. Some people repress or deny their past and insist they had a happy childhood to avoid painful or confusing truths.

Denial affects future generations and can cause families and entire groups to endure decades of shame, which can be extremely difficult to resolve. But when you face the truth, seeking help and interrupting that agonizing legacy becomes much easier.

BUILD AWARENESS

Once you acknowledge that you're not able to change your narcissistic partner, the next phase is to become aware of the dynamics in your interactions. Dispassionately collect and analyze data as if you were a scientist conducting an experiment, observing both your partner's and your behavior. If you have any denial remaining, heightening your awareness will help you get a clearer perspective and prepare you for action. Keep a journal to record your observations.

> ### Innercises: Observe Your Partner's Behavior

For several weeks, keep a record of the following behaviors:

- List ways in which your partner devalues you, or your family and friends. For example, if you're criticized, called names, blamed, threatened, undermined, or ignored — not all abuse is verbal.
- List ways in which your partner manipulates or exploits you and others. Review the types of manipulation in chapter 3. What is the typical pattern? How does it make you feel?
- What does your partner do when you react passively or aggressively? Does their behavior escalate or diminish? Do you feel better or worse?

- What are your partner's express or implied rules about how they want to be treated?
- What are your partner's triggers? Do they involve feeling shame or loss of control?
- What does your partner need most from you? (e.g., attention, sex, praise, companionship)
- List ways in which your partner attempts to dominate or control you and others, such as:

  ✓ Interrupting or blasting you with an onslaught of words or statistics
  ✓ Ordering you to do things
  ✓ One-upping you
  ✓ Mentioning allies in support of their position
  ✓ Making unilateral decisions that affect you
  ✓ Telling you what opinions to hold
  ✓ Telling you how to dress or whom to associate with
  ✓ Telling you how to behave
  ✓ Restricting your freedom
  ✓ Undermining your efforts, interests, or friendships
  ✓ Interrogating you about your conversations with others
  ✓ Preventing you from seeking outside help or talking to others
  ✓ Restricting your access to finances

> ### Innercises: Observe Yourself

Keep a daily record of your experience and your feelings.

- Notice when you feel insecure or unloved. What triggered your feeling, and what was your reaction?
- Notice when you feel shame or guilt. What triggered your feeling, and what was your reaction?
- Notice when you feel afraid or intimidated. What triggered your feeling, and what was your reaction?
- Notice when you feel angry and resentful. What triggered your feeling, and what was your reaction?
- Write about your physical, emotional, and sensory feelings.
- When you're abused, dominated, or manipulated, what is your reaction — your thoughts, words, and behavior? What are your underlying beliefs?
- What are your rules about how you want to be treated? How do you communicate them?

- Do you avoid doing things by yourself or with friends in order to accommodate your partner's needs?
- Is giving and receiving balanced in your relationship? If not, how does it make you feel?
- Identify your needs and wants (see my blog, "Need-Fulfillment is the Key to Happiness,"[79] and chapter 9 in *Codependency for Dummies*).
- List your needs that are and aren't being met. Do you sacrifice your wants and needs?
- Do you believe that your partner's needs are more important than yours? Why?
- Have you changed since you've been in this relationship? If so, how?

ACCEPT REALITY

Before change is possible, you must face reality and accept it on its terms. It doesn't mean you're okay with your partner's behavior or the relationship. It doesn't imply that you approve of or want the status quo or even feel peaceful about it. Nor does acceptance equate to passivity or resignation. In fact, it's the opposite.

In practice, acceptance means that you must learn all you can about narcissism and accept the truths about yourself, your partner, and your relationship. Acceptance does *not* mean you accept that being abused or manipulated is acceptable, only the fact that it's happening.

Expectations

You may have already requested change, only to have your pleas ignored or only half-heartedly acknowledged. Some people will make the changes that you ask of them; others won't. Continuing to expect someone to change when they keep disregarding your requests is denial. Such expectations also lead to feelings of disappointment, hopelessness, and resentment. On the other hand, if *you* change your words *and behavior* as suggested in this book, the chances are greater that your partner will change, too.

For starters, you are more empowered if you have no expectations for your partner. Positive and negative expectations are usually based on hope or fear; you'd be wise to base your thinking on all the available facts. By not expecting your partner to change, you let go of the hope that they will be empathic to your feelings and needs, express praise and genuine warmth, and not manipulate or take advantage of you. It's also a form of denial to expect a narcissist to support your requests for change, put you first, or reliably be there for you. They may have no interest in developing empathy or meeting your needs. You're a more effective agent for change if you're grounded in reality. Although paradoxical, lowering your expectations may lead to change in your partner, provided *you alter the way you react.*

› *Innercises: Lowering Expectations*

Here are some innercises that can help you lower your expectations:

- List your expectations of your partner.
- Are your expectations reasonable in light of your experience? It's reasonable to expect your partner not to lie to you, but if they have in the past, it's unreasonable to assume the future will be any different unless you've witnessed clear signs of remorse *and* amends *and* efforts at self-reformation.
- List ways you've tried to change him or her. What were the consequences?
- List ways you've tried to change yourself to better the relationship. What were the consequences?
- How do you feel when you think about the fact that your partner may not change?
- Are you willing to accept your powerlessness over your partner and put effort into changing yourself?
- What is the most important behavioral change you'd like to see happen? What would be a small sign that it had taken place?

Grieving

Acceptance also entails grieving the dissolution of your illusions and unrealistic hopes for you and your partner. For example, accepting that your partner is an alcoholic might mean accepting not only that you cannot keep him or her sober but also that your life together won't be as you hoped it would have been and that your partner may die from the effects of addiction.

Many partners of narcissists stay in painful relationships because of an unconscious desire to heal a past relationship with a narcissistic, unavailable, or abusive parent. You may have been unhappy in your childhood family and yearn to create a better one with your current partner. This is an unconscious fantasy. Accepting that your wished-for outcome won't happen is doubly sad because you're grieving not only that you won't achieve your wish in your present relationship but also what you missed growing up (see chapter 11 – Stages of Grief). This may entail re-experiencing the suffering of your childhood, but it doesn't mean you can't make a better life or find happiness as an adult. However, expecting someone with NPD to make big changes and become vulnerable and empathetic while still being abusive keeps you stuck in an illusion.

Once victims of abuse come out of denial, it's common for them to mentally want to redo the past. They're often self-critical for not having trusted themselves and stood up to the abuse. *Don't do this!* Instead of perpetuating self-abuse, practice stopping self-criticism and start raising your self-esteem.

DETACH

It's hard to feel safe when you're afraid of being criticized. It's bold to ask for your needs or to share your feelings when they're ignored or dismissed. It's painful to hunger for closeness and never know if or when you might experience it. Feeling unimportant or uncared about are signs your relationship is out of balance. You want to feel loved and desired, but instead, you feel insecure. You're nervous about asking for your partner's reassurance, help, or cooperation. This emotional insecurity fosters anxiety and an unhealthy preoccupation with your relationship.

You may be overly attached to your partner because you're watching the narcissist's moods and reactions to avoid conflict and abuse and to maintain a positive connection. Your thinking can become consumed with analyzing, reacting, worrying, and obsessing over your partner's needs and wants. You can become myopic and an extension of the narcissist. Meanwhile, your life disappears without a trace like Echo, who spent her whole life trying to get Narcissus' attention. The antidote is to detach and let go.

Additionally, often narcissists' partners give up independent activities just to spend the little positive moments they have with them. They might drop friends or hobbies that the narcissist doesn't like or not pursue a class or career that their partner disparages.

> ### *Innercises: Are You Over-Involved?*

Ask yourself whether:

- You try to get your partner's praise, attention, or validation
- Your moods depend on your partner's mood
- You're afraid of making a mistake or being criticized
- You spend time wondering about what your partner is thinking, intending, or doing
- You try to analyze your partner's motives
- You're afraid of your partner's disapproval
- You have strong emotional reactions to your partner's opinions, judgments, and behavior
- You neglect your career, hobbies, activities, or friends due to your relationship

- You drop other activities if your partner won't join you or disapproves
- You try to please your partner because you're afraid of rejection
- You become anxious while doing things alone

Learning to Detach

Attachment and caring are normal. It's healthy to be attached to people you love and care about, but an unhealthy attachment to a narcissist causes pain and problems. Changing that pattern calls for detaching, but that doesn't mean physical withdrawal or leaving someone. Although physical space or separation may be useful as a means of setting boundaries and centering yourself, detaching isn't based on proximity. Nor is detaching emotional withdrawal, such as ignoring someone or being aloof, disinterested, or shutdown.

You can be detached and right next to the person or very enmeshed and reactive 3,000 miles away. You might dwell on a conversation for days, even if it occurred only in your mind! Some divorced couples are more emotionally attached and reactive to one another than most married couples. Detaching is about refocusing and taking charge of yourself. It's your attitude and state of mind that inform your behavior.

Detaching involves not reacting to things that other people say and do, not obsessing, and not worrying. It means letting go of expectations for other people and not entangling their problems and affairs with your own. In other words, you take control of your feelings and thoughts and mind your own business. But detaching doesn't take away your feelings, needs, and concerns; it healthily channels them. In practice, it's more compassionate and loving than codependent attachment. Detaching involves four key concepts:

1. Accepting reality
2. Having appropriate boundaries
3. Being in the present, not lost in the past or the future
4. Taking responsibility for your feelings and needs

Benefits of Detaching

Detachment enables you to get a wider perspective on your relationship's dynamics. It allows you to be more separate and therefore more yourself. Detachment also frees you from worry and obsession. It provides you time to develop yourself and engage in rewarding activities and friendships. Letting go brings you profound benefits, not only in relationships, but in personal growth, inner peace, and all areas of life. Some of the advantages to detaching with compassion are:

- You diminish your reactivity.
- There is less conflict in your relationship.
- You're better able to truly love your partner.
- You become a better listener.
- You gain serenity and become less anxious.
- You have more time and energy for developing and enjoying yourself.
- You gain independence and self-responsibility.
- You gain peace, freedom, and power.
- You become more resilient to loss.
- You encourage autonomy and responsibility in others.

You're responsible for your thoughts, feelings, actions, and the consequences of those actions. Other people are responsible for theirs; their feelings and behavior emanate from *them*, even if they blame you, as most narcissists do. You can't make any narcissist happy or fill their emptiness. Constantly being someone's cheerleader or punching bag deprives both partners of the opportunity to be self-responsible.

How to Detach

Learning to detach isn't easy, but with practice, you stop taking things personally. When you detach, you stop your knee-jerk reactions. Your emotions are no longer dependent upon those of your partner. Instead, you take charge of yourself. You decide how you'll respond. You redirect your efforts to changing what you can: your attitude, words, and behavior.

This means that you take your eyes off the narcissist and focus on your own feelings, beliefs, and behavior, which are the only things that you can change. Even when the narcissist is angry, you can be calm and composed. When you're angry and resentful, your reactive emotions work against you and heat up the conflict, which your partner probably enjoys. By practicing detachment, you gain control over your mind, feelings, behavior, and self-esteem.

When you first learn to detach, you will probably turn off your feelings or use walls of silence to refrain from codependent behavior, but with persistence, understanding, and compassion, you'll soon let go with equanimity. By understanding your partner's cognitive and emotional limitations, you're better able to respond. At the same time, you'll develop compassion for the frightened and fragile child behind the narcissist's grandiose, needy, and difficult persona.

As you detach, your investment in your partner will gradually fade even as you become more compassionate and encouraging. Rather than argue, please, or persuade, be curious about the differing points of view you two have. This shows respect and honors boundaries and separateness. For example, instead of offering solutions, you can say, "It must be upsetting to be so frustrated." Instead of trying to change someone's need for space or silence, you can enjoy time alone or with friends. This may sound impossible, but you can succeed and benefit from it.

Despite your relationship troubles, it's possible to enjoy life, which becomes more probable when you stop looking to your partner for your happiness.

› *Innercises: Practicing Detachment*

Take these steps to practice detaching:

- Ask yourself whether you're living in reality or denial.
- Examine whether your expectations of your partner are reasonable, given that they have a personality disorder. Or are you expecting something they're incapable of?
- Honestly examine your motivations. Are you coming from anger or revenge?
- Practice allowing and accepting reality in all aspects of your life.
- Allow and honor your feelings.
- Practice meditation to be less attached and reactive.
- Practice compassion for others and yourself.
- Be authentic. Make "I" statements.
- Practice listening without reacting. If you feel emotionally charged, write about your feelings instead of acting on them.
- A good slogan to remember is QTIP, "Quit taking it personally!"
- When your partner is being obnoxious or abusive, picture him or her as a lonely, frightened child up on stage while you're in the audience. You wouldn't get on stage with the actors, would you?
- Allow yourself time to think about and grieve your losses, such as your illusions and unrealistic hopes about your relationship. Write about what you're letting go of.
- Repeat the wise Serenity Prayer, known worldwide and used in twelve-step programs:
    "God, grant me the *serenity* to accept the things I cannot change, the *courage* to change the things I can, and the *wisdom* to know the difference."
- Repeat these mantras:
    "Let go, let God"
    "Live and let live"

- Remember the three C's:
  You didn't *Cause* your partner's feelings, narcissism, or problems.
  You can't *Control* them.
  You can't *Cure* them.
- Beware of the five don'ts:
  Don't watch.
  Don't expect.
  Don't judge.
  Don't obsess.
  Don't react.

Finally, have a plan B. If your partner is unreliable or often changes their mind, be prepared. Follow through with your arranged plans and have a backup plan you can readily execute. This way, you empower yourself and won't feel like a victim. It also alerts your partner that you won't be manipulated by their whims. You may even enjoy yourself more on your own! For example, it may be wise to drive a separate car to avoid abuse or your partner's sudden change of plan. You can honor invitations that your partner refuses to attend. Planning ahead to read a book or work on a personal project can ease your mind.

For more about detachment, see chapter 12 in *Codependency for Dummies*.

A Warning about Empathy

Beware that you may be using empathy for your partner as a defense against your own pain in the relationship. If you typically think in terms of black and white, you may find it hard to hold two contradictory thoughts. Empathy for someone doesn't excuse abuse and shouldn't replace empathy for yourself. These are subtle, but very important distinctions. You can empathize *and also* not justify, minimize, or rationalize your feelings or your partner's actions. Furthermore, you should not confuse compassion with the false belief that you can rescue or save him or her through accommodation, self-sacrifice, or love. It's not within your power, nor is it your responsibility, to change your partner. It only causes more dysfunction in the relationship and perpetuates your denial and unhappiness.

GAIN AUTONOMY

Autonomy is a fundamental human need. The word comes from the combination of two Latin words: *self* and *law*. Construed together, it means that you govern your own life and that you endorse your actions. Although you're still influenced by outside factors, overall, your behavior reflects your choice.

People who control their lives and destinies are happier and more successful. They report higher levels of functioning, psychological health, and have a greater sense of well-being and self-esteem. Autonomy and self-esteem are important in all relationships, but especially with a narcissist for several reasons:

1. To preserve your identity and individuality, which the narcissist often doesn't acknowledge and pressures you to relinquish.
2. To change the power dynamics in the relationship.
3. To maintain your self-respect and self-worth.
4. To not lose yourself by over-focusing on the limitless needs of the narcissist.
5. To heal codependency.

When you value yourself, you're better able to claim your autonomy. It's a feeling of both individuality and wholeness that permits you to feel separate in a relationship and complete when on your own. Rather than feel like a victim of fate or others' actions, you're motivated from within and believe that your efforts generate results for better or worse. Both belief and experience then enable you to function autonomously.

You feel independent and can set limits despite pressure from others. Your beliefs, needs, and values determine your actions, which gives you more control over your thoughts and emotions. It's the opposite of being a rebel or people-pleaser. They're not autonomous but merely oppose or comply with an external authority. Autonomy allows you to listen non-defensively and modify your views to incorporate new information.

Internalize Your Locus of Control

Of course, a narcissist wants to be the decision-maker and the center of your focus. If you grew up in an environment where your feelings and desires were similarly ignored or criticized or your voice and actions didn't have an impact, you can lose motivation and develop a sense of futility — a "What's the use?" attitude. This shows that your locus of control is external. You may even believe that you're controlled by fate, outside forces, or your partner. Your inner voice may represent the voice of a parent who talked you out of what you wanted. As a result, you feel powerless to achieve your goals and influence your life.

Without autonomy, you're controlled by what others do, say, think, and feel. That attitude reflects a passive stance toward your life and stems from and reinforces low self-esteem. Lack of autonomy and self-esteem can cause many symptoms, such as stress, addiction, domestic violence, emotional abuse, communication problems, worry and anxiety, depression, guilt, and anger.

> ### Innercises: Developing Autonomy

Consider the following questions:

- What are your yearnings and passions beyond your relationship? (See chapter 16 in *Codependency for Dummies*).
- Is there something you've always wanted to do? What are you waiting for?
- What are your goals? Are you pursuing them? If not, why not?
- Does focusing on your partner or your relationship problems distract you from pursuing your goals?
- Do your relationship problems distract your partner from pursuing their goals? If not, what if you were to pursue your goals like your partner does?
- If you're not self-supporting, what stops you?
- How would it feel to be self-supporting? What steps can you take to achieve that?
- There are also suggestions for developing autonomy in chapter 12 – Practical Steps.

NURTURE YOURSELF

It's frustrating and sad to repeatedly be denied understanding and nurturing. In addition to physical nourishment, including touch, care, and food, you have the following emotional needs:

- Love
- Play
- Respect
- Understanding
- Acceptance
- Empathy
- Comfort
- Reliability
- Guidance
- Encouragement

By all means, experiment with asking your partner to meet those needs according to the guidelines outlined in chapter 9, but don't be surprised if you still feel like you're trying to squeeze water from a stone. There's a saying, "Don't go to the hardware store for milk." This has been your pattern. Remember that the Serenity Prayer counsels to "accept the things I cannot change," and to "change the things I can."

Stop looking to your partner to provide what they can't or won't, and do what *you* can to nurture yourself. Even in the best relationships, self-responsibility includes self-love and self-nurture. It's up to you to be your own parent and meet those emotional needs, regardless of whether you're in a relationship. If you decide you'd rather leave and be single, you still must nurture yourself. Of course, there are times when we all need support, touch, understanding, and encouragement from others, but the more you practice self-nurturing, the better your relationships will be.

Your Support System

Friendships outside your relationship are essential to maintaining a healthy partnership. It's unrealistic to expect anyone to share all your interests or meet all your needs for companionship and support.

If you're being abused, shame may motivate you to hide what's going on from family and friends. Some cultures also encourage this. Your partner may even have threatened you not to talk to anyone about what's going on. It's imperative that you nonetheless reach out for support. Remaining silent about abuse perpetuates the problem. You need to get help, understand your options, and ensure your safety.

Seek the services of a professional to support you in overcoming PTSD reactions, in building self-esteem, in learning effective, assertive communication, and in taking risks to set boundaries and improve your relationship. This builds self-confidence and autonomy.

If you're experiencing physical abuse, expect it to continue or escalate. Get help immediately. In case of violence, the 24/7 number for the national hotline is 1-800-799-SAFE (7233). Also keep handy the numbers of other services, including local police and shelters in your town.

Support groups can play an important role. Hearing the stories of other abuse survivors can provide hope, strength, and wisdom. There are support groups that deal specifically with divorce and with narcissistic relationships. Join one in your area, an online forum, or social media group for abuse survivors, such as MovingForward, Victims of Narcissistic Abuse, and Out of the FOG.

Twelve-step meetings can play an important role in helping you change your habits and attitudes. You'll get tools to protect yourself and improve your self-worth and how you feel whether you stay or leave. Find the online directory for Codependents Anonymous' phone, zoom, and in-person meetings. There are specific twelve-step programs for partners of addicts, such as Al-Anon Family Groups, Gam-Anon, or Nar-Anon for relatives and partners of alcoholics, gamblers, or drug addicts, respectively.

Self-Acceptance

Self-acceptance works wonders. It includes honoring your feelings and needs, accepting your appearance and shortcomings, and forgiving yourself[80] to overcome guilt about the past. Once you start accepting yourself, you gradually stop worrying about what others think and become more spontaneous and natural. Self-acceptance allows you to be authentic. You can finally relax and let the inner, real you be seen. You have no shame or fear of revealing yourself when you accept yourself unconditionally. This is the key to intimacy and spiritual relationships that also enables you to accept others.

Self-Love

Self-love is more than just a word. It requires patience, awareness, and action. When you love someone, you try to understand their experience and worldview even though it differs from your own. You offer your attention, respect, support, compassion, and acceptance of your beloved's feelings, thoughts, and actions with understanding and caring. Self-love involves all that as well but is directed toward yourself. You may find it easier to love others than it is for you to love yourself.

You develop the ability to see yourself objectively and Love requires knowledge. Spending time alone with yourself is essential to developing the ability to identify and listen to your feelings with sensitivity and empathy. However, if you suffered alone as a child, doing so as an adult merely repeats your past abandonment trauma. Instead, you need to share your pain with someone you trust.

When most people are stressed or overwhelmed, they attempt to do even more instead of stopping to refocus and care for themselves. If you weren't nurtured as a child, self-nurturing can be challenging to learn as an adult, but it can be learned in psychotherapy over time. Nurturing is expressed with gentleness, tenderness, and generosity of spirit—the opposite of self-criticism, perfectionism, and pushing yourself. Self-compassion differs from self-pity, which is an angry judgment about your situation.

Psychoanalyst Eric Fromm states that self-love entails the faith and courage to take risks and overcome life's setbacks and sorrows. Faith in yourself enables you to comfort yourself and face challenges and failures without lapsing into worry or judgment. You know that you'll survive despite the storms of your present emotions. If you constantly seek validation and reassurance from others, you miss the opportunity to develop those internal functions.

Learning self-love isn't easy, but it can heal shame and improve self-esteem. You have opportunities to learn self-love all the time. Throughout the day, you're confronted with many opportunities to either disregard or attune to your feelings, to judge or to honor them, to abandon yourself or keep commitments and be responsible to yourself, and to ignore or meet your needs, values, and feelings. Every time you talk yourself down, doubt yourself, exhaust yourself, dismiss your feelings or needs, renege on plans for yourself, or act against your values, you undermine your self-esteem. The reverse is also true. You might as well make healthier choices, because you, your life, and all your relationships will benefit from it.

➤ *Innercises: Self-Nurturing*

There are many aspects to self-care. Of course, nurture yourself with healthy food and sufficient sleep and exercise. Allow yourself leisure that's not goal-oriented and time for pursuing interests, hobbies, and socializing. Develop a daily practice to nurture yourself spiritually such as through prayer, spiritual reading, meditation, or martial arts.

You can nurture yourself through doing something creative, whether it's cooking, woodworking, sewing, painting, or dancing. Make time for play and pleasure, which are antidotes to both physical and emotional pain.[81] Pleasure is enhanced through the enjoyment of the senses, including self-touch or massage, listening to music, looking at art, aromatherapy, spending time in nature, and taking time to literally "smell the roses." Here are some suggestions:

- Create a playlist of the most uplifting or relaxing music for your digital devices.
- Attend a meditation group.
- Take weekly walks in nature.
- Spend time on hobbies and activities you enjoyed as a child.
- Take a class on something you enjoy or find interesting.
- Do something playful or creative with a friend.
- Spend time playing with a pet.
- Make a list of fun activities and spend a few hours each week doing one.
- Write about your feelings. Journaling can alleviate depression and increase your self-knowledge.
- Express your feelings to someone safe.
- When you have painful feelings, with your hand on your chest, say aloud, "You're (or I'm) feeling ____ (e.g., angry, sad, afraid, lonely), and it's okay." This accepts and honors your feelings.
- Meeting your needs is good parenting. Identify, honor, and your needs, rather than diminish or dismiss them.

- Once you discover the cause of uncomfortable feelings, think about what will make you feel better.
- If you're angry, practice martial arts or meditation. Doing something active, like hiking, dancing, tennis, swimming, or playing a team sport, is ideal for releasing anger.
- If you're anxious, practice yoga or martial arts, meditation, or simple breathing exercises. Slowing your breath slows your brain and calms your nervous system. Exhale 10 times while making a hissing ("sss") sound with your tongue behind your teeth.
- Write a comforting, supportive letter to yourself. Write what an ideal parent would say.
- Have a warm drink. Studies show this elevates your mood.
- Swaddle yourself like a baby in a blanket or sheet. This soothes your body and nervous system.
- Write a list of things you're grateful for each day, and read it to a friend.
- Write at least three things you did well each day and three things you like about yourself.
- Throughout the day, praise and encourage yourself, especially when you don't think you're doing enough. Remind yourself of what you have done, and allow yourself time to rest and rejuvenate. Your brain doesn't distinguish between validation by you or from someone else.
- Listen to my *Self-Love Meditation*,[82] and practice talking to yourself in the same way.
- Watch my free Youtube video, "Three Exercises for Self-Love, Confidence, and Relaxation."

Chapter 9

COMMUNICATING EFFECTIVELY

Communication with abusers requires detachment, presence, and assertiveness. Additionally, a special approach is necessary because to them communication is not about listening to understand but is used to get their needs met, boost their ego, and enhance their control and power. Exchanges are a win-lose game and they use abuse to win. Therefore, you must be strategic in how you communicate and confront them effectively to get what you want in the relationship.

Codependents have low self-esteem and dysfunctional communication that was learned in childhood, where the communication style was probably passive and/or aggressive. Anyone can learn healthy and assertive communication techniques. Assertiveness and self-esteem go hand-in-hand. Being assertive raises your self-esteem, and vice-versa. You can gauge people's self-esteem by the way they communicate.

BE ASSERTIVE

Assertive communication is a response to what's going on within you — your feelings, needs, and wants — rather than a reaction to someone else. This requires you to control your emotions. It's a big challenge to maintain your composure without reacting to your partner because your emotions trigger your reactions. It's always helpful to take *time to think* when your usual reactions are triggered. If you need a time-out, let your partner know that their feelings matter and that after more consideration, you'd like to talk about the issue later (say when).

Elements of Assertiveness

When you're assertive, you stay present and in charge of your communication. You're able to think about what you want and what you're saying. The stronger your self-esteem, the more confident and sure of yourself you are.

Perhaps, you equate assertiveness with aggression, but it's not. Assertive communication is *respectful, concise, courteous,* and *calm*, while at the same time, firm. You want to impart honest information and feelings, not to vent, avenge, or scold. When you're being assertive, there's no need to raise your voice.

Assertiveness also requires *directness.* Indirectness is unclear, vague, and nonassertive. For instance, a simple "Yes" or "No" is a complete, concise, clear, and direct assertive statement. In other words, assertiveness requires you to *take a position.* When someone blames or criticizes you, that's not taking a position, it's aggression. Assertiveness entails taking responsibility for yourself and asserting your opinions, thoughts, feelings, and needs. *Using "I" messages is the cornerstone of assertive communication.* It doesn't involve analyzing or judging someone, but it does require you to stand up for yourself. This can be difficult because it challenges your fears and anxieties. To be able to address the problems in your relationship assertively, you also must know and believe you're entitled to what you think, need, want, and feel.

Listening is an essential part of good communication. If you want to be listened to and if you want to hear the truth, you must be willing to listen and wait your turn to respond. It's not helpful to keep listening to abuse; that's when boundaries become essential.

I recommend reading more about assertiveness and doing the exercises in *How to Speak Your Mind—Become Assertive and Set Limits*[83] to communicate your boundaries and bottom line. You can also get the webinar, *How to Be Assertive.*

▸ *Innercises: How to Be Assertive*

When communicating with a super-sensitive narcissist, don't blame or criticize. Otherwise, you'll escalate conflict and soon be on the defensive. You must also avoid passivity and concessions when dealing with demands or abuse. Bad behavior must be confronted assertively, as explained in the next sections.

Doing the following exercises will help prepare you to be assertive:

- Practice identifying your feelings and needs every day.
- Journal about your feelings during interactions with people each day.
- Analyze your communication. Were you authentic? Did you use "I" statements? Did you take positions?
- Write about fears that stop you from being honest.
- How honest are you with your partner? If you remained silent or misrepresented your truth, how did that make you feel? What was the consequence?

- On the other hand, did you interrupt, accuse, criticize, or blame? How did your partner react? Did your behavior get you what you wanted? How did that make you feel? What was the consequence?
- Are you a good listener? Are you thinking about your response before the other person has finished?
- If you're being verbally abused, what are you feeling and thinking? What does your body want to do?
- Does your partner listen to you? If not, what feelings emerge in you?
- Are you more or less assertive with people other than your partner? What's the difference?

When you're ready to express what you want, feel, think, or need, write it down using only "I" statements. ("I feel that *you're...*" isn't an "I" statement; it's a judgment that will provoke defensiveness and conflict.) You can practice aloud. Be aware of any nonverbal communication that might conflict with your words. Remember not to explain or justify. Make eye contact, don't fidget, and remain calm.

In the beginning, practice active listening. You can also ask for clarification and repeat the words you just heard. This can be very effective and can often diffuse arguments because it shows your partner that they have made an impact, something your partner was probably unable to do in childhood.

STOP REACTING

Most victims *react* to abuse irrationally. Assertiveness isn't a reaction; it's a conscious, proactive response. When you react to a provocation without thinking, you cede your power to the narcissist who now knows how to control you. The abuser has won at that point and deflected responsibility for any abuse.

To achieve change, you must begin by not *reacting* in the same old way. Responding to a situation requires you to be thoughtful about what you want, need, and say. You consider the impact of your words, maintain your boundaries, and stay present. You're conscious of what you want to achieve rather than react to the emotions of the other person. That's a tall order, and it takes dedication and practice, but eventually, you communicate more effectively.

Think of your reactions as habits that reflect your personality and past experiences, often from childhood. They may be trauma reactions or learned behavior. They're also based upon beliefs, which may bear no correlation to the present facts.

Reactions to Abuse

To achieve your communication goals, it's essential to avoid making your partner defensive so that they will listen to your needs and feelings and appreciate that your relationship requires reciprocity. As they say, it takes two to tango. If you react and conflict develops, you not only lose an opportunity to initiate change, you also defeat your objective, feel more negative emotions, and give your partner reasons to justify unwanted behavior.

The following is a list of typical reactions and mistakes people make in dealing with abuse:

- **Appeasement:** If you placate to avoid conflict and anger, it empowers the abuser, who sees it as weakness and an opportunity to exert more control.
- **Defending:** When you're wrongly blamed or attacked, trying to defend yourself beyond a simple denial of a false accusation leaves you open to more abuse. It sends this message: "You have power over my self-esteem. You have the right to approve or disapprove of me. You're entitled to be my judge (i.e., parent)." This dovetails with the narcissist's motive to have power over you.
- **Silence:** In some cases, silence may be a helpful tactical response, but when it's habitual and automatic, it's a trauma freeze response and disempowering.
- **Explaining:** You may mistakenly believe or hope that your partner is interested in understanding you. However, most narcissists aren't interested in truly knowing or understanding you. Depending on the degree of narcissism, sharing your feelings may also expose you to more hurt or manipulation. It's better to share your feelings with someone safe who cares about you. Narcissists are interested in winning a conflict and having the superior position. Facts can get in their way because they want only to justify their position and avoid responsibility. As with defending, you endorse an abuser's right to judge, approve, or abuse you. Your reaction communicates that you want their validation.
- **Pleading:** This sends the same message as placating. It shows weakness, which narcissists despise in themselves and others. They may react dismissively with contempt or disgust.
- **Withdrawal:** This is a good temporary tactic to collect your thoughts and emotions, but not an effective strategy to deal with abuse unless combined with stating a boundary.

- **Arguing and Fighting:** Arguing over the facts wastes your energy. Arguments with an abuser can quickly escalate to fights that drain and damage you. They lead to more resentment on both sides. As anger intensifies, so does abuse. You gain nothing. You lose and can end up feeling more victimized, hurt, and hopeless.
- **Criticizing and Complaining:** Because abusers are insecure, they may act tough even though they're fragile inside. They can dish it out, but can't take it. Instead of getting the love you want, complaining or criticizing an abuser can provoke rage and vindictiveness. It's more effective to be assertive and communicate your needs.
- **Threats:** Making threats can lead to retaliation or backfire if you don't carry them out. Never make a threat you're not ready to enforce. Boundaries with direct consequences are more effective.
- **Denial:** Don't fall into the trap of denial by excusing, minimizing, or rationalizing abuse. And don't fantasize that it will go away or improve in the future. The longer it goes on, the more it grows, and the weaker you can become.
- **Self-Blame:** Don't blame yourself for an abuser's actions and try harder to be perfect. Doing so is delusional. You can't cause anyone to abuse you. You're only responsible for your behavior. You will never be perfect enough for a narcissist to stop abusing, which stems from their insecurities, not you.
- **Blaming Your Partner:** Reacting with blame when something goes wrong discharges shame and anger without being constructive. When you say, "It's your fault that I...," it puts them in charge of you. It's as if you're saying, "I can't control myself (or manage my affairs), and you have power over what I say and do." Blaming your partner denies your power to make yourself happy, which is your responsibility. (The reverse is also true when you're blamed by your partner.)

Less typical reactions include distraction with antics or jokes, playing the martyr, or intellectualizing by responding with analysis, abstractions, and data.

Identify Your Trauma Reactions

Abuse can cause a PTSD trauma response that is connected to prior abuse or shaming and abuse. Research has identified five trauma reactions. (See my blog, "How Trauma Reactions Can Hi-Jack Your Life.")[84] Not reacting to those powerful emotions may seem insurmountable. It's likely your partner's behavior has precipitated a toxic shame attack in you because it triggered deep feelings of rejection or abandonment. Shame produces a visceral response of the autonomic nervous system that sets off a flight-or-fight-or-freeze reaction, which affects your entire body and mind. It can produce temporary paralysis so that you can't think clearly. It affects your pulse, skin, respiration, and muscle tone.

When you have a powerful reaction, generally it's because your current situation has provoked a memory. This limits your choices and prevents you from responding effectively in the present. When your partner blames, criticizes, or manipulates you, you may react like the scolded child you once were. It may trigger shame about feeling flawed and unlovable. You will probably rebel (fight) or retreat (flight), dissociate (freeze), or try even harder to win their approval (fawn).

To illustrate, if your partner calls you sloppy, you might not mind so much, but if your partner calls you selfish and you were criticized for that as a child, it hits a nerve, and you might feel ashamed and guilty or even blow up. It might trigger toxic shame, and the natural tendency is to attack or back off and have self-deprecating thoughts, feelings of inadequacy, alienation, and depression. Because you're trapped in a shame reaction, you can't see that it's your partner who was the selfish one and who projected that onto you as perhaps your self-centered, critical parent once did. You won't be able to set a boundary concerning such critical remarks. If you had a domineering parent, you might react obediently to your partner as if to your parent. For example, if your partner cross-examines you, instead of deciding not to answer, the child in you automatically answers every question. To refuse to answer wouldn't occur to you.

If you were emotionally or physically abandoned as a child, you'd be hypersensitive to that in adult relationships. Due to childhood trauma, you will over-react to your partner if they're unaffectionate, stay out later than expected, ignore you or your feelings, or give attention to someone else. For example, if your partner's behavior triggers feelings of being ignored and emotionally abandoned, you might withdraw in hurt or anger instead of trying to connect by addressing the lack of connection, stating what you want, or by being playfully affectionate.

> ### Innercises: Changing Your Reactions

You've collected data on your triggers and reactions in the *Innercise: Observe Yourself*. Here are some exercises to help you change your reactions:

- From your self-observations in chapter 8, and the preceding discussion of reactions, identify your style(s) of reacting.

- Are your strongest reactions when you feel insecure, anxious, afraid, angry, or hurt?
- Experiment with different responses. How does it make you feel? How does your partner react?
- How do your thoughts, feelings, and reactions affect your self-esteem?
- Choose an incident where you reacted strongly. Go deep into your physical and emotional reactions. Exaggerate them in your imagination. What do they remind you of from your past? Visualize and then write about experiences from childhood when you felt and reacted similarly. What does your body want to do — run, fight, freeze, please, or hide? Allow yourself to do this in your imagination. What do you wish would have happened? If it's to clobber an abusive adult in your life, picture yourself doing that. If you wish for protection, imagine a loving and trustworthy adult (your adult self or a loving relative, therapist, friend, or teacher from the present or past) entering the scene, advocating on your behalf, and protecting you. Visualize that person comforting the child you.
- Write about your feelings and reactions as a child to experiences involving criticism, scolding, and punishment.
- Thinking over your experiences. What beliefs did you form about yourself and your relationships? For example:
  - "I'm bad, and no one will love me."
  - "I'm all alone, and no one can help me."
- How do your beliefs from the past inform your current perceptions and behavior? What would be more accurate and constructive thoughts and beliefs? For example:
  - "My parents' words and actions reflected their problems. I was an innocent child, acting as all children do. I have positive and negative traits like everyone else and am just as worthy of love."
  - "I'm an adult now and have friends and relatives to whom I can talk. I can ask for and receive help from professionals and other people."
- Imagine that your partner throws you a ball of fire that represents anger or verbal abuse. See yourself dropping the ball and walking away. If you catch the ball, you're accepting your partner's pain. If you throw it back, your hands are still burned, and your pain increases with each toss. You have a choice not to play that game.

CONFRONT ABUSE

It's vital to remember that the narcissist's goals are domination and avoidance of responsibility. Narcissists are highly sensitive to any sign of dominance by another person. They react with aggression.[85] Some victims will even provoke physical abuse to stop their anxiety and get the abuse over with because their anxiety and fear are so great.

Allowing abuse damages your self-esteem. Thus, it's important to confront it. That doesn't mean to fight and argue. To be effective you must design your strategy (explained in the following sections), not react, and thereby not reward the abusive behavior. It means standing your ground and speaking up for yourself clearly and calmly and having boundaries to protect your mind, emotions, and body.

Setting boundaries and asking for change requires confidence and assertiveness. You must honor yourself and feel entitled to be treated with respect. You must deeply know that you have specific rights, such as the right to your feelings, the right not to have sex if you decline, a right to privacy, and a right not to be yelled at, touched, or disrespected.

Confronting an abuser, especially in a long-term relationship, is challenging. This is especially true if you've been abused for any length of time. Usually, both you and your partner have experienced shaming in childhood that impaired your self-esteem. You may no longer trust yourself or have the confidence to be able to consistently stand up to abuse. It generally takes the support and validation of a group, therapist, or counselor who can validate your experience. Without it, you may doubt your reality, feel guilty, and fear loss of the relationship or reprisal. Your compromised self-esteem leads to self-doubt, insecurity, isolation, and increased dependency on the abuser.

Without practice, it's difficult to confront abuse while under attack. The best time to deflect violence is in the build-up stage. It's fine to confront abuse fine later when things are calm; you're also more likely to be heard then. Afterward, your partner may express regret or promise never to repeat it. Don't be surprised if it recurs. Lasting change requires continual boundary setting. As you become more confident and skilled, you become more effective.

During this learning period, it's helpful if you avoid conflict and don't react to provocation. If your partner says something abusive or provocative, you can merely say, "I hear you. I'll think about it." Notice what happens when you don't take the bait. By not engaging or by responding in an unpredictable way, such as with humor, you can throw an abuser off-guard. It puts you on equal footing and deprives the abuser of the power they seek by belittling you.

Pay attention to your feelings, reactions, and the responses they provoke. Write them down, and add other possible responses as well. Repeating what you just heard also has an impact, followed by calmly stating a boundary. For example, "Did you say you think that I don't know what I'm doing?" You may get a defiant repetition of the insult. Then follow up with, "I disagree," or "I don't see it that way," or "I know exactly what I'm doing."

Respond to Projection

As discussed in chapter 3 – Projection and Blame, projection is a favorite defense of narcissists to rid themselves of unwanted traits and feelings. Projecting them onto you comes naturally to them since they see you as an extension of themselves and are convinced about their faulty perceptions. Because of this, they will exert enormous pressure on you to accept the projection. If you have a strong sense of self and healthy self-esteem and boundaries, when your partner projects something onto you, it bounces off. You don't take it personally, because you realize it's untrue or merely a statement about the speaker.

Understanding how projective identification works is crucial for self-protection. Recognizing the defense can be a valuable tool, for it's a window into the unconscious mind of an abuser. You can experience what your partner is feeling and thinking or the way that they were treated as a child. Armed with this knowledge, realize that your partner is projecting and reacting to their shame. It can give you empathy, which is helpful, provided you have good self-esteem and empathy for yourself!

Still, you may feel baffled about what to do. When someone projects onto you, simply set a boundary. This creates a force field, an invisible wall, and returns the projection to the speaker. Say something like:

- "I don't see it that way."
- "I disagree."
- "I don't take responsibility for that."
- "That's your opinion."

Remember not to argue or defend yourself, which gives credence to the narcissist's false reality. If they persist, you can say, "We simply disagree," and leave the conversation. Your partner will have to stew in their negative feelings.

Ask for Change

In chapter 8, you identified your feelings, needs, wants, and rules about how you'd like to be treated. Those are your boundaries. You've identified your needs, but it may be harder to identify what you really want. Do you ever wonder how your partner never hesitates to ask or even demand that their needs and wants be fulfilled, while yours go unspoken, ignored, or dismissed? Maybe at some point, you stopped asking; perhaps it was even long before you two met. Self-denial may be so natural that you believe that if you asked for what you want, you'd appear selfish. That concern doesn't stop a narcissist. Remember, by squelching your needs and wants, you inevitably become more unhappy and resentful.

Some needs you can meet yourself, such as physical, intellectual, and spiritual needs. You can also become financially self-supporting and get some social and emotional needs met by friends and others. Our needs for sex and intimacy are best filled by an intimate partner. However, remember that narcissists are reluctant to be open and vulnerable. Your intimacy might be limited to sex or spending quiet time together.

If you're going to stay in your relationship, you owe it to your partner to communicate your boundaries, needs, and desires, and you owe it to yourself to at least try to have them met. Then you'll know what you can expect from your relationship. Don't expect him or her to read your mind or gestures. When I tell this to couples, some women object, saying, "If I have to tell him, it doesn't count." Another way of looking at it is that your partner cares enough to be willing to listen to you and make an effort to change his behavior.

Employ a Strategic, Transactional Approach

Because narcissists are highly defensive and lack empathy, you need to adapt your requests to him or her to be effective in having them met.

In chapter 8, you observed the needs of your partner. Narcissists take a transactional approach to relationships and need-fulfillment by always considering what's in it for them. In knowing their needs and wants, you can have a greater impact using the transactional approach outlined below. The best method is to think as they do. Remember, you're dealing with someone mentally ill. You must educate a narcissist as you would a child. Explain the impact of their behavior and provide incentives and encouragement for different behavior *that will benefit their needs*. This may involve communicating consequences. It also requires planning what you're going to say without being emotional.

Your goal is to communicate in a way that will motivate change, not conflict. It's not about proving that you're right and that your partner is wrong or to blame. An educative approach is thus the most effective. To ask for what you want, use the following 8-step outline:

1. Prepare.
2. Describe your partner's behavior.
3. Describe how it makes you feel about yourself (limit this with callous narcissists, who don't care how you feel and use your vulnerability against you).
4. Describe how it makes you feel about your partner and the relationship.
5. Request the desired behavior.
6. Describe how you will feel individually and especially about your partner and the relationship if your partner makes the change you want.
7. Give your partner support for making the change.
8. Provide positive feedback for compliance.

Step 1: Prepare.

- Write what you need and want in your relationship in the form of requests.
- Write the specific behavior that impairs your needs and wants. Be brief.
- Write the new desired behavior and previous time(s) your partner has behaved that way.
- Experiment with giving your partner positive reinforcement for the behavior you want. Whenever they happen to do or say something you appreciate, enthusiastically communicate that you notice and are pleased about it. For example:
    - "Thank you. It makes me very happy when you compliment how I look."
    - "I'm very grateful that you're so generous."
    - "I appreciate it that you're taking the time to help me solve this problem."
- Prioritize your needs and wants. Select one that you'd like to discuss with your partner. Because narcissists are highly defensive, don't bring up more than one need or behavior at a time, and stay focused on it.
- Write a script based on Steps 2-8. Practice them aloud before speaking to your partner.

Steps 2 and 3: Describe your partner's behavior and how it makes you feel about yourself.

- Describe the unwanted behavior and how it affects you. For example:
  - "I'm sure that it wasn't your intention, but I've been unhappy (or insert the specific feeling you've had) because of _____."
  Be specific about what behavior they're doing or not doing and how it makes you feel. (See modification in Step 4 about sharing your feelings.)
- Don't label your partner (e.g., mean, cold, self-centered), which puts him or her on the defensive. Your goal is to encourage him or her to listen to you. For example:
  - "I'm sure you don't intend this, but when you turn on the light to read during the night, I wake up and can't get back to sleep. When I ask you to turn it off, you refuse. I'm tired the next day, and I become hurt, feel uncared about, angry, and resentful, because I'm not rested and because my request and needs were ignored. I know you like to read in bed, but I have needs, too."
  - "I think you don't intend to hurt me, but sometimes, I feel _____ (criticized, scolded, ignored, etc.) when you _____. (Be specific: belittle me, order me, put me down, roll your eyes, make unkind jokes about me, use that tone of voice, etc.) I'm very saddened that you act (speak) without regard for my feelings."

Step 4: Describe how it makes you feel about your partner and the relationship.

- Describe how the behavior affects your feelings *about your partner and the relationship*. Don't blame.
- With some narcissists, sharing vulnerable feelings isn't productive. They likely won't care and your disclosure can be used against you. Instead of "I feel hurt or uncared about," it would be better to say, "My loving feelings for you go away." In this way, it shows how your changed feelings *affect your partner*, and they care about that! For example:
  - "When you wake me up and ignore my requests, in my mind, I imagine that me and my needs are unimportant to you. Then I feel not only angry but also disconnected from you. My loving feelings go away, and I get hopeless about our relationship." (Note that the speaker takes responsibility for the hypothesis by saying, "In my mind, I imagine that…")

- You can also add a consequence that impacts your partner. Emphasize the relationship has to work for both of you — it's transactional:
  - "When my needs are ignored, I have no desire to _____ (state a need that your partner would like filled.) Our relationship has to work for both of us. It's a two-way street, because frankly, even though I care about you and your feelings, when you don't seem to care about mine, it's difficult for me to feel _____ (considerate, loving, kindly, sexual, affectionate) toward you."

Step 5: Request the desired behavior.

- Ask for what you want. Specifically, describe the behaviors you'd like to see.
- When you complain saying, "You didn't (or worse, "never") do X," you sound like a victim, and your partner will feel criticized and tune you out or react defensively. *Don't express only what you don't want or don't like.*
- It's more powerful and effective to state exactly what you do want. Make it concrete and visual and emphasize mutuality. For example:
  - "Once we're asleep, please don't turn on the reading light. I understand if you wake up and feel that you must read to get back to sleep. So that we both can get our needs met, I'd appreciate it if you would use a flashlight or go into the other room to read or sleep."
  - "How we treat each other matters so that we're both happy. I'd appreciate it if you'd be more _____ (cooperative, helpful, thoughtful, considerate, gentle when you speak to me, etc.)."

Step 6: Describe how you will feel individually and especially about your partner and the relationship if they make the change you want.

- Describe how compliance will make you feel individually and about him or her and the relationship. This gives your partner incentive.
  - "If you do this little thing, I'll feel much closer to you and happy to spend time with you."
- Emphasize the importance of reciprocity in your relationship. Remember, to a narcissist, it's a transaction, not based on empathy and concern.
  - "I know what you want is important to you and that what I'm saying is upsetting, but we each have responsibilities in our relationship. How we talk to each other is important, too."

- Describe how loving (grateful, impressed) you'll be when your partner makes the change you want.
    - "This is important to me, and if you're willing to compromise on this, it would make me very glad. I'd feel respected and respect you more. I'd also feel like being closer to you because I'd feel cared about. And because I'd see that you took my request seriously and tried to compromise, I'd be more inclined to happily accommodate your needs and requests, too."

Step 7: Give your partner support for making the change.

- Reassure your partner that you know they can do this.
- Give examples of past changes in how they have treated you or others or examples of specific goals they have accomplished. For example:
    - "I know you can do this because I noticed that some nights you leave the bedroom and read in the living room. Sometimes, when you wake up during the night, you don't read at all, but you fall back to sleep."

Step 8: Provide positive feedback for compliance.

- If your partner complies, let him or her know you appreciate it. Communicate the positive consequences that you promised.
- Say and demonstrate that you feel closer and want to meet their needs, too. For example:
    - "Thanks for sleeping on the couch. It meant a lot to me that you considered my needs. Would you like me to make you breakfast?"
    - "I appreciate your telling me what happened at work today. It helps me to understand the pressure you're under and feel closer to you."
- If your partner dismisses you and/or doesn't comply, prepare a script about being dismissed and ignored. Repeat your request at another time. If repeated requests fail, you may have to initiate consequences, discussed below.

The above script may seem long and tedious. It's designed to communicate exactly what you want and don't want and to provide incentives for making change. You're being careful not to put your partner on the defensive. It's also demonstrating that their behavior has an impact on you and that it has a boomerang effect. Remember that narcissists need enlightenment about the impact of their behavior because they lack empathy. They learned that they were either bad or wonderful without getting specific feedback about their actions. When they learn that pleasing you benefits them in the long run, they're more likely to try to do so, but you must spell out the steps. It doesn't come naturally. (This technique is also very effective in shaping children's behavior.)

Practice your script aloud a few times, and choose a time to speak to your partner when they're relaxed or receptive to you. In all likelihood, you relish those moments and don't want to make waves, but be aware that a storm is coming, and now is the time to prepare for it. Here are some examples of openers:

- "I understand that _____is very important to you."
- "I love and care about you."
- "I'm sorry that I_____; however..." Only apologize for things you take responsibility for, such as blaming, breaking an agreement, or forgetting something.
- "I see the problem this created for you."
- "I know that you have other things on your mind."
- "I know that you're under a lot of stress right now."

SET BOUNDARIES

Once you've mastered being assertive, you're ready to attempt the more difficult task of setting boundaries. Boundaries are rules that govern the way you want to be treated. People will treat you the way you allow them to. You must know what your boundaries are before you can communicate them. This means getting in touch with your feelings, listening to your body, knowing your rights, and learning assertiveness. The boundaries must be explicit. Don't hint or expect people to read your mind. If you've followed these suggestions and found that they're not working, you probably haven't invoked consequences.

Boundaries are especially important in close relationships, where inevitable conflicts of needs arise. Love cannot exist without boundaries, even between parents and children. Relationships with narcissists and abusers have weak boundaries. An abuser violates your boundaries because you don't enforce them.

Boundaries aren't meant to punish but are imperative for your well-being and protection. If you feel resentful, used, disrespected, unappreciated, exploited, or burned out you probably haven't been setting boundaries and need to act. If certain behavior hurts you or causes mistrust or anger, let your partner know. This is being responsible to you and your relationship.

When you set a boundary passively by withdrawing communication or affection, you contribute to relationship dissatisfaction. It doesn't solve the problem, and you're missing an opportunity to effect change. When boundaries are violated repeatedly, trust and goodwill are undermined and the relationship suffers. You feel unloved or exploited. By not saying anything while harboring negative feelings, you're being dishonest and risk erecting emotional walls that destroy love.

To help you understand and identify your boundaries, read my blog, "The Power of Personal Boundaries."[86]

Give Yourself Permission to Set Boundaries

Codependents typically feel guilty setting boundaries and resentful when they don't. Telling someone "no," especially in close relationships, brings up anxiety. If this is true for you, your boundaries were likely violated within your family growing up. The fundamental belief you learned is that others' needs and wants are more important than your own. You may not believe that you have a right to say "stop" or "no" to what your partner or other people do or ask of you. If you (incorrectly) believe that people will like and even love you if you're always agreeable, you almost certainly don't feel likable or lovable for who you are. It indicates that you need validation from others to feel worthy.

Even if you *feel* guilty setting boundaries, that doesn't mean you are guilty. Remember, even if you *can* do what's asked, that doesn't mean that you *must*. You have a right to your preferences. Your feelings and needs are of equal importance to those of anyone else.

People-pleasing helps neither you nor your relationships. Kindness and helpfulness are wonderful traits, but not when they're continually at the expense of your own needs, wants, or feelings. When you feel guilty asserting yourself, you risk becoming a doormat and exploited. Being always available to others or being the "go-to" person on the job might ensure you're needed so that you won't be abandoned or fired, but there's a price you pay and it doesn't necessarily mean *you're* valued.

On the other hand, once you get practice setting boundaries, you become empowered and feel less anxiety, resentment, and guilt. Generally, you receive more respect, and your relationship improves. You no longer feel like a victim. You build self-esteem and integrity.

> ➤ *Innercises: Claiming Your Rights*

To establish boundaries, you must know what you feel and believe you have rights. Do you believe you have a right to respect? To be heard? To feel safe? Here are a few suggestions about setting boundaries:

1. Make a list of your rights.
2. Identify which ones make up your bottom-line boundaries, those that are non-negotiable, such as a right to nonviolence.
3. What specific behaviors (including words) of your partner violate your boundaries? How does it make you feel about yourself, your partner, and your relationship?
4. What benefits will there be to you and your relationship if you set a boundary?
5. What detriments will there be to you and your relationship if you don't set a boundary?

How to Set Boundaries

When narcissists are physically or emotionally abusive, they're violating your boundaries to exercise power over you. They aren't interested in communicating. Before any discussion of the facts, you must address the matter of the boundary violation. If you ignore this principle, your partner has already won and will feel entitled to continue violating your boundaries.

There's an art to setting boundaries. If it's done in anger or with criticism or nagging ("I've told you a hundred times..."), you won't be heard. Boundaries are most effective when you're assertive, calm, firm, and courteous. Speak in a matter-of-fact tone. Don't invite questions that encourage a response and more discussion, unless you're trying to compromise on a matter. When it comes to abuse, your boundaries aren't negotiable. You can repeat what you said and state, "I have nothing more to say on this topic." Before setting boundaries, think through the effect it will have on you and your relationship if you do or if you don't set them. Then use the 8-step formula (above) for describing the behavior that you want to stop and the behavior you desire. Remember to be specific in describing the behavior you want and don't want.

Narcissists and abusers will ordinarily resist boundary setting and often become defensive when anyone says "no" or asserts a position that is contrary to what they want. When confronted, narcissists usually escalate abuse, further obfuscate the facts, or threaten to wage greater abuse or violence. But you must continue to address the abuse in the same manner. You might say, "If you continue, I'll leave the room," and do so if the abuse continues.

What You Can Say

Boundary-setting can also apply to simple encounters where all that's needed is for you to assert your position. Examples include statements, such as the following:

1. "No."
2. "I don't take responsibility for that."
3. "Thank you for your_____ (offer, request, input, suggestion), but I think not."
4. "Thank you, but that doesn't work for me."
5. "Now isn't a good time for me."
6. "I don't want to listen to (or discuss) that."
7. "I don't see it that way," or "We just disagree."
8. "That's your opinion." You can add, "I disagree," or "I don't see it that way."
9. "I'll think about it." (This may postpone setting another boundary; don't use it to replace "no.")
10. "I hear what you're saying (repeat it)," and respond to the abuser by saying, "I see," and walk away.

When someone is violating your boundaries, it may be best to curb their behavior with one of the below forceful statements. In this way, you set a boundary of how you want to be treated and take back your power. The abuser may respond with "Or what?" and you can say, "I will not continue this conversation." Other useful phrases are:

1. "Stop it."
2. "I don't like that."
3. "Please don't..."
4. "I won't talk to you if you (describe abuse, e.g., raise your voice, belittle me, etc.)." Then walk away.
5. "Don't talk to me that way."
6. "That's demeaning,"
7. "Don't call me names."
8. "Don't raise your voice at me."
9. "Don't use that tone with me."
10. "I don't respond to orders."

Here are some useful phrases to deal with put-downs, blame, or pressure:

1. "I know X (spell it out) is important to you. I need to think things over and consider the impact on both of us and our relationship."
2. "I know you're upset about ____, but don't blame me." Then walk away or, if appropriate, you can redirect the discussion toward finding a solution.
3. When criticized, you can agree to the true part: "You burned the dinner," and ignore the rest: "You're a rotten cook."

4. "I don't like it when you criticize me. Please stop." Then walk away and don't explain or argue.
5. "You're right. I'm not perfect."
6. "Why don't you take your car, and I'll meet you there."
7. If you're good at it, humor is a great solvent for intense emotions. For example, "You're very cute when you get annoyed."
8. "I'll never be the good enough wife (husband) that you hoped for."

Create Consequences

People often say that they've set a boundary, but it didn't help. (See my blog, "Ten Reasons Why Boundaries Don't Work.")[87] If your partner ignores your boundaries, it's important to communicate and invoke consequences. These aren't threats, but actions you take to protect yourself or meet your needs.

If making repeated requests doesn't work, you need to communicate consequences to encourage compliance. My mother always said, "Actions speak louder than words." This is absolutely true when dealing with a narcissist or any uncooperative person, including toddlers! You may believe what your partner says, but they only believe what you *do*. Be explicit and tie the consequences to your partner's behavior, rather than be passive-aggressive. Remember that a narcissist doesn't realize that their selfish behavior redounds to their detriment.

Thus, there's a good chance that a narcissist will ignore your verbal boundary. If it happens twice, this in itself is a new undesirable behavior to also address. Overlooking being ignored condones being ignored. Bring it out in the open with a gentle reminder. For example:

> – "I've asked you to please not leave your dirty clothes on the floor, but you ignored my request. Maybe you forgot, but in my mind, I imagine that my needs don't matter to you. (You can add that you feel angry, insignificant, disrespected, hopeless about the relationship, etc.) I don't feel like being close or listening to you any longer when you refuse to listen to me. (Again, make this specific to your feelings.) But when you consider my needs, too, I feel_____."
> (Add language about the positive impact of honoring your requests per the 8-step formula, above.)

When your partner continues to ignore your requests, it's time to initiate consequences. This will take courage on your part but remember *consequences are for your well-being and not to punish* anyone. Think about a consequence for when your partner ignores your request. It might be how you're going to feel, an action you might take, or the natural consequence of their failure to listen to you. If the consequence is an action or inaction on your part, you must be willing to follow through. Hence, don't ever make empty threats or threaten a consequence that you're not fully prepared to carry out.

Move slowly and choose a reasonable consequence that you can both comfortably carry out and stay connected to your partner unless you're willing to end the relationship. You can first address the fact that you've been ignored by stating how that affects you and your relationship, as above, and then add a consequence. For example:

> – "I've asked you several times to please not leave your dirty clothes on the floor, but you continue to ignore my requests. I'm starting to feel _____. Our relationship must work for both of us, where we both feel respected and that our needs matter. If it happens again, they'll stay where you left them."

You can start with a simple consequence. If that doesn't work, raise the stakes, such as, "I'm going to hire a maid," or "I'm no longer willing to wash your clothes." Ideally, consequences are the natural effect of the other person's behavior. For example, "Next time, you're not ready, I'll leave without you," or "If you're late to the restaurant again, I'll wait ten minutes and then order (or leave)."

It's important to hold your partner accountable, especially if this is something new for you. Keep in mind that you're not punishing tit for tat, but guiding and educating your partner about the consequences of one-sided behavior, emphasizing that cooperation is a two-way street that benefits you both.

❯ *Innercises: Setting Limits*

Here are some things to think about before setting boundaries:

- Think about times you said "yes" when you wanted to say "no." What motivated you?
- How do you feel when you'd like to set a boundary or say "no," but don't? Do you feel resentment?
- Recall if there were times you said "no" and felt guilty.
- What were your needs? What were the other person's needs?
- Write about what makes you believe your partner's wants, feelings, or needs supersede yours.
- What are you afraid will happen if you set limits or say "no" to a request?

It takes time and practice to learn to value your needs and feelings and to be able to set boundaries without feeling guilty. When someone makes uncomfortable requests or demands, try saying, "I'll think about it." This gives you the time to consider your feelings, needs, wants, and the consequences of your choices. Keep in mind that *you can't set a boundary and take care of someone else at the same time.*

EXPECT PUSHBACK AND SLIPS

Relationship satisfaction can improve when only one person begins to change. Narcissists are used to making the rules, but not respecting them. They may experience your rule-setting as criticism or loss of power. Expect continued pushback on your limits. A narcissist will likely try to manipulate you to go back to your permissive ways. Things may get worse before they get better, or they may continue to deteriorate as you start standing up for yourself. They might even have a tantrum and go on the offensive. Don't relent. This isn't failure. It demonstrates your strategy is working! It shows how scared and powerless the narcissist feels. Pushbacks are another reason support is essential. You will need courage and consistency.

Compare setting boundaries and consequences to training a dog or young child. It may take many repetitions of taking a position with negative consequences applied before the unwanted behavior fades away and new habits emerge. If a toddler begs for candy at a store, and his mother says "no," he might throw a tantrum. After a few shopping trips like this, she might institute a consequence. After a while, the child will be taught that his tantrums don't manipulate his mother, and he'll stop asking for candy. But if she relents, he'll surely resume crying and begging for candy if he's learned that tears change her mind.

When your partner reacts emotionally, it may tempt you to do so as well. But if you do, you lose. Remain calm and assertive. If you cave under continual pressure, threats, or other tactics, your partner is back in control. They have learned that you will bend, and so they feel empowered to ignore your interests. You must be steadfast. When you're certain about your boundary, others will listen.

When threats are used to intimidate you, they're abusive. One way to deal with threats after you've stated a consequence is to hand back the choice to the abuser, such as saying, "It's up to you" and then walking away. Threats of physical violence, however, should be taken very seriously and shouldn't be allowed. Get outside help immediately, including legal advice, if you've been harmed.

Remember you're educating an immature adult. Good parenting includes rewarding good behavior. Just as in the above example of the boy, the mother might reward her son with loving words for his good behavior, saying, "I enjoy taking you places when you behave and don't cry." It's the same with your partner. So, it's necessary to reinforce compliance and any signs of effort. For example:

– "I know you've tried to be more _____ (helpful, caring, respectful).
I've noticed and appreciate your changes."

Expect you and your partner to slip up from time to time because changing behavior is even harder for a narcissist than it is for you! If you see that your partner is trying, you might joke about a slip and praise their effort. Forgive yourself, too. Remind yourself that you'll certainly have another opportunity to respond differently.

COUPLES PSYCHOTHERAPY

Only a small minority (2-16%) of narcissists seek individual therapy[88] because the vast majority sees the cause of their problems as external due to their defenses and limited ability to be introspective. They also don't want to be exposed or criticized. Eventually, however, you might insist on couples counseling when asking for what you want. Some narcissists want to become better parents. Hence, parent counseling can be a backdoor to marital counseling. The changes you've instituted can make participation more likely. Additionally, the assertiveness and courage you've gained will make the therapy more effective.

Suggested goals of couples therapy are that you both attain more realistic and empathic perceptions of one another and learn to tolerate each other's failure to meet each other's needs. Your partner can learn that defensive tactics erode good feelings and damage the relationship. Counseling can facilitate improved communication and cooperation when both partners want to stay and work together in therapy.

The therapist can ask each of you to talk about how you protect yourselves when you're hurt, what you need and want from each other, and the effects of your current behavior. This can open a dialogue about feelings, wishes, needs, your communication, and how they impact one another.

It's important that you feel safe and supported by the therapist and that your partner isn't allowed to abuse you there. You also must speak up about your reactions in the session both to your partner and to the therapist. Use some of the phrasing exemplified in the 8-step formula, above. That way the therapist will see how your partner responds. Your partner will likely attempt to persuade the therapist of their innocence and make you the perpetrator. This is an opportunity for you to point out that your partner is demonstrating how they practice DARVO (see chapter 3 —Manipulation: DARVO), denigrates you, and how, if true, your partner incites other people to side against you.

Continue to practice assertiveness in sessions. Calmly discuss how your partner's behavior affects you and request change using the scripts you developed using the 8-step formula.

When your partner becomes defensive, the therapist should interrupt the conversation, stating something like, "Something just happened that hurts both of you and is triggering strong reactions." They can mirror the underlying hurt, emotions, and needs and guide each of you to express yourselves in a nonthreatening way. Then, you can connect with your past pain, which provides space between you both for mutual understanding. It allows projections to be withdrawn and not taken personally by the recipient. The relationship can be strengthened, abuse can diminish, and the past be forgiven. However, don't expect that someone diagnosed with NPD will turn into an empathetic, attentive partner.

Although tempting, it's unwise to seek couples counseling from your personal therapist, who may be biased toward you. More importantly, your partner will perceive your therapist as biased regardless of whether that's the case and use that as a justification for being uncooperative or abandoning treatment. If they do abandon treatment, this isn't a reason for you to discontinue individual therapy.

Finally, don't try to be a therapist to a narcissist. This is not only dangerous and impossible, but it can backfire and damage you and your self-esteem. If your partner refuses to attend counseling, individual therapy can still have a positive effect on you and the interpersonal relationship dynamics.

POINTS TO REMEMBER

Change is a process. Be patient with yourself. It may take at least six months or more of concerted effort to detach, become less reactive, and identify your feelings, needs, and wants. This lays the foundation for assertiveness, which requires practice. By trial and error, you'll refine your communication and gain the courage to set boundaries. Equally important is building your autonomy through other activities and goals.

Without support, you may languish in self-doubt and succumb to abuse and denigration. It's challenging to change your reactions, let alone those of anyone else. A twelve-step program and assertiveness class can be extremely helpful and speed things up, as can a therapist to encourage and help you apply the principles and techniques suggested in this book (see chapter 8 – Your Support System).

Your partner will notice your transformation, and the dynamics of your relationship will necessarily change. Eventually, they will get the message that manipulation and abuse aren't effective, and initial resistance to preserve the status quo can give way to reform. But you must stay firm during this phase by consistently maintaining your boundaries and repeating the same message. Once that comes more naturally to you, give your relationship at least six months to readjust to the new rules.

Remember these guidelines:

1. Boundaries aren't meant to punish but rather to protect and help you.
2. Avoid becoming angry or judgmental. No matter what, refuse to fight.
3. Be calm and compassionate, remembering that a narcissist is afraid and vulnerable.
4. Your attitude must be educative, not punitive.
5. You're establishing new ground rules for reciprocity in your relationship.
6. Go slow, escalating consequences, but only those you're ready to carry out.
7. Consequences are actions that you will take.
8. Expect pushback. This is natural, so don't give up or become discouraged.
9. Outside support will give you courage, and get help if there is physical, emotional, or verbal abuse.
10. Give positive reinforcement for the behavior you want, and provide positive feedback in words and actions for compliance.

Chapter 10

LEAVING A NARCISSIST

L eaving an abusive relationship, especially one with a narcissist, is harder than you'd imagine. Reason doesn't make it any easier to leave! Even when the relationship turns out to be toxic, once attached, ending the relationship is just as hard as falling in love was easy!

When you fall in love, becoming attached and forming a romantic bond is natural. But once in love, it's not easy to leave, even despite the abuse from a narcissist. Family and friends who see that you are in pain might urge you to "just leave." Those words can feel shameful, especially because you also think you should. On the other hand, some people who never witnessed the abuse or who are also under the spell of the narcissist will encourage you to stay. They're more dangerous because they side with the narcissist and challenge your wiser instincts as you come to grips with reality and develop the courage to leave.

You may want to leave, but feel stuck and don't understand why. This is because, unlike in other relationships, deeper reasons keep you bonded. If, however, you have come out of denial, detached, stopped reacting to your partner, and recovered your self-esteem and autonomy, you will have changed the dynamics of the relationship. When narcissists can no longer control or manipulate their partners, they feel abandoned. They don't feel safe without their usual source of narcissistic supply from your codependency, in which case, they may do the leaving for you. It's as if you've thrown water on the Wicked Witch of the East in *The Wizard of Oz*, and she dissolves into a puddle.

MAKING THE DECISION

Although you're unhappy, you may be ambivalent about leaving because you still love your partner, have young children, lack resources, and/or enjoy lifestyle benefits. If you haven't tired of it, your partner can still be charming, interesting, and enlivening to be around. Of course, you planned on being with your partner forever and became attached. This bond isn't easily broken. Even more to your disadvantage, narcissists turn on the charm if you threaten to leave; but just remember, it's another temporary ploy to reassert control. If you're unsure whether you want to leave, practice speaking up and self-care, and develop support and activities in your life beyond the relationship.

Why Leaving Is Hard

There are multiple reasons why victims of abuse stay in toxic relationships. Do you relate to any of the following reasons?

- Fear of retribution and threats made by your partner
- Financial insecurity
- Nowhere to live
- No outside emotional support
- Childcare problems and fear of losing custody
- You're swayed by your partner's charm, promises to change, and attempts to win you back
- You take the blame for problems and feel guilty
- You deny, minimize, and rationalize the abuse
- Your self-esteem and confidence have been lowered
- You still love your partner
- You feel shame for staying and/or guilt for leaving and worry about what others will think
- You're afraid of losing friends and relatives who will side with your partner

If you're being physically abused, it's imperative to protect yourself and your children and seek counseling immediately. Without intervention, abusers don't keep their promises to stop.

There are deep psychological reasons why you stay, including codependency, shame, isolation, trauma bonds, and learned helplessness.

Codependency

Codependents don't have easy emotional lives. They look for security and love and struggle to get into or out of relationships. They may remain in unhappy or abusive relationships and keep trying to make them work. Codependents have difficulty letting go. They're often indecisive, ambivalent, fearful, and loyal to a fault. Breakups affect their self-esteem more than they do for people who are secure and confident. This is because breakups trigger hidden grief and cause irrational guilt, anger, shame, and fear.

Codependency may have helped you cope and evade responsibility for your life and happiness by focusing on your relationship. The excitement and lifestyle of a narcissist can do just that for a while. But this strategy leads not only to relationship problems but also masks personal emptiness and loneliness. You may want to leave but feel stuck. Filling those voids with self-love and building your self-esteem and autonomy will help you leave and thrive once you do. See chapters 5 and 11 – Codependency.

Shame and Isolation

Victims of abuse feel shame and become isolated. You've been humiliated by your partner and your self-esteem has been undermined. Abuse, betrayal, and gaslighting have damaged your confidence and autonomy. Your trust in yourself, reality, and your perceptions, and your openness to love again have suffered. Abuse and intimidation over time have made you more dependent and fearful. You may have hidden the abuse from people close to you to protect the reputation of your partner and because of your shame about the truth. As discussed in chapter 3, your partner may have also isolated you from friends, family, and professional support by criticizing them. Leaving feels like a Herculean task.

Additionally, you probably have the belief that no one else would want you. You must realize the fallacy of your beliefs and remarks such as: "You'll never find anyone as good as me"; "The grass isn't greener"; "At your age, you'll never meet anyone else if you leave;" or "No one else would put up with you."

Trauma Bonds

You may have become trauma-bonded as described in chapter 7. Trauma bonding was coined by Patrick Carnes, Ph.D., to describe an attachment occurring in the presence of danger, shame, or exploitation in order to survive. Before recovery, it operates beneath your conscious control. So don't judge yourself.

Consideration from your partner may now be rare, especially if the relationship has become abusive. You're hopeful and accommodating and keep trying to win back crumbs of loving attention. Meanwhile, your self-esteem and independence are undermined daily with emotional abuse. When you object, you're attacked, intimidated, or confused by manipulation. You may have been gaslighted and have begun to doubt your perceptions due to blame and lies.

Over time, you attempt to avoid conflict and become more deferential. As denial and cognitive dissonance between reality and your beliefs and perceptions grow, you do and allow things you wouldn't have imagined when you first met. Your shame increases as your self-esteem declines. You wonder what happened to the happy, self-respecting, confident person you once were. This behavior is common for victims of abuse who become attached to their abuser as described in chapter 7. This worsening trend parallels the chronic progression of codependency and makes it harder to leave.

You're especially susceptible to this if the relationship dynamics are repeating a pattern you experienced with a distant, abusive, absent, or withholding parent. The trauma bond with your partner outweighs the negative aspects of the relationship. You not only fear retaliation but also the loss of the emotional connection with your partner, which can feel worse than the abuse.

Learned Helplessness

You can feel hopeless and helpless when you experience chronic abuse or repeated obstacles and develop *learned helplessness,* a term coined by psychology professor Martin Seligman in the 1960s. It describes a mindset where you don't try to get out of a negative situation because in the past you learned that you were helpless. In Seligman's experiment, he rang a bell and then gave a dog a light shock to condition it to expect a shock after hearing the bell. He discovered that after a while when hearing the bell, the dogs reacted fearfully as though they'd been shocked, although they hadn't been.

Human behavior is similar. For example, if you were lied to or betrayed, you become distrustful. You might imagine you're being deceived when you're not. Then you might react to your thoughts, become angry, and falsely accuse your partner. You may be confused as to whether you're reacting to your past trauma or reality. Sometimes, both can be true!

Seligman went further and put these dogs in a divided crate so that the shock would affect only one side. The dogs could easily step over a low fence to the other side and avoid the shocks. However, the dogs did not! Instead, they gave up and lay down. Then he shocked different dogs who hadn't previously been conditioned with the bell and shock. These dogs quickly jumped to the other side of the fence to avoid the shock. This proved that the conditioned set of dogs had learned helplessness. Similarly, young elephants are trained by chaining them to a post. As adults, when the chains are removed, they don't run.

We attribute causation to internal and external factors. How you interpret events matters. If you consistently make global internal attributions to negative events, meaning that you blame yourself regardless of the situation, you can develop learned helplessness.[89] When you believe you're always the problem, you lack the motivation to improve, to try again, or to try new things. This negative self-talk reflects internalized shame and also perpetuates it. Narcissists blame their behavior on you and other people. When you've been blamed over and over, you absorb those interpretations of reality and begin to doubt and blame yourself.

The undermining of your self-esteem, trauma-bonding, and relentless abuse create learned helplessness. Over time, you accommodate the abuser to feel safe. When at first you might have become angry and protested, eventually you realize that this tactic is usually counterproductive. You may have numbed your feelings, become anxious and/or depressed, and developed physical symptoms. As fear and shame grow, you don't believe you have any options or that you can leave. You may believe that leaving would be futile and no one would want you. Indeed, you may have been told as much. Hopelessness and powerlessness can lead to resignation. When leaving doesn't seem a viable option, it's essential to get outside support and counseling.

‣ Innercises: Making The Decision

After a reasonable amount of time has passed and you're satisfied with your efforts in changing your attitude and behavior in your relationship, go back and review the checklists in chapters 3 and 4 to evaluate the changes you've made. To evaluate whether your relationship is salvageable, look at the facts. Try to decide based on your experience, rather than based on hope, fear, or guilt. Give yourself credit for your hard work, which has strengthened you as an individual. Regardless of your decision, it's important to redeem your autonomy and self-esteem for your mental health.

Then consider whether or not your partner has made progress in the following areas:

1. Acknowledges responsibility for their behavior, including dishonesty
2. Willingness to participate in individual or couples therapy
3. Listens and is more respectful
4. Reciprocates more in your relationship
5. Cares about the impact of their behavior on you and others
6. Continues to be dishonest and won't admit it
7. Violates the law or ethical standards without remorse
8. Continues to be emotionally abusive without remorse
9. Continues to be grossly irresponsible

It isn't necessarily bad if your partner has made little or no change because you can now clearly see whom you're dealing with and can let go of any false hope of getting what you want from the relationship. You may, however, still decide that there are aspects of your partner you enjoy and that there are adequate benefits to staying. Alternatively, you may conclude that you'd rather be on your own. Regardless of whether you stay or leave, your efforts aren't without reward. By working on yourself, you grow stronger and will enjoy greater autonomy and self-worth.

You may have tried to get your partner into therapy, you may have threatened to leave, or even done so in the past but never finally broke off the relationship. You may vacillate between whether the blame lies with you or your partner and how much satisfaction you can squeeze out of the relationship. The most important factor is emotional unbonding — when you no longer engage in the old patterns and change the dynamics of your relationship. Once the relationship dynamics are altered from following the suggestions in this book, even if you don't leave, the relationship is forever changed. (See my article, "The Stages of Divorce,"[90] describing the five stages of divorce; and emotional unbonding is the most important and most difficult.)

HOW TO LEAVE

Deciding to leave usually follows a long period of frustration and unhappiness. Your intention may not be expressed or even consciously acknowledged, but usually long precedes your final decision. Generally, people set goals before they're emotionally and physically ready to carry out major decisions, such as changing jobs or moving. Your intent sets the keel in a direction for events to follow.

Before planning an exit, strengthen yourself and prepare for your future. As discussed in chapter 8, develop autonomy, assertiveness, self-esteem, self-trust, self-love, and a support system. Whether you stay or leave, you need a fulfilling life to supplement or replace your relationship. Don't make empty threats. When you decide to leave, be certain you're ready to end the relationship and not be lured back.

Gray Rock Strategy

One strategy for dealing with a narcissist is to act like a "gray rock," meaning that you become dull and unresponsive and blend into the background like a gray rock. Your objective is to make your partner lose interest in you. You don't feed their need for drama and attention. This withholds narcissistic supply from your partner and eliminates any distraction that you otherwise might serve from their emptiness. You don't show emotion, say anything interesting, or disclose any personal information. Nor do you ask questions or participate in conversations, except for brief factual replies. Limit your answers to a few syllables or a nod. Say "maybe," or "I don't know."

Additionally, make yourself plain and unattractive, so your partner gains no pleasure in showing you off or being seen with you. You become so boring that your partner has no interest in you and will look elsewhere to get their needs met. Even if you're accused, you might agree or say nothing. Your nonresistance makes it hard for them to project onto you.

Although she did not use the "gray rock" strategy, a client I'll call Monica achieved similar results by repeatedly explaining that after feeling criticized and unsafe for so long, she had changed. By unbonding, her feelings had gone and she was unable to accommodate her husband's demands. Monica didn't withhold communication but expressed her sadness about their marital state. By not reacting yet refusing to give the narcissist the attention he craved, he reluctantly gave up. They both looked forward to finding new partners and had an amicable separation.

When To Be a Gray Rock

The gray rock strategy is most effective before ending a relationship and afterward when you want no contact. If you try gray rock but want to stay married, be prepared for your partner to get needs met outside the marriage. Consider how you will feel if your spouse openly takes a lover. Not reacting to adultery permits your spouse to "have his (or her) cake and eat it too." On the other hand, if you're ready to break up and escape your partner's attention, they will tire of your lack of response and leave you alone.

The Risks of Going Gray Rock

Going gray rock isn't without risks. If you want more attention and love from your partner, this tactic may achieve that in the short term, but will eventually cause the opposite. Moreover, narcissists will up the ante to elicit a response from you to regain control and reassure themselves that you have feelings for them. It's essential that you practice detachment and not respond to seduction, anger, putdowns, outrageous accusations, slander, or jealous provocations. Like childish having a tantrum, once you give in and react, they believe they have the upper hand. But if you're persistent, eventually they tire of not getting a reaction.

If you're with a violent partner, you may be in harm's way regardless of whether you react, because violent abusers don't need an excuse to take out their rage on you. They may easily manufacture unfounded justifications. In fact, some abusers may interpret your non-reaction as abandonment and escalate the abuse. It's better to confront abusive behavior, set boundaries, and take steps to protect yourself.

Unless you unequivocally want to leave or are already living apart, there is a hidden danger that few mention. I've witnessed it with clients who have lived with narcissists for years. You risk losing connection to your feelings, wants, and needs. By not expressing yourself and suppressing your thoughts and feelings, you become alienated from your real self. This can be traumatic. Beware that you don't become depressed and withdraw in other relationships, too.

Being a gray rock requires you to suppress your natural needs for love, attention, companionship, empathy, sex, and affection. As you become more invisible, your behavior feeds codependency. Rather than becoming more assertive as Monica did, you may be replaying the dynamics from your childhood. It may be a re-traumatization of how you felt growing up if your needs and feelings were ignored. This tactic is based upon self-denial and self-sacrifice. It isn't a good strategy to feel safe and get your needs met.

Splitting up and going no contact is a far better option. If you're unable to do that for emotional reasons, examine your vulnerability to being drawn back in. Are you still hoping for love and commitment? If so, deep yearnings will sabotage your gray rock performance. It's far better to set effective boundaries on bad behavior and learn strategies to get your needs met, as described in this book.

Prepare and Plan Ahead

Often threats of abuse or violence occur when it appears to the narcissist that you're planning to leave. It can be helpful if your partner initiates the idea of leaving in order to protect their fragile ego. If you're physically threatened or harmed, immediately seek shelter. Physical abuse repeats itself. If you're afraid for your safety, follow these suggestions.

1. Find local shelters. Arrange for a safe place to go: the home of a friend or relative, a local shelter, etc.
2. Alert neighbors to call the police if they suspect violence.
3. Remove weapons from your home.
4. Pack a bag to leave in a rush with important legal and financial papers, your passport, money, phonebook, credit cards, plus bags for your children.
5. Make an extra pair of house and car keys. Hide a car key outside in case your partner takes yours.

You're wise to be seeking information. It's crucial to prepare yourself for the battle and emotional rollercoaster of leaving. Planning is important in leaving any long-term relationship, but more so with a narcissist who will not gently fade from your life. You will be hurt and disappointed if you assume everything will be settled without anger or that you can count on your ex's friendship. Ask yourself whether your partner considered your needs in the past. It's better to expect conflict and manipulation, but try not to react to it. Think of the tremendous force required to split the atom. Often it takes anger or the firm resolve of at least one spouse to break up an enmeshed marriage. Anger, jealousy, guilt, fear, and hurt can interfere with your judgment and escalate the conflict.

There are exceptions. If you consistently practice assertive communication and build your support system and self-esteem, eventually a narcissist realizes that they cannot get their needs met by you and may look forward to dating and moving on. To detach with equanimity, you must truly undergo an internal shift so that you no longer desire to try to get love, approval, and attention from an abusive partner, as Monica did. Once unbonded from the toxic emotional dynamics in the relationship, you won't react in the same old ways. This "emotional divorce" is the most difficult stage, but you can do the majority of the work while still together. If your partner is a concerned parent, parenting counseling can enhance cooperation in co-parenting during and after a divorce.

If you're planning to divorce, obtain legal advice as soon as you can. Although mediation can be an effective alternative to divorce proceedings; a mediator, however, is neutral and will not protect your interests. Moreover, mediation isn't advisable if your spouse intimidates you and/or if there is a history of abuse or current addiction. If you do mediate, review what you discuss in mediation with your attorney.

WHAT TO EXPECT

Narcissists and abusers are basically codependent. If you distance yourself from them, they do what it takes to pull you back in because they don't want to be abandoned. Narcissists want to keep you interested to feed their ego and fulfill their needs. Being left is a major humiliation and blow to their fragile self. How could anyone leave them!?! As you become more confident and autonomous, the power dynamics in the relationship reverse. You become stronger and the narcissist appears more codependent.

Narcissists react differently as their independent and grandiose self-image crumbles. They will distort reality and use defenses, such as blame, denial, and projection to avoid any responsibility. They may attack with rage or direct it toward themselves, withdraw, and behave self-destructively. Others act needy and dependent or paranoid. The main goal is to stop you with kindness and/or charm, blame and guilt trips, threats and punishment, or neediness, promises, and pleas – whatever it takes to control you so that they "win" and restore their wounded illusion of grandiosity.

You might feel guilt, pity, or tell yourself that your ex really loves you and that you're special to him or her. Who wouldn't want to think that? You're vulnerable to forgetting all the pain you had and why you left. If you resist their attention, it fuels their ambition. But once you fall into their trap and they feel in control, they'll return to their cold and abusive ways. When you feel weakened and isolated, it's then that a narcissist may alternate between threats of revenge and expressions of affection and promises of reform to convince you to stay. Only consistent, firm boundaries will protect you and disincentivize them.

Hoovering

Breakups with narcissists don't always end the relationship. If you succeed in leaving, although some narcissists move on, many won't let you go, even when they're the ones who left the relationship or even if they're with a new partner. Just when you think you've moved on, you're reeled back in. They don't want to be forgotten and keep you waiting and hoping. They may intentionally space out when they contact you. Whenever they're lonely or bored, your attention feeds their narcissistic supply when they need a fix.

This behavior is called hoovering after the famous Hoover vacuum because when you're finally free of the abusive relationship, they suck you back in. They hoover and try to stay friends after a breakup or divorce or rekindle the relationship. They'll pull out all the stops to lure you back.

Motivation for Hoovering

Narcissists who attempt to win you back are trying to regain their self-esteem and power. They're not necessarily motivated by love. Just knowing you think about them or will talk to them soothes their injured ego. If you go back, as soon as they feel secure, they put you down or break up to reverse the narrative.

They might continue their games to exert their power and control you. They're not concerned with your feelings at all and have disdain for weakness and dependency, refusing to acknowledge their own. In their mind, you're their property and have no right to leave. If you do, it mortifies their sense of grandiosity, entitlement, and superiority. They hoover to stay in your life, keep the relationship going, and/or seduce and convince you to come back. In this way, hoovering compensates for their hidden insecurities.

A study showed that some narcissists and psychopaths tend to stay friends with their exes for selfish reasons.[91] Especially after a short relationship, narcissists may not be interested in the relationship for sentimental reasons. They're out for themselves, looking for access to resources, such as sex, money, information, status, or love. Their impetus is pragmatic. They're dependent on their narcissistic supply. Their weak ego needs constant reassurance and attention to avoid feeling their inner emptiness.

They may not want to be with you, but they don't want you to let go or be with anyone else either. They want to dominate you and feel solely entitled to your affection. They may keep in touch merely to distract you from falling for someone else, or in some cases, to punish you for leaving. The fact that you respond can give them enough satisfaction and fuel their fantasy that they still control you. Even if you show anger or hatred, it shows that you're hurt and still attached. Malignant narcissists take pleasure in causing you pain — the pain they feel inside. Vindictiveness soothes their pain of abandonment, shame, and humiliation.

Signs of Hoovering

It starts with unobtrusive behavior, such as liking your social media posts. Your ex may send veiled messages via social media posts or try to make you jealous with photos of fun times with someone else. They may send you a friendly text or email a joke, song, or link directly, followed by phone calls.

Hoovering narcissists aim to engage you in conversation and to meet up. If you refuse, they arrange "fortuitous" encounters in your neighborhood or usual haunts where you shop, worship, work out, or play a sport. They might get your friends and relatives to lobby on their behalf. The less you respond, the more they up the ante. They may start love-bombing all over again with gifts, seduction, expressions of love, guilt, contrition, and false promises about the future.

Being expert manipulators, narcissists know your vulnerabilities. They appeal to your emotions. Be alert when they express guilt and love, ask for help, want assistance from your expertise, make romantic gestures, or send messages, cards, or gifts on significant dates or anniversaries. They attempt to seduce you with financial support, feigned compassion, pleading, jealousy, sex, loving words, or promises to reform.

If you still love or have affection for your ex and are hopeful that the relationship could improve, you're vulnerable to being sucked back in. You now hear everything you've always wanted, perhaps including willingness to attend or return to therapy with you. You're made to feel loved, valued, heard, and wanted. These tactics are hard to resist, especially on the first go-round. Even victims of violence return frequently, only to be abused again.

But don't be fooled. Be prepared for a bait-and-switch maneuver. When hoovering doesn't work, narcissists reveal who they are with threats, guilt, and shame to wear you down. Alternatively, once narcissists realize that they've won, that they've recaptured you, their positive behavior diminishes, and the cycle of abuse starts over until you walk away or get discarded.

Coping with Hoovering

Hoovering can be very damaging. Narcissists lie and distort reality to confuse you for their own ends, perpetuating the abuse that you've endured. Because of the prior relationship dynamic, they may easily succeed with positive or negative manipulation. You may succumb because you've been made to feel so unworthy and lucky to have your ex back in your life. Employ these strategies to protect yourself:

1. When they contact you, remember the abuse, your unhappiness, and that they're incapable of giving you what you need.
2. The best way to deal with hoovering is to ignore it. No contact both protects you and helps you recover from a breakup. That includes not looking at photos or social media accounts of your ex. A narcissist may escalate hoovering, and then lose interest after a while, only to reappear a year or more later when they're in need. Don't give in to sweet talk that they miss you.
3. If you must communicate — for example, you have business matters or children in common — practice the gray rock strategy. This removes any incentive for a narcissist to pursue you romantically. Preferably, communicate only in writing. Stay on point, be brief and impersonal, and don't laugh or smile at their jokes or attempts to flirt and cajole you.
4. Beware of idealizing your ex or romanticizing the relationship. Arm your psyche against falling for fake expressions of love, seduction, or lies about you and the relationship. Remember your unhappiness and any abuse you suffered.
5. It's important to tease out the truth from lies so that you learn to trust yourself again and not question your perceptions. Resist any attempt to distort the past. Write a story about what happened and why you were unhappy.
6. Get professional help to restore your self-trust and heal PTSD and wounds from the relationship and those triggered from your childhood.
7. Write your feelings about the narcissist's behavior and associate them with family members and memories from your past. If you can make a connection, then when you miss your ex, shift your mind to feelings from your childhood.
8. Remember that narcissism is a personality disorder. A narcissist will not change for you and certainly not without years of focused therapy. Put yourself first and focus on your healing.

Character Assassination

Narcissists cannot tolerate rejection, especially when you were the one who left the relationship. They find it humiliating. When narcissists are unable to change your mind on their own, more aggressive and malignant narcissists may initiate a smear campaign. This bolsters their fantasy that they're flawless and faultless to protect themselves from experiencing their underlying shame and insecurity. Rather than accept that you "quit," they go on the offense and "fire" you. Their crusade is designed to punish you, get what they want, and make you doubt yourself and your perceptions.

Narcissists do this behind your back so that you cannot challenge their lies and denial. They spread gossip, lies, and assassinate your character to turn family and friends against you and elevate themselves in others' eyes. Their emails malign you to make them appear to be innocent victims of your so-called bad behavior. They even convince themselves of their fabricated truth and eventually, they get other people to believe their version of reality. Character assassination is excruciating because you feel powerless against false incriminations.

Flying Monkeys

In the process of denigrating you, many narcissists rally friends and relatives to act on their behalf as allies, known as "flying monkeys," named after the winged monkeys spellbound by the Wicked Witch of the East. You may have already experienced this tactic of triangulation if your partner has sought an ally of a relative or child in a campaign against you or to get their way.

Generally, flying monkeys unwittingly succumb to the narcissist's manipulation, often trying to be helpful to rescue the narcissist and the relationship. Others may have their own biases and agenda and so readily take sides against you. When confronted, narcissists deny these tactics and play the innocent victim to you and everyone else, all the time blaming the real victim: YOU.

They employ their minions to spread their lies and gossip and/or spy on you personally or on social media. The monkeys assist in hoovering by letting your partner know your plans and arranging events or "accidental" run-ins so you'll see each other. Their scheme is effective because you stand to lose not only your relationship with your partner and your reputation but also other relationships. Years of abuse and lowered self-esteem have made you accustomed to doubting yourself and taking the blame. Their tactics are designed to further undermine your reality-testing, courage, self-esteem, and support system.

There are several strategies for dealing with flying monkeys:

1. Ignore what they say. Be calm and impersonal. Maintain firm internal boundaries by not reacting.
2. Remind yourself of the truth and that they're speaking for the narcissist based on their lies.
3. Don't judge them. Remember that they were deceived as you once were. Reflect silently on the truth: the speaker has been manipulated, and this is another abuse strategy.
4. Be careful about whom you allow access to your social media. Put up privacy guards so only those whom you trust can view, share, or comment on your page or profile.
5. Take the high road. Be polite and calmly act surprised by these astonishing stories that have no resemblance to your experience. Send best wishes to your ex appearing to have no ill feelings. Your kindness will confuse the messenger, who may then wonder about the truth of the message.
6. Keep asking questions about the information and arguments they make until they reveal exactly what was said to them. Question how they know it is true. What evidence do they have? This will make them self-reflect on the veracity of what they've heard. Ask how they can be so convinced when they have never asked or heard your side of the story. It may be wise to end the conversation there, rather than tell your side, which either they or the narcissist will refute. You also risk showing your anger once you recount what's happened and your emotions may feed into their version of events.
7. Try to educate them. If the person is close to you and you're okay with revealing facts about your relationship and the abuse you've suffered, explain to them the narcissist's abusive tactics. If they lack empathy for you or refuse to listen, you know they're not a friend.
8. Express how disappointed you are that they've not asked to hear how you're feeling and what you need, but have only spoken to your ex. Let them know you need their support. Ask them not to speak to your ex if your relationship with the person is stronger than your ex's.
9. Don't react emotionally, instead set boundaries when flying monkeys blame or shame you. You can change the subject, ask that they not judge you, give unsolicited advice, or meddle in your relationship, and then agree to disagree.
10. If someone ignores your boundaries, bullies, nags, or harasses you, block them and don't communicate with them.

The Divorce Game

Some narcissists care about parenting and rather preserve their assets rather than waste money on legal costs. However, many narcissists love battles. These are the most aggressive types who need to win to avoid humiliation and shame. It's all about having power over you, just like it's been in the relationship. Stay alert for familiar abuse, such as blaming you for the failure of the marriage and the divorce, gaslighting with fabrications and denials, projection, DARVO, and attempts to charm you and the court. Don't fall into the trap of self-blame, reacting or defending yourself. Since narcissists believe rules don't apply to them, keep strong boundaries, preferably in writing.

Find a CFLS, or Certified Family Law Specialist, with trial experience. (Nine states, including California and Texas, provide specialty certification in family law.) An attorney familiar with the judges in your jurisdiction can give you an important advantage. Listen to your attorney, but also listen to yourself. If standing up for yourself is still difficult in your marriage, find a strong attorney to stand up for you. Find someone experienced with high-conflict divorces who has tried cases against disturbed individuals, such as narcissists. You can read reviews of lawyers online and contact your local bar association for referrals. Some have a low-fee referral service; however, in some cases, the court may order attorney fees to be paid by one spouse. Ask about that and pro bono services if you cannot afford an attorney. Don't rack up legal fees recounting horror stories to your attorney. Instead, ask questions about your rights and find out what information you must provide to prevail in court.

Narcissists try to game the system by spreading lies about you and playing the role of victim to win the sympathy of others and the court. They run up attorney's fees and court costs with frivolous claims, needless motions, and mounds of paperwork to delay the case and overwhelm you into submission.

Ignore false promises or seduction, such as, "You can trust me." Instead, pay attention to your partner's actions and trust your experience. You know your spouse and may have witnessed belligerence, threats, and dishonesty, or your partner's hostile battles with adversaries. Don't delude yourself to believe that they will treat you any differently. Some narcissists will do anything to win, including defying court orders and lying about you and their assets in court and in documents without a scintilla of guilt.

Don't be surprised when your spouse hides or misrepresents financial information. Deceit is fueled by fear and it heightens conflict. When you must make legal decisions, stick to the facts and gather necessary evidence if you can. Don't play tit for tat with a narcissist. Disclosure is the best approach since deception or concealment is likely to backfire and breed resistance, contempt, and loss of credibility with the court when the truth comes out. Although a narcissist might do this, try not to over-control everything out of fear or anger. It's hard to accept that you won't get all you want, particularly control over your children. It's challenging but helpful to be assertive and kind.

Document everything. Eleven states, including Florida and California, make it illegal to record a call without the other party's permission. Thus, it's best to communicate through your lawyer, email, or preferably through a controlled website, such as the ones listed below. You can videotape child abuse or behavior that violates court orders. Use your documentation in court to combat your spouse's lies.

Remember that your spouse is fighting to protect a fragile ego. For example, to some narcissists, actual parenting isn't important, but demanding shared custody to save the expense of child support or to appear to be a good parent might be essential to them. Use that weakness to your advantage by reassuring your spouse that you appreciate how hard they're trying to be a great parent despite their busy schedule and that you want to help in that regard. When your ex has custody but wants to work or socialize, you can suggest that they leave the children with you (or share your babysitter). After a while, your ex may tire of this scenario and parenting responsibilities and ultimately forego visitation or physical custody.

Here are some guidelines:

1. Open a bank account and credit cards in your name if you don't have them. Start saving money for a lawyer, childcare, and new residence, if necessary.

2. Change passwords on your online accounts, email, phones, computers, and children's phones.

3. Gather information about your combined assets, how title is held to real property, all bank accounts, retirement and credit union accounts, and liquid assets, such as stocks, pensions, annuities, and bonds. Make copies of deeds and all financial instruments. Depending on the law in your state, once you're separated, income isn't usually considered joint marital property, nor are expenditures considered a joint liability. After a petition for dissolution has been filed, money taken from joint accounts or received from a unilateral sale of any marital property must be repaid by the spouse who withdrew the funds or sold the property.

4. Because of "no-fault" divorce laws, itemizing emotional abuse or infidelity is largely irrelevant and could backfire by making you look bad unless a police report has been filed about domestic violence as it relates to parenting your children or to substantiate a restraining order. If you have evidence of illegal behavior, however, such as lying to the court, the IRS, or in response to a subpoena, the court will look unfavorably upon that. Discuss this with your attorney.

5. If your spouse lies about you in settlement negotiations, don't retaliate. Instead, maintain your composure, simply deny the false allegations, and focus on the settlement plan that you want. Ask your attorney whether and how to rebut lies told to the court. Not all lies are relevant.

6. Beware of emphasizing your primary need; it will be seen as a weakness that a narcissist can exploit for control and revenge. For example, if cash is more important to you than keeping your residence, emphasize keeping the residence and then reluctantly negotiate it away for cash. The narcissist will believe they won the battle and got revenge, but you get what you want. Of course, discuss this and all legal strategies first with your lawyer.

7. Protect yourself from stress, abuse, and manipulation by not discussing the settlement alone with your ex. Ask that all settlement and custody and visitation negotiations be conducted through your attorney or with your attorney present.

8. Websites such as talkingparents.com and ourfamilywizard.com offer services for co-parenting communications that provide an online calendar, messaging, journaling, and banking and expense data that is secure and can be downloaded. These apps generate accurate, unalterable records that are accessible to courts, if so ordered. Talkingparents records calls without revealing your phone number.

9. It's preferable to communicate in writing so that you have documentary evidence. Keep a log of in-person exchanges with your spouse, including the date, time, subject, and who was present.

10. Record the time(s) you and your spouse spend with your children and which of you take responsibility for meeting their needs. In court, your spouse may brag about what a great parent they are, despite the reality that they're neglectful of parental responsibilities, miss visitations, and don't show up for school meetings and other important events in your children's lives. The data you collect can be used to discredit your spouse's court testimony and also demonstrate to the court that awarding you custody is in the best interest of your

children.

11. If your children reside with your spouse, document every time you're denied access to them and vital communications regarding school notices, events, and medical information. Act promptly to confront any attempts by your spouse to alienate your children.

12. In court, expect your spouse to lie. Don't be provoked or react. Stay cool and calm and serene, regardless of what your spouse says. Let your lawyer defend you.

13. Make a list of witnesses that can be called to court, detailing what they might know and testify about.

14. Be prepared for a lengthy and expensive divorce because narcissists typically pull out all the stops to "win." Discuss the cost with your lawyer and whether your spouse might be ordered to pay for your legal expenses.

Chapter 11

LETTING GO

L etting go and healing involve acceptance of yourself and your partner as separate individuals. Usually, relationships end because partners have individual issues with self-esteem and shame, are ill-matched, or have needs that they're unable to communicate or have met.

Breakups usually happen over time. Couples frequently reunite one or more times, especially when they haven't unbonded emotionally. You can fluctuate between attachment and separation, sometimes being compliant, then resistant. For partners of narcissists, cooperation can stir up the fear of going back. You might feel like you're giving up a part of yourself. To a narcissist, compromise means losing. For example, one couple had everything worked out: the father would pay for the children's daycare, named in the agreement. But when the facility unexpectedly went out of business, he refused to pay for an alternative daycare and instead wanted to take custody. Endless struggles for control over every last detail represent last-ditch efforts to avoid the finality of divorce and the pain of separation, loss, and abandonment. To a narcissist, it's also a humiliation. Don't be tempted to fight over insignificant items and issues.

ISSUES THAT MAKE IT HARDER TO LET GO

Often your own experiences and mindset can make breakups and letting go harder. Other factors include the length of your relationship, the degree of intimacy and commitment, the ending's predictability, and cultural and family judgments about the breakup. Some additional factors listed below may be true for you and may have contributed to the unhealthy dynamics in your relationship. Working through them can help you move on.

Codependency: For codependents, it usually takes longer to get over a breakup, sometimes years for even a short relationship. There are several reasons. It can be hard to let go if you haven't let go of the childhood hope of having the love you missed from your parents. You yearn to be cared for, loved, and accepted unconditionally by a partner in the way your parents didn't. No partner can make up for those losses and disappointments.

Parents aren't perfect, and even those with the best intentions disappoint their children. Part of becoming an independent adult is realizing and accepting this fact, not only intellectually, but also emotionally. Acceptance usually involves sadness and sometimes anger.

It's not unusual for codependents to drop their friends, interests, and hobbies, if they had any, once they're in a relationship. When you focus all of your energy on the relationship and adapt to your partner's life, a breakup can make your world crumble, especially if you're left without hobbies, goals, and a support system. This is why building autonomy as described in chapter 8 is so important.

Codependents typically seek someone to fill their inner emptiness and make them feel lovable. You can evade responsibility for your life and happiness by focusing on your relationship and your ex. The excitement and lifestyle of a narcissist can do that for a while. This strategy leads not only to relationship problems but also when you break up, you may uncover depression and feelings of loneliness and emptiness that you've been avoiding all along. Until you address your deepest pain, you may keep recycling codependency. The adage, "Happiness begins within," is apt.

Recovery from codependency helps people assume responsibility for their happiness, and although a relationship can add to your life, it won't make you happy in the long run if you can't do that for yourself. It's important to have a support network of friends and/or twelve-step meetings as well as activities that bring you pleasure, whether you're in a relationship or not.

An Insecure Attachment Style: Many codependents have an anxious attachment style, which makes you less resilient than someone with a secure attachment style who can rebound more quickly. Breakups are harder because they trigger feelings of abandonment. Anxious attachers are prone to obsess, have negative feelings, and attempt to restore the relationship.

Low Self-Esteem, Blame, and Shame: Rejection can devastate you if your self-worth is low, reinforcing beliefs such as, "I'm inadequate (not enough)," or "I didn't try hard enough." Shame fosters feelings of failure, unlovability, and irrational guilt, which can be hard to shake. Shame and low self-esteem make you absorb your partner's blame and actions as if they were true comments about you and your value. Even though you left the narcissist's abuse, you may continue to believe your partner's criticism and blame after the relationship is over. You might unreasonably blame yourself and any personal defects to explain the breakup. It's not unusual for victims of abuse to blame themselves and feel guilty for leaving and/or for not leaving sooner. You may vacillate between the two. You may judge yourself for not standing up for yourself, for accommodating your ex, or for perceived "mistakes" in the way you handled the breakup.

You might feel guilty and responsible not only for your shortcomings and behavior but also for the feelings and actions of your partner; i.e., blaming yourself for your partner's affair rather than realizing the cause was their insecurity or fear of intimacy. No one is responsible for someone else's actions. Both your and your partner's behavior reflects individual issues and are part of a bigger picture of why the relationship didn't work. If you feel guilty, take the suggested steps in my e-workbook: *Freedom from Guilt and Blame - Finding Self-Forgiveness.*[92]

Self-blame is a symptom of the problem and works against your healing and moving on. It's part of the reason you were in the relationship in the first place. Take steps to change your negative self-talk. You have lots of opportunities to honor yourself, to be assertive, and to set boundaries presently and in the future.

Anger at Your Ex: Of course, you're angry. It's best to allow your feelings and think about how you will act differently going forward. Letting anger at your ex fester keeps you connected emotionally. You might think it's helping you keep your boundaries, and you may be right. Shame and grief can cause you to blame your partner, which protects you from feeling the loss and any guilt. Feelings are neither good nor bad, but resentment, blame, shame, and guilt are unhelpful and can keep you stuck in the past. Get to the root of your feelings, express them to someone trustworthy, and uncover how you can act differently and protect yourself in the future.

Fear of Loneliness: You might fear being alone and never meeting anyone else, but remember you were in a lonely relationship in which you were abandoned emotionally all the time. Codependents fear being alone because they believe they're unworthy of love. Underlying shame can make you fear that you won't be accepted and loved. This is why you were with a narcissist. By recognizing your worth, you have a real opportunity to create supportive relationships. Building a life that you enjoy prepares you to both live single and be in a healthier relationship where you're less dependent upon someone to make you happy.

Denial about the Relationship: Recovery from a breakup or divorce is more difficult when you've been in denial about the problems in the relationship. Denial can continue even after the truth comes out. It takes time to reinterpret your experience in light of all the facts once you recognize them. It can be quite confusing due to splitting, because you may love the charmer, but hate the abuser. This is especially true if all the bad behavior was out of sight, and memories of the relationship are mostly positive.

Depression: If you've ever received a diagnosis of depression, you're more susceptible to suffering from it again. Your vulnerability increases with the number of times you've had depression. Shame causes depression, so stop any negative self-talk. Seek medical help if you're having prolonged signs of depression.

Lack of Closure: It's challenging to get a narcissist to acknowledge and discuss problems in the relationship without using the discussion as an opportunity to blame you and avoid responsibility. Some narcissists can be motivated to start individual or couples therapy, where the two of you can address the issues in your relationship. Even if the narcissist continues to blame you, at least you can air mutual complaints. You can agree that the relationship isn't working for either of you. This can smooth the path of separation and can help extinguish any lingering doubts or denial about what could have been. Generally, however, letting go includes accepting that "closure" can't come from the narcissist.

Staying in Contact: It's axiomatic that staying in contact with an ex extends the relationship and can postpone the process of grieving and letting go. Professionals agree that the quickest way to get over an ex is no contact. If you're co-parenting, maintain strict boundaries, abide by your visitation agreement, and keep contact impersonal, to a minimum, and only about the children. With that exception, if you talk, text, or see each other, you haven't really broken up. See hoovering as manipulation and continued abuse to help extinguish any false hopes you may have for a better relationship.

Staying connected with your ex on social media, playing your special song, and/or looking at pictures prolongs letting go and recovery. This might be natural in the early stages of a breakup, but after that, it can be an imaginary way to stay connected.

Prior Losses or Trauma: Psychologists know that each loss recapitulates prior losses. You may have had other losses as an adult that compound grief about the current one. A breakup or divorce frequently rekindles pain associated with past losses, such as an abortion, a death, prior breakups, immigration, or your own parents' divorce. The breakup can trigger feelings of rejection and emotional abandonment in childhood. If you were neglected, blamed, abused, betrayed, or rejected in childhood, current events can reactivate those traumas. Such past traumas may cause you to incorrectly interpret a breakup as rejection because you expect to be treated the way you were previously.

Unhealed past trauma can also keep you stuck. Working through it helps you sort out your emotions and know what you feel about the ending of the present relationship. Many times, there have been both a prior loss and lack of individuation from a parent. The threat of going through the losses associated with divorce can be overwhelming.

This was the case for a woman who was overly close with her mother following the death of her father. She hadn't finished grieving her father and hadn't separated emotionally from her mother. This made "letting go" of her marriage nearly impossible. She created disputes and obstacles to settlement to postpone the divorce, thereby avoiding grief, feelings of helplessness, emptiness, and abandonment. In such cases, anger helps to separate, yet ongoing fighting is a way of staying in contact.

PSYCHOLOGICAL DISTRESS

All change is stressful. Going through a breakup, particularly a divorce, is a major life stressor. The tension is enormous because so many important elements of one's life are in transition all at once. Facing the unknown and anticipated losses provokes anxiety. Additionally, you're dealing with real loss, momentous decisions involving property, children, living arrangements, and legal and financial matters. You're also faced with creating a new life for yourself. When you have young children, the difficulties and trauma loom even larger. You may have to deal with lying, infidelity, concealment of assets, parental alienation, and the vindictiveness and abuse mentioned in the previous chapter.

Leaving the relationship can be a huge relief and provide you the peace and safety necessary to heal, but it isn't the end of your problems. After initially rejoicing and reveling in newfound freedom, there's often grief, regret, and sometimes guilt.

Even with "no contact," the trauma of abuse isn't over. Your self-esteem has surely suffered. Breakups are harder on the spouse who is less prepared or feels "left." The blow to your self-esteem can be particularly hard if the breakup was unexpected or the relationship ended because your ex loves someone else. You may lack confidence or feel unattractive. You've lost not only the relationship and person you loved and/or shared a life with, but also trust in yourself and future relationships.

Sometimes, the abuse continues by family members, by your ex with whom you co-parent, or through your children who've been alienated, damaged, or weaponized by your ex. There are support groups for parents victimized by parental alienation, such as International Support Network of Alienated Families (ISNAF).[93]

As hard as it was to end your relationship, it may still haunt you (sometimes even after the abuser is dead). Decades later, you might learn that you have scars from post-traumatic stress disorder (PTSD) brought on by the abuse you thought you'd left behind. You might have nightmares, become risk-averse, and be hesitant to love again. It's not easy to "leave" for good. It's essential to address the damage from your relationship even if you're feeling better after leaving.

GRIEVING

Ending a relationship involves loss, and romantic rejection especially hurts. The pain of feeling lonely and missing someone serves the evolutionary purposes of survival and reproduction. A UCLA study confirmed that sensitivity to emotional pain resides in the same area of the brain as physical pain — that is, they hurt equally.[94] Your reaction to pain is influenced by genetics. If you have increased sensitivity to physical pain, you're more vulnerable to feelings of rejection. Moreover, love stimulates such strong feel-good neurochemicals that rejection can feel like withdrawal from a drug, says anthropologist Helen Fisher.[95] It can compel you to engage in obsessive thinking and compulsive behavior. This proved true even for tsetse flies in lab experiments.

A divorce, even if you want it, entails even more inevitable losses. Aside from the ending of the marriage and a future with your spouse, you may be losing your home, time with your children, and relationships with in-laws. You may no longer speak to estranged friends or relatives, even children you love or worry about. There are also unavoidable financial losses, loneliness, a change of lifestyle, imagined losses of what might have been, and of memories of what once was. It may involve a move to a different city, a change of jobs or schools, or a homemaker entering the workforce for the first time. Another loss not usually talked about is the loss of identity as a wife, a husband, and possibly as a father or mother.

You might feel so desperate that you relent and go back to avoid the withdrawal symptoms of loneliness, insecurity, depression, and emptiness. It's natural to long for your ex more when you're lonely. You may do this a few times before realizing that the relationship isn't getting better (unless your ex is serious about getting long-term treatment). To move on successfully, you must embrace and mourn each loss. Facing each fear and loss squarely can help you accept reality and move forward.

Stages of Grief

Much of the grief work can precede the physical and legal divorce and smooth the way. It can be useful to recognize stages of grief. Psychiatrist and author Elisabeth Kübler-Ross identified the following five stages, but many people also experience a sixth stage — guilt:

1. Denial
2. Anger
3. Bargaining
4. Depression
5. Acceptance
6. Guilt

Also not mentioned is fear, which is a predominant emotion in times of transition. As Kübler-Ross so famously recognized, letting go and grieving are part of a process. You might still love your ex even though you're grateful you left. Expect to go through withdrawal afterward. You might feel angry in the morning and believe you've moved on, only to break down in tears by the afternoon. This is normal as you process your emotions. Don't be ashamed or feel confused that you may still miss and love the abuser, but not the abuse. Letting go is difficult because you've been addicted to intermittent reinforcement. Don't allow friends and family to judge you for missing your ex or not letting go at their speed. They can't comprehend the bond that you might still feel.

Grief is part of letting go, but it's important to maintain friendships and life-affirming activities in the process. The worst will pass, and you will be stronger.

➤ *Innercises: Letting Go*

- List all your fears. Write a paragraph describing your feelings about each one. Typical fears would include financial insecurity or living alone. Include beliefs as well, such as, "My children will be damaged," or "I'm too old to meet anyone." Take your time and allow yourself to feel each fear. Read the list to someone you trust and challenge the credibility of your worries.
- List all anticipated losses. For example, losing your home, loss of daily contact with your children, and loss of relationships with your ex's family. Include other losses mentioned above under the above section, Grieving. Write a paragraph describing your feelings about each one. Read the list to someone you trust and discuss solutions to minimize your pain and support your needs.

- Are you feeling guilty and blaming yourself? Were you blamed or criticized as a child? Don't continue to do it to yourself. Confront negative self-talk with the facts. If you made mistakes, forgive yourself like you would anyone else.
- Do you miss your ex and what they represent, or just miss being in a relationship.
- What function did your ex serve for you? (e.g., humor, motivation, inspiration, fun, a social life, status, or a certain lifestyle)
- How can you improve your self-care and provide those functions for yourself?
- When you feel inflexible or angry about something you're negotiating or didn't get in negotiations, ask yourself what it represents, and what it means to your future life. How important it is in the big picture? Allow yourself to experience the feeling of not getting your way.
- If you feel your grief, depression, or anxiety are unmanageable, seek a support group and/or a therapist to help you. Talk to a doctor about getting medication to help you during this stressful period. Don't listen to friends who judge you or attack your ex.
- Listen to my seminar on *Breakup Recovery*.[96]

Chapter 12

MOVING ON

The two biggest challenges to moving on are setting boundaries with your ex and balancing grieving with moving forward in your life. If you haven't unbonded emotionally, there are more reactivity and fights, weak boundaries, and too much contact that keeps you from moving on.

Social support is especially important. Newly single people may not be ready to date or feel awkward dating after married life. Creating a single lifestyle takes time. Perhaps you never lived alone. You may not be used to attending cultural and social events alone or to not having a companion with whom to go.

So, now's the time to take care of you and your children. The losses and changes you go through during divorce are overwhelming and stressful. Most parents emotionally neglect their children during a divorce. It's hard to be emotionally available and present for them, but they're sad and scared, too, including savvy teenagers. Adolescence is a vulnerable period, especially for boys. You won't be able to be there for your children if you're not getting your needs met. Get all the support you can from lawyers, accountants, therapists, family, friends, and spiritual groups.

Spend quality alone time with each one of your children and listen to them. Don't talk negatively to them about your ex or use them as confidants. Both behaviors are very destructive. It's also a mistake to let children of any age decide with whom they want to live. Listen to their feelings, but make that decision with your spouse. It's too big of a responsibility, even for a 17-year-old.

NEW RELATIONSHIPS

New relationships pose new problems. Fearful of re-experiencing abuse, abandonment, or loss of your autonomy, you might isolate or erect walls of distrust when dating again. Isolation isn't healthy and can cause you to depend too much on your children for companionship. On the other hand, loneliness and/or impaired self-esteem lead you to continue to make poor partner choices. Out of fear you may settle for someone "safe," not right for you, unavailable, or to whom you'd never commit.

But despite your intentions, you might nevertheless reattach to someone new and find it difficult to leave. Relationships aren't easy. When you're dissatisfied, you don't trust yourself and ponder whether the problem lies in you or your new partner. And although you've vowed to never again let anyone abuse you, you might once more be betrayed, abandoned, or mistreated in ways you haven't experienced before.

This cycle of repeated abandonment can make you fearful of intimacy. If you opt for being alone, your needs for love and closeness go unmet. Loneliness can trigger toxic shame from childhood when you felt alone and unloved or unlovable. It may seem like there's no hope or escape from your misfortune. But there is a good reason for hope, and healing is always possible.

Reevaluate what attracted you to a narcissist, your present needs and wants, and to what extent you were driven by childhood longings (see chapters 4 and 6). Did you undervalue your needs for understanding, consideration, support, and empathy? When dating, pay attention to how you feel, express your feelings and needs, and be authentic. This is how you'll separate the wheat from the chaff.

HEALING AND THERAPY

Unless you've followed the recommendations outlined in this book and have understood, detached, and unbonded from the narcissist, you'll likely spend time reviewing your relationship to help you understand what you went through from a perspective informed about NPD. This can help you move out of victim mode and feeling hurt, ashamed, abandoned, betrayed, angry, confused, and afraid.

It's not advisable to discuss your relationship with anyone judgmental or who will plant doubt in your mind. Some friends and family won't see your ex through the same lens as you. Remember that they may have only known the charming Dr. Jekyll side of the narcissist. Even if they're not flying monkeys, often mutual friends want to stay neutral, hear "both sides," and stay connected with your ex. Don't try to convince them otherwise. You may feel betrayed, angry, and hurt, and choose to limit contact with them. Talk with compassionate people who validate your experience and don't blame you. People who understand narcissism and a therapist are more supportive listeners.

Do be gentle with yourself, and nourish yourself with sleep, healthy food, relaxation, pleasurable activities, and time with loved ones. Don't add to your problems with self-recriminations. Instead, congratulate yourself for your courage, whether or not the breakup was your choice. Remind yourself of your innocence.

Stages of Recovery

Studying this book and others about NPD can help you gain more understanding to not feel so personally injured by your partner. You need to reappraise events and your partner's manipulative tactics, abuse, rejection, and motives in the context of their mental illness and not allow them to undermine your self-worth. Rather than blame either yourself or your ex, this can help you let go of any illusions and accept the reality of what happened and why.

Healing requires that you then turn your attention inward and learn to become your own best friend. Your relationship with yourself is the template for all your relationships. You may have to get to know yourself again after having accommodated your partner for so long. Focus on rebuilding your self-esteem. People with healthy self-esteem tend to have more secure relationships with greater longevity. You may discover that you've been quite self-critical and lack self-compassion. You may even have been abusing yourself all along. This is a positive revelation. Your mission is to relate to yourself in positive, healthy ways.

In time, you become more comfortable being authentic, meeting your needs, and setting boundaries with your ex, co-workers, family, and friends. This helps you to regain your confidence and trust yourself again. You may not yet or ever be ready to forgive, but your anger will lessen as you turn your attention toward the future rather than the past. Nurture yourself and develop a fulfilling single life that includes a support system. This stage may also include recovery from codependency and childhood trauma. Healing shame, abuse, and loss helps you move forward, take responsibility for yourself, and improve your relationships.

What You Can Do

Your tasks are to reconnect to your internal cues – your guidance system – and to take responsibility for your pain, safety, and pleasure. This involves learning to trust and parent yourself, which may be new concepts for you. Here are some suggestions:

1. Nurture and comfort yourself (see the Self-Nurturing Innercises in chapter 8).
2. Identify your feelings. If this is difficult, pay attention to your inner dialogue. Notice your thoughts. Do they express worry, judgment, despair, resentment, envy, hurt, or wishing? Notice your moods. Are you irritable, anxious, or blue? Try to name the *specific* feeling ("upset" is not a specific feeling). Do this several times a day to improve recognition of your feelings. You can find lists of hundreds

of feelings online or can use the one in chapter 9 of *Codependency for Dummies*.

3. Heal your shame and affirm your authentic self. Follow the recovery plan laid out in *Conquering Shame and Codependency: 8 Steps to Freeing the True You*.

4. Find pleasure, e.g., read or watch comedy, look at something beautiful, go for a walk, sing or dance, create something, or stroke your skin. Pleasure releases chemicals in the brain that counterbalance pain, stress, and negative emotions. Discover what pleasures you (read about the neuroscience of pleasure in my article, "The Healing Power of Eros").

5. Adults also need to play. This means doing something purposeless that fully engages you and is enjoyable for its own sake. The more active the better, e.g., play with your dog vs. walking him, sing, or collect seashells vs. watching television. Play brings you into the pleasure of the moment. Doing something creative is a great way to play, but beware not to judge yourself. Remember the goal is enjoyment, not the finished product.

6. Forgive yourself. Good parents don't punish or constantly remind children of their mistakes, and they don't punish willful wrongs repeatedly. Instead, learn from mistakes and make amends when necessary. If this is difficult, do the exercises in *Freedom from Guilt and Blame Finding Self-Forgiveness*.

7. Honor commitments to yourself as you would to anyone else. When you don't, you're in effect abandoning yourself. How would you feel if your parent repeatedly broke promises to you? Love yourself by demonstrating that you're important enough to keep commitments to yourself.

8. Building your self-esteem is essential for your well-being and to confront abuse. (Watch the webinar *How to Raise Your Self-Esteem*.)[97]

9. Stopping self-criticism is the first step in building self-esteem, self-acceptance, and self-love. Notice your self-judgment. Write it down to build self-awareness.

10. Become a positive coach. Disarming your inner critic is also your first defense against projection. (See my e-workbook, *10 Steps to Self-Esteem: The Ultimate Guild to Stop Self-Criticism*.)[98]

Therapy

From both my personal and professional experience, it's hard – impossible, really – to make these changes on your own. Find a psychotherapist who both understands narcissism and is trained in healing abuse and trauma to help you change the relationship dynamics and reclaim yourself. A therapist can help you detach from the narcissist, build your self-esteem, be autonomous, express your needs, and set boundaries. Therapy can improve your capacity to witness and contain your emotions. You'll learn to be with your feelings and to give yourself the acceptance and empathy you receive from your therapist.

Once you leave, therapy can be useful to work through losses and fears of separation. You learn to distinguish between the present and any earlier trauma and to resolve grief and anger towards your ex. This helps you heal and move on. A therapist can aid you in de-idealizing your partner and accepting the reality of your partner's limitations. It's helpful to connect your relationship interactions to pain in your childhood. This way, you can work through past trauma and shame to increase self-worth and self-compassion.

You may have left the toxic relationship yet still experience the effects of trauma and PTSD. They don't resolve on their own. Seek trauma counseling to recover from abuse and help you to trust yourself and your perceptions. You also need help in learning new skills, such as self-nurturing and assertiveness. There are many different modalities, but cognitive-behavior therapy (CBT) should be in your therapist's toolkit. There is also specific TF-CBT (Trauma-Informed CBT) for working with children. If your emotions are unmanageable, dialectical behavioral therapy (DBT) or DBT group therapy can be helpful. Eye Movement Desensitization and Reprocessing (EMDR), Emotional Freedom Technique (EFT), Sensory Experiencing (SE), and Brain-Spotting might also be helpful forms of therapy.

There is no magical prince or princess or unconditionally loving parent who can make up for what you didn't get in childhood. You can, however, do the work of recovery, grieve, accept your past, parent yourself, and feel worthy of love. Then you're ready to love and be loved, not by a god or goddess, but by a flawed-yet-loving partner. To learn more about healing from codependency, do the self-healing exercises in *Codependency for Dummies* and *Conquering Shame and Codependency: 8 Steps to Freeing the True You.*

PRACTICAL STEPS

Here are more tips to practice that will help you increase your autonomy and sense of well-being:

1. Don't expect your ex to take care of your needs.

2. Learn something new about your goals and passions. Take action. Actions today create your future.
3. Accept the reality that you're single. It's your responsibility to create happiness in your life. It's okay to be angry about it. That's a step toward acceptance.
4. Establish new, clear boundaries with your ex.
5. Journal and write every day about the things you did well, even small things; i.e., "I resisted the urge to call my ex and called a friend instead." Also, jot down and date small signs of healing, such as crying less, trying new things, and socializing more.
6. Don't ruminate about the past. It saps your energy and can turn fatigue or sadness into hopelessness. Don't let depression take over. Get professional help if you feel stuck.
7. Avoid any temptation to isolate. Ideally, loneliness should encourage you to reach out to others and maintain your relationships. Balance alone time with activities with friends.
8. Make plans and don't wait for invitations on holidays, including your birthday. As a single adult, now you must make plans to honor yourself.
9. Take time out from stress. Find activities that involve and relax you.
10. Engage in an exercise that is fun, such as dancing, surfing, squash, or biking that double your benefits.
11. Find a creative hobby that is fun and fulfilling.
12. Review chapter 8 – Innercises for Developing Autonomy.
13. Meetups and religious, spiritual, twelve-step, and other support groups, such as Parents Without Partners and New Beginnings, all can provide both support and a social network (see chapter 8 – Your Support System).
14. To make new friends, join classes and groups centered on your interests.
15. Attend weekend retreats.
16. Vacation on your own.
17. Go to events, movies, activities, museums, etc. on your own. Buy season tickets that force you to get out even when you don't feel like it.
18. Take risks that challenge your abilities. Taking risks, including interpersonal risks, enhances your competence, autonomy, and effectiveness. This in turn raises self-esteem and gives you the motivation to take more risks.

*　*　*　*

In sum, change is a process. Be patient with yourself. If you've practiced the suggestions in this book, you've inevitably made progress in reclaiming your Self. Don't despair if your efforts didn't improve your partner's behavior. You have gained clarity and will reap the reward of greater autonomy and self-esteem whether you choose to stay or leave.

ENDNOTES

1   American Psychiatric Association. (2013). *Diagnostic and Statistical Manual of Mental Disorders: DSM-V.* American Psychiatric Publishing.

2   Ovid. (2004). *The Metamorphoses* (David Raeburn, Trans.). Penguin Classics. (Original work published 8AD)

3   Ovid. (2004). Book III, 386-392.

4   Dhawan, N. K. (2010). Prevalence and treatment of narcissistic personality disorder in the community: a systematic review. *Comprehensive Psychiatry,* 51(4), 333-339. https://doi.org/10.1016/j.comppsych.2009.09.003; and McClean, J. (2007, October). Psychotherapy with a narcissistic patient using Kohut's self psychology model. *Psychiatry,* 10, 40-47.

5   Horton, R.S., G. Bleau, & B. Drwecki. (2006). Parenting narcissus: What are the links between parenting and narcissism? *Journal of Personality,* 74(2), 345-376. https://doi.org/10.1111/j.1467-6494.2005.00378.x

6   Horton, R. S. (2010). On environmental sources of child narcissism: Are parents really to blame? In Barry, C. T., Kerig, P. K., Stellwagen, K. K., & Barry, T. D. (Eds.). (2011). *Narcissism and Machiavellianism in youth: Implications for the development of adaptive and maladaptive behavior* (pp. 125-143). American Psychological Association. http://www.jstor.org/stable/j.ctv1chrxxt

7   Cramer, Phebe, (2011). Young adult narcissism: A 20 year longitudinal study of the contribution of parenting styles, preschool precursors of narcissism, and denial. *Journal of Research in Personality,* 45(1), 19-28. https://doi.org/10.1016/j.jrp.2010.11.004

8   Luo, Y.L.L. & Cai H. (2018). The etiology of narcissism: A review of behavioral genetic studies. In A. Hermann, A. Brunell, & J. Foster (Eds.) *Handbook of Trait Narcissism.* Springer. https://doi.org/10.1007/978-3-319-92171-6_16

9   Raskin, R., & Terry, H. (1998). A principal-components analysis of the Narcissistic Personality Inventory and further evidence of its construct validity. *Journal of Personality and Social Psychology,* 54(5), 890-902. https://openpsychometrics.org/tests/NPI. See also Glover, N., Miller, J. D., Lynam, D. R., Crego, C., & Widiger, T. A. (2012). The Five-Factor Narcissism Inventory: A five factor measure of narcissistic personality traits. *Journal of Personality Assessment,* 94, 500-512. https://psychology. uga.edu/sites/default/files/CVs/FFNI_shortform.pdf; Pincus, A. L., Ansell, E. B., Pimentel, C. A., Cain, N. M., Wright, A. G. C., & Levy K. N. (2009, Sept.). Initial construction and validation of the Pathological Narcissism Inventory. Psychological Assessment, 21(3),365-379. https://doi.apa.org/

doiLanding?doi=10.1037%2Fa0016530, https://www.researchgate.net/
publication/26779097_Initial_Construction_and_Validation_of_the_
Pathological_Narcissism_Inventory; and https://psytests.org/darktriad/
pni.en.html

10 Battaglio, S. (2017, April 11). "I really did it for my daughters": L.A. Radio
host Wendy Walsh on why she spoke out against Bill O'Reilly. *Los Angeles
Times*. https://www.latimes.com/business/hollywood/la-fi-ct-walsh-fox-
20170411-story.html

11 Masterson, J. (1993). *The Emerging Self: A Developmental, Self, and Object
Relations Approach to Treatment of the Closet Narcissistic Disorder of the
Self*. Brunner Mazel.

12 Kaufman, S. B., Weiss, B., Miller, J. D., & Campbell, W. K. (2020).
Clinical correlates of vulnerable and grandiose narcissism: A personality
perspective. *Journal of Personality Disorders*, 34(1), 107-130. https//doi.
org/10.1521/pedi_2018_32_384

13 Houlcroft, L., Bore, M., & Munro, D. (2012). Three faces of narcissism.
Personality and Individual Differences, 53, 274-278. https://doi.
org/10.1016/j.paid.2012.03.036

14 Mandal, A. (2019, Feb. 27). Narcissism variations. *News-Medical Life
Sciences*. https://www.news-medical.net/health/Narcissism-Variations.aspx

15 Big five personality theory posits that the five hereditable traits are
extroversion, agreeableness, openness, conscientiousness, and neuroticism.
These are the essential, building blocks of personality.

16 Wai, M. & Tiliopoulos, N. (2012, May). The affective and cognitive
empathic nature of the dark triad of personality. *Personality and Individual
Differences*. 52(7):794-799. https://doi.org/10.1016/j.paid.2012.01.008

17 Wei & Tiliopoulos, (2012). The affective and cognitive.

18 Jones, D. N. & Paulhus, D. (2017). Duplicity among the dark triad: three
faces of deceit. *Journal of Personality and Social Psychology*, 113(2), 329-42.
https://doi.org/10.1037/pspp0000139

19 Muris, P., Merckelbach, H., Otgaar, H., & Meijer, E. (2017). The malevolent
side of human nature: A meta-analysis and critical review of the literature
on the dark triad (narcissism, Machiavellianism, and psychopathy).
Perspectives on Psychological Science, 12(2), 183-204.
https://doi.org/10.1177/1745691616666070; http://www.craiganderson.
org/wp-content/uploads/caa/Classes/Readings/17DarkTriadMeta.pdf

20 Campbell, W. K., & Miller, J. (2017, August 1). Trifurcated Model of
Narcissism. https://doi.org/10.31234/osf.io/8nd95; CC-By Attribution 4.0
International 10.31234/osf.io/8nd95. Miller, J. D., Lynam, D. R., Hyatt, C.
S., & Campbell, W. K. (2017). Controversies in narcissism. *Annual Review
of Clinical Psychology*, 13, 291-315. https://doi.org/10.1146/annurev-
clinpsy-032816-045244

21 https://www.truity.com/view/tests/big-five-personality.

22 Kaufman, et al. (2020). Clinical correlates.

23 Kerzan, Z. & Herlache, A. D. (2018). The narcissism spectrum model: A synthetic view of narcissistic personality. *Personality and Social Psychology Review,* 1(29). https://doi.org/10.1177/1088868316685018

24 Edershile, E. & Wright, E. (2019). Fluctuations in grandiose and vulnerable narcissistic states: A momentary perspective. https://doi.org/10.31234/osf.io/8gkpm

25 Lancer, D. (2014). Loving a Borderline. *What is codependency.* https://whatiscodependency.com/bpd-borderline-personality-disorder

26 University at Buffalo. (2015, March 4). Men tend to be more narcissistic than women, study finds. *ScienceDaily.* https://www.sciencedaily.com/releases/2015/03/150304104040.htm

27 Walsh, S. (2010, June 28). 20 identifiable traits of a female narcissist. *Brainsyntax.* http://www.brainsyntax.com/Home/MessageDetail/1219

28 Lancer, D. (2015). What is Toxic Shame. *What is Codependency.* https://whatiscodependency.com/what-is-toxic-shame

29 Alliance of Psychoanalytic Organizations. (2006). *Psychodynamic Diagnostic Manual,* 46.

30 Rothstein, A. (1984). *The Narcissistic Pursuit of Perfection.* Routledge.

31 Stoeber, J. (2014). How other-oriented perfectionism differs from self-oriented and socially prescribed perfectionism. *Journal of Psychopathology and Behavioral Assessment,* 36(2), 329-38. https://doi.org/10.1007/s10862-013-9397-7; https://core.ac.uk/download/pdf/18530042.pdf

32 Epstein, Z. (2018, June 15) Ex-Apple employee: Working for "Giant Jerk" Steve Jobs was a nightmare. *Yahoo!finance.* https://bgr.com/general/what-its-like-to-work-for-steve-jobs-4671636/

33 Birch, J. (2018, Aug. 16). Knowing your "attachment style" could make you a smarter dater. *Washington Post.* https://www.washingtonpost.com/news/soloish/wp/2018/08/16/knowing-your-attachment-style-could-make-you-a-smarter-dater. See also Kinnison, J. (2014). *Bad Boyfriends: Using Attachment Theory to Avoid Mr. (or Ms.) Wrong and Make You a Better Partner.* Author. https://jebkinnison.com/bad-boyfriends-the-book. All estimates of prevalence of attachment types are from these two sources.

34 Fraley, R. C. & Shaver, P. R. (1998). Airport separations: A naturalistic study of adult attachment dynamics in separating couples. *Journal of Personality and Social Psychology,* 75(5), 1198-1212. https://doi.org/10.1037/0022-3514.75.5.1198.

35 Mikulincer, M. & Shaver, P.R. (2012, Feb.). An attachment perspective on psychopathology," *World Psychiatry,* 1(1). 11-15. https://doi.org/10.1016/j.wpsyc.2012.01.003

36 Miller, J. D., Hoffman, B. J., Gaughan, E. T., Gentile, B., Maples, J., & Campbell, W. K. (2011). Grandiose and vulnerable narcissism: A nomological network analysis. *Journal of Personality,* 79(5), https://onlinelibrary.wiley.com/doi/10.1111/j.1467-6494.2010.00711.x; https://www.academia.edu/download/27676006/Miller_et_al._-_2011_-_Grandiose_and_vulnerable_narcissism_A_nomological_network_analysis.pdf

37 Dickinson, K. A., & Pincus, A. L. (2003). Interpersonal analysis of grandiose and vulnerable narcissism. *Journal of Personality Disorders, 17,* 188-207. https://doi.org/10.1521/pedi.17.3.188.22146

38 Dickinson & Pincus, (2003). Interpersonal analysis.

39 Rohmann, E., Neumann, E., Herner, M. J., & Bierhoff, H. W. (2012). Grandiose and vulnerable narcissism: self-construal, attachment, and love in romantic relationship. *European Psychologist, 17*(4), 279-290. https://doi.org/10.1027/1016-9040/a000100

40 Lancer, D. (2014). *Conquering Shame and Codependency: 8 Steps to Freeing the True You.* Hazelden Foundation.

41 See Lancer, D. (2019) Sons of narcissistic mothers. *What is codependency.* https://www.whatiscodependency.com/sons-narcissistic-mothers; (2015) Sons of Narcissistic Fathers. *What is codependency.* https://www.whatiscodependency.com/sons-of-narcissistic-fathers; and (2017). Daughters of Narcissistic Mothers. *What is codependency.* https://whatiscodependency.com/daughters-narcissistic-mothers)

42 Lancer, D. (2012). What is Emotional Abandonment? *What is codependency.* https://whatiscodependency.com/what-is-emotional-abandonment

43 Lancer, D. (2014). *Conquering Shame and Codependency.*

44 Miller, J. D., Lynam, D. R., Hyatt, C. S., & Campbell, W. K. (2017). Controversies in narcissism. *Annual Review of Clinical Psychology, 13,* 291-315.

45 Grapsas, S., Brummelman, E., Back, M. D., & Denissen, J. J. A. (2020). The "why" and "how" of narcissism: A process model of narcissistic status pursuit. *Perspectives on Psychological Science, 15*(1) 150-172. https://doi.org/0.1177/1745691619873350

46 American Psychiatric Association. (2013). *Diagnostic Statistical Manual.*

47 Schultze, L., Disiobek, I., Vater, A., Heekeren, H. R., Bajbouj, M., Renneberg, B., Heuser, I., & Ropeke, S. (2013). Gray matter abnormalities in patients with narcissistic personality disorder. *Psychiatric Research, 47*(10), 1363-1369. https://doi.org/10.1016/j.jpsychires.2013.05.017

48 Ritter, K., et. al. (2010). Lack of empathy.

49 Ritter, K., Dziobek, I., Preißler, S., Rüter, A., Vater, A., Fydrich, T., Lammers, C. H., Heekeren, H-C., Roepke, S. (2010, Nov). Lack of empathy in patients with narcissistic personality disorder. *Psychiatry Research.* https://doi.org/10.1016/j.psychres.2010.09.013; https://pdfs.semanticscholar.org/2fe3/32940c369886baccadb14fd5dfcbc5f5625f.pdf.

50 Lancer, D. (2015). Dealing with a Passive-Aggressive Partner. *What is codependency.* https://whatiscodependency.com/passive-aggressive-codependent-partner)

51 Lancer, D. (2012). *Codependency for Dummies.* John Wiley & Sons.

52 Irwin, H. J. (1995) Codependence, narcissism, and childhood trauma. *Journal of Clinical Psychology 51*(5), 658-65. https://doi.org/10.1002/1097-4679(199509

53 Lancer, D. (2010). The Dance of Intimacy. What is codependency. https://whatiscodependency.com/the-dance-of-intimacy.

54 Lancer, D. (2017). *"I'm Not Perfect–I'm Only Human:" How to Beat Perfectionism*. Carousel Books. https://whatiscodependency.com/product/im-not-perfect-im-human-beat-perfectionism

55 Lancer, D. (2014). *Conquering Shame and Codependency.*

56 Delič, L., Novak, P., Kovačič, J. & Avsec, A. (2011). Self-reported emotional and social intelligence and empathy as distinctive predictors of narcissism. *Psychological Topics*, 20(3), 477-488. https://www.semanticscholar.org/paper/Self-reported-Emotional-and-Social-Intelligence-and-Deli%C4%8D-Novak/0fe02aba217382005c8289b4607dc721a16e11e7

57 Back, M., Schmuckle, S. C., & Egloff, B. (2010, Jan.). Why are narcissists so charming at first sight? decoding the narcissism-popularity link at zero acquaintance. *Journal of Personality and Social Psychology, 98*(1) 132-145. https://doi.org/10.1037/a0016338; https://www.researchgate.net/profile/Mitja-Back/publication/40869027

58 Lancer, (2014). *Conquering Shame and Codependency.*

59 Campbell, W.K. & Foster, C.A. (2002, April). Narcissism and commitment in romantic relationships: An investment model analysis. *Personality and Social Psychology Bulletin 28*(4), 484-495. https://doi.org/10.1177/0146167202287006; https://www.researchgate.net/publication/247747057_Narcissism_and_Commitment_in_Romantic_Relationships_An_Investment_Model_Analysis

60 Campbell, W. K., & Foster, C. A. (2002, April). Narcissism and commitment.

61 Strutzenberg, C. Wiersma-Mosley, J., Jozkowski, K.N., & Becnel, J. N. (2017, Sept.) Love-bombing: A narcissistic approach to relationship formation. *Discovery, The Student Journal of Dale Bumpers College of Agricultural, Food and Life Sciences, 18*(1), 81-89. https://scholarworks.uark.edu/discoverymag/vol18/iss1/14

62 Goff, B. G., Goddard, H. W., Pointer, L., & Jackson, G. B. (2007). Measures of expressions of love. *Psychological Reports, 101,* 357-360. https://doi.org/10.2466/pr0.101.2.357-360; and Swenson, C. (1972). *The behavior of love.* In H.A. Otto (Ed.) *Love Today* (pp. 86-101). Dell Publishing.

63 Branden, N. (1980). *The Psychology of Romantic Love.* J.P. Tarcher.

64 Fromm, E., (1956). *The Art of Loving.* Harper & Brothers.

65 Campbell, W. K., & Foster, C. A. (2002, April). Narcissism and commitment.

66 Lancer, D. (2014). *Conquering Shame and Codependency.*

67 Rohmann, E., et. al. (2012). Grandiose and vulnerable narcissism.

68 Ritter, K. et al. (2010). Lack of empathy.

69 Ritter, K. et al. (2010). Lack of empathy.

70 Lancer, D. (2017). *"I'm Not Perfect."*

71 SafeLives. (2015). Getting it right first time: Policy report. https://safelives.org.uk/policy-evidence/getting-it-right-first-time

72 Lancer, D. (2014). *Conquering Shame and Codependency.*

73 Ishida, D. (2019, June 21) Brains of pairs of animals synchronize during social interaction. *Scienmag.* https://scienmag.com/brains-of-pairs-of-animals-synchronize-during-social-interaction

74 See Lancer, D. (2011). Your Intimacy Index: How to Have More Intimacy. *What is codependency.* https://whatiscodependency.com/overcoming-fear-of-intimacy

75 Campbell, W. K., & Foster, C. A. (2002, April). Narcissism and commitment.

76 Lowen, A. (1985) *Narcissism: Denial of the True Self.* Simon & Schuster.

77 Carey, B. (2017, Nov. 20.). Denial makes the world go round. *The New York Times* https://www.nytimes.com/2007/11/20/health/research/20deni.html

78 Lancer, D. (2017). Secrets and lies: the damage of deception. *What is codependency.* https://whatiscodependency.com/secrets-betrayal-lies-deception-infidelity

79 Lancer, D. (2019) Need-fulfillment is the key to happiness. *What is codependency* https://whatiscodependency.com/need-fulfillment-is-the-key-to-happiness

80 See my workbook, Lancer, D. (2015). *Freedom from Guilt and Blame: Finding Self-Forgiveness.* Carousel Books. https://whatiscodependency.com/product/freedom-guilt-blame-finding-self-forgiveness

81 Lancer, D. (2006, Winter) The healing power of Eros. *Somatics, XV*(1) http://www.whatiscodependency.com/wp-content/uploads/2011/12/Eros-2015.pdf

82 Lancer, D. (2018). Self-Love Meditation. [Audio file]. *What is codependency.* https://whatiscodependency.com/product/self-love-meditation

83 Lancer, D. (2015). *How to Speak Your Mind: Become Assertive and Set Limits.* Carousel Books. https://whatiscodependency.com/product/how-to-speak-your-mind.); Lancer, D. (2016). How to Be Assertive. [Webinar] https://whatiscodependency.com/product/how-to-be-assertive

84 See Lancer, D. (2022). How trauma reactions can hi-jack your life. *What is codependency.* https://whatiscodependency.com/trauma-reactions-ptsd

85 Wright, A. G. C, Stepp, S. D., Scott, L. N., Hallquist, M. N., Beeney, J. E., Lazarus, S. A., & Pilkonis, P. A. (2017, Oct). The effect of pathological narcissism on interpersonal and affective processes in social interactions. *Journal of Abnormal Psychology, 126*(7), 898-910. https://doi.org/10.1037/abn0000286

86 Lancer, D. (2016). The power of personal boundaries. *What is codependency.* https://whatiscodependency.com/the-power-of-personal-boundaries

87 Lancer, D. (2015). Ten reasons why boundaries don't work. *What is codependency.* https://whatiscodependency.com/setting-boundaries-limits-codependency)

88 McClean, J. (2007, Oct.). Psychotherapy with a narcissistic patient using Kohut's self psychology model. *Psychotherapy Rounds*, 40-47. See also Lancer, D. (2019). Therapy for NPD and narcissists. *What is codependency*. https://www.whatiscodependency.com/therapy-for-npd-and-narcissists

89 Hiroto, D. S., & Seligman, M. E. (1975). Generality of learned helplessness in man. *Journal of Personality and Social Psychology, 31*(2), 311-327. https://doi.org/10.1037/h0076270

90 Lancer, D. (2003). The Stages of Divorce. *What is codependency*. https://whatiscodependency.com/the-stages-of-divorce

91 Mogilski, J. K. &Welling, L. M. (2017, Sept.). Staying friends with an ex: Sex and dark personality traits predict motivations for post-relationship friendship. *Personality and Individual Differences, 115,* 114-119. https://doi.org/10.1016/j.paid.2016.04.016Get

92 Lancer, D. (2015). *Freedom from Guilt and Blame.*

93 International Support Network of Alienated Families https://isnaf.info.

94 Healy, M. (2011, April 4). Heartache or headache, pain process is similar, studies find. Los Angeles Times. https://www.latimes.com/health/la-xpm-2011-apr-04-la-he-mood-pain-20110404-story.html

95 Hendrick, B. (2010, July 9). Losing love has similarities to addiction. *WebMD.* See also Aron A., Fisher, H., Mashek, D.J., Strong, G., Li, H., & Brown, L.L. (2005). Reward, motivation, and emotion systems associated with early-stage intense romantic love. *Journal of Neurophysiology, 94,* 327-337. https://doi.org/10.1152/jn.00838.2004

96 Lancer, D. (2016). Breakup Recovery. [Audio file]. https://whatiscodependency.com/product/breakup-recovery-2

97 Lancer, D. (2016). How to Raise Your Self-Esteem. [Webinar]. https://www.whatiscodependency.com/product/how-to-raise-your-self-esteem

98 Lancer, D. (2012). *10 Steps to Self-Esteem: The Ultimate Guild to Stop Self-Criticism.* Carousel Books. https://whatiscodependency.com/product/10-steps-to-self-esteem

Printed in Great Britain
by Amazon

44408361R00116